IRREVERENT

guide to

Amsterdam

Frommer's®

IRREVERENT

guide to

Amsterdam

6th Edition

By
George McDonald

WILEY

Wiley Publishing, Inc.

other titles in the

IRREVERENT GUIDE

series

About the Author

George McDonald is a former deputy editor of and current contributing writer for *Holland Herald*, the in-flight magazine of KLM Royal Dutch Airlines. He has written extensively about Belgium and the Netherlands for international magazines and travel books such as *Frommer's Amsterdam* and *Frommer's Europe*.

Published by:
Wiley Publishing, Inc.

111 River St.
Hoboken, NJ 07030-5774

ISBN-13: 978-0-471-77337-5
ISBN-10: 0-471-77337-9

Interior design contributed to by Marie Kristine Parial-Leonardo

Editor: Stephen Bassman
Production Editor: Heather Wilcox
Cartographer: Tim Lohnes
Photo Editor: Richard Fox
Production by Wiley Indianapolis Composition Services

For information on our other products and services or to obtain technical support, please contact our Customer Care Department within the U.S. at 800/762-2974, outside the U.S. at 317/572-3993 or fax 317/572-4002.

Wiley also publishes its books in a variety of electronic formats. Some content that appears in print may not be available in electronic formats.

Manufactured in the United States of America

5 4 3 2 1

A Disclaimer

CONTENTS

gezelligheid *(32)* • *Taking care of business (33)* • *For travelers with old money (33)* • *For travelers with new money (34)* • *Dowdy but lovable (35)* • *For those who hate surprises (36)* • *Luscious love nests (37)* • *Rooms with a view (37)* • *Home away from home (38)* • *Convention hotels with flair (38)* • *To relive the Golden Age (39)* • *In search of the perfect pool (39)* • *The royal treatment (39)* • *For cheap sleeps (40)* • *Lavender lodgings (40)* • *Party scenes (41)* • *Family values (42)* • *When everything else is filled (43)*

Maps

2 DINING   56

Basic Stuff   58

The Lowdown   63

Going Dutch (63) • *Dutch on the run (64)* • *Real rijsttafel (64)* • *Mumbai on the Amstel (65)* • *Thai me up (66)* • *Asian delights (66)* • *Utopian Ethiopian (66)* • *Multi Mediterranean (67)* • *The French connection (68)* • *For that special moment (69)* • *Overrated (70)* • *See-and-be-scenes (71)* • *Landmarks (72)* • *Cheap eats (72)* • *Isn't it romantic? (73)* • *Tourist traps (73)* • *Something fishy (74)* • *Can you put that out, please? (75)* • *When the play's the thing (75)* • *Kid pleasers (76)* • *For a quiet tête-à-tête (77)* • *Vegging out (77)* • *When the boss is paying (78)* • *Alfresco (79)* • *Take me to the river (79)* • *Best cafe food (79)*

Maps

INTRODUCTION

Wonderful, wild, more than a little woolly, too-good-to-be-true Amsterdam and its self-consciously cool, cultivated denizens lend themselves to tongue-in-cheek treatment. Few Europeans are so forthright, so eager to make fun of themselves, their history, language, and customs as the inhabitants of this small, flat, watery capital of a small, flat, watery country—they just don't want *you* to make fun of them (or, heaven forbid, Queen Beatrix). "Our hearts are on our tongues," goes an old Amsterdam saying. So much for the stereotype of the dour Dutch: Amsterdammers are disarmingly friendly, fun—and irreverent.

In fact, the Dutch as such do not exist; The Netherlands is a collection of 12 provinces with distinct personalities (like Friesland, which fancies itself to be a nation, distinct from the rest of the country). Amsterdammers are as different from their countrymen as a Scotsman is from a Londoner, or a Milanese from a Sicilian. The governmental capital, The Hague, is stiff and conservative; Rotterdam, home of the world's busiest port, is industrial and hard-edged (the people there are said to be born with their sleeves already rolled up); Maastricht, in the Catholic south, is elegant as well as exuberant. Amsterdam, the symbolic capital, where Dutch figurehead monarchs from the House of Orange have been inaugurated (Dutch monarchs aren't uppity enough to be crowned) since 1813, is casual and liberal, with an anything-goes spirit. Stunningly well preserved—though plenty

2

Map 1: Amsterdam Maps Overview

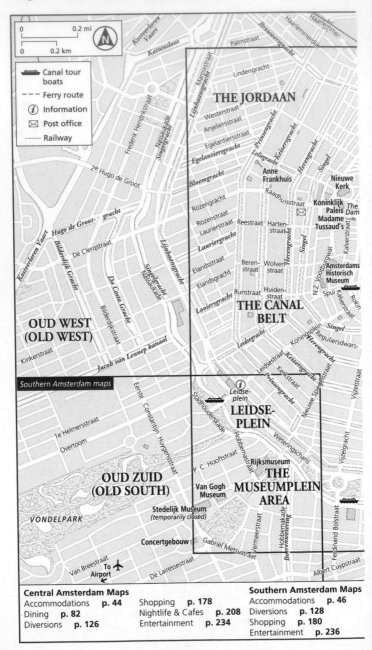

Central Amsterdam Maps		Southern Amsterdam Maps	
Accommodations **p. 44**	Shopping **p. 178**	Accommodations **p. 46**	
Dining **p. 82**	Nightlife & Cafes **p. 208**	Diversions **p. 128**	
Diversions **p. 126**	Entertainment **p. 234**	Shopping **p. 180**	
		Entertainment **p. 236**	

3

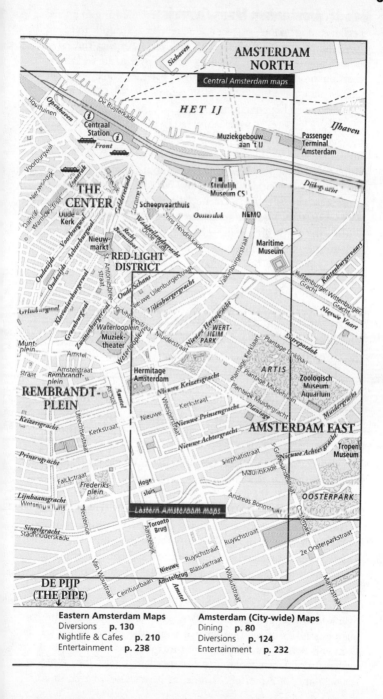

Eastern Amsterdam Maps
Diversions   **p. 130**
Nightlife & Cafes   **p. 210**
Entertainment   **p. 238**

Amsterdam (City-wide) Maps
Dining   **p. 80**
Diversions   **p. 124**
Entertainment   **p. 232**

grimy in places, and speckled with what is something of a local specialty: dog poop—Amsterdam revolves around tourism, conventions, and high tech, with Schiphol Airport the city's second-largest employer. The biggest employer is the seemingly recession-proof government, whose tolerant quality-of-life policies help make this city so livable and so loved, even by visitors who detest big government.

Like Florence, Amsterdam is a city of art. Truth be told, only half a dozen of its 40-plus dynamic and ever-expanding museums are world-class: the Rijksmuseum, Van Gogh Museum, Stedelijk Museum, Rembrandt House Museum, Amsterdam Historical Museum, and Maritime Museum—still an impressive roster for a cosmopolis of just 750,000 souls, a city so compact you can stroll across it in a couple of hours. Within the Centrum alone—the center-city bounded by the 19th-century Singelgracht canal—are 6,800 centuries-old canal houses (which give the old center of Amsterdam its timeless character) that are historical monuments, many of them dating from the city's 17th-century Golden Age squeezed into a semicircle that you can easily amble across in an hour. Their bricks stand balanced on wooden pilings driven through the mud into more-or-less solid ground, constantly reminding people of the city's precarious situation below sea level.

Though most locals are proud of their showcase city, which has modernized while maintaining its monuments, they manage to poke fun at its founding. There is no illustrious Roman pedigree ("Here a wretched race is found," noted Pliny the Elder, "inhabiting either the more elevated spots or artificial mounds," where no Romans in their right minds would set foot); there's not even a lost Viking to pep up the history books. The whole thing started, it seems, when some fishermen and their dogs drifted down the Amstel River sometime in the early 1200s. The city's original coat of arms depicts the founding tale of two fishermen and a dog arriving onboard a small boat. It is said that the dog promptly threw up, thereby marking the spot. The fishermen slogged up a muddy bank and had a stiff drink, thus laying the foundations of a tavern around which the entire metropolis would grow.

And grow it did: Bright, beaverlike fishermen dammed the river (doubtless they damned it too, on occasion), reclaiming huge quantities of mud, at what is today the square called the Dam. Their brilliant, inspired, and imaginative name for their settlement? Amstellodam (or Amstelledamme, or Aemstelledamme, or Amestelledamme, as it was also written in an age that lacked spelling bees), which means Dam on the Amstel River. Archaeological remains show that by 1204, local big wheels were moving in on what the peasants had created. The lord of Aemstel, Gijsbrecht II, made the first power play, building a castle at the settlement and lording it over the locals. (In the 1990s, archaeologists uncovered the foundations of the castle under a tiny side street called Nieuwezijds Kolk.) But Gijsbrecht had to watch his back constantly, as others began maneuvering for position. In 1275, Count Floris V of Holland granted this previously unknown fishing village special trading privileges. Count Gijsbrecht IV of Aemstel didn't appreciate Floris's efforts to win friends and influence people on his patch, and in 1296 he murdered Floris in his castle at Muiden.

Gijsbrecht didn't have long to enjoy his victory. Two years later Floris's brother, Guy of Hainaut, defeated Gijsbrecht in battle and hauled him up in front of the bishop of Utrecht for judgment; Gijsbrecht's land was confiscated and he was imprisoned and later exiled. In 1300, the bishop granted Amstelledamme its town charter and in 1317 ceded the town to the counts of Holland.

Things really got going when the founding fathers and their dog were joined by a few founding mothers bearing *jenever* (gin) and salted herrings. The humble herring was responsible for the city's early prosperity: Local fishermen knew how to catch, preserve, and market it better than anyone else in Europe. Tobacco arrived a few centuries later, and soon the institution of the tobacco-stained, fly-blown *bruine kroeg*—or brown cafe, as visiting Anglo-Saxons called it—was born. Brown cafes worth their stains haven't been washed or painted since—thus their name—and are marvelous time tunnels to the Golden Age of Rembrandt's Amsterdam, since these places have been haunts of *every* Amsterdam generation since then. This includes during the hippie heyday of the 1960s, which was apparently a kind of alternative Golden Age for the city, though the hippie scene is now about as dead and buried as Count Floris V.

The talents and resources of the early immigrants fueled everything from diamond polishing (still an important industry) to shipbuilding and international trade. The 1602 creation of the United East India Company (V.O.C.) by natives and immigrants ushered in the so-called Golden Age of the 17th century, when Amsterdam briefly reigned as Europe's most populous and powerful city. As the company's headquarters, Amsterdam in effect ruled a vast commercial empire, with satellites in South Africa, Indonesia, Sri Lanka, Goa, China, and

Japan. As the company grew embarrassingly rich, so too did Amsterdam. Today, the East India Company is reviled by young Amsterdammers guilty about their checkered colonial past, but like it or not, the corporation helped make Amsterdam the handsome, prosperous, cosmopolitan capital it is today. It also helped create the city's signature Red-Light District: Practical-minded city governors saw this bawdy-house district as the best means to prevent sailors from molesting the wives and daughters of locals (and it helped that it also generated considerable income, as it still does today).

During its heyday in the 17th century, the city burst through its medieval corset of walls and spilled outward in concentric semicircles; the Grachtengordel—literally, the "girdle of canals"—was built to handle this midriff bulge. First came the grandest canal of all, the Herengracht, whose Golden Bend (between Leidsestraat and Vijzelstraat) sprouted scores of mansions. The slightly less grand Keizersgracht followed, then the notably less grand Prinsengracht. The word "Grachtengordel" came to signify both the canals (a noun) and the fat-cat society living there (an adjective); it still does. Along these picturesque arteries, thousands of opulent palaces, churches, and public buildings sprang up. Miraculously, most are still there, and some members of the same merchant-prince dynasties—notably the Six family—still live in them.

At the same time, beyond the Grachtengordel to the northwest, the helter-skelter Jordaan neighborhood grew, its name a corruption of the French *jardin* (garden), left behind by Protestant French Huguenots, refugees from Catholic persecution back home (though today the district isn't a garden at all, but it does contain some handsome small gardens). Another Frenchie, Napoléon Bonaparte, later forced the Amsterdammers to name and number their canals and streets, thus making obsolete the city's endearing gablestones. The gablestones, of which some examples survive, were sculptures or tiles that depicted a picture-book bas-relief image relating to the trade or profession of the householders. These had been used instead of street numbers—which made it difficult to find your way around unless you were in the know, which must have been infuriating to a control freak like the little Corsican. Poetically, the Jordaan's urban garden—its streets and canals—bears the names of flowers: Rozengracht, Egelantiersgracht, Bloemstraat, and so on.

Unless you're an architecture buff, the rest of the city is so-so but unremarkable, a study in variations on a handful of themes—counterclockwise, the Old West, Old South, New South, and East quarters, all added in the 19th and early 20th centuries.

Amsterdam may look like a museum, but it lives in the present like no other European city. The economy is slowly recovering from the substantial knock it took from the fallout of the September 11, 2001, terrorist attacks. Expansion on other fronts continues apace: A major focus of ongoing redevelopment work is the old harbor area fronting the IJ channel, and farther out to the east at IJburg on the IJmeer lakefront, where vast new residential and infrastructure projects are sprouting like tulips in springtime. It seems likely that water transportation will be increasingly important in the future, as this redevelopment continues to turn the city's collective gaze back toward the harbor, where it had been fixed during the Golden Age. In a related activity, the Passenger Terminal Amsterdam cruise-ship port facility is handling an increasing number of seagoing visitors (and riverborne visitors from Europe's inland waterways).

Furthermore, Amsterdam deserves its reputation as both the sex and drugs, if not rock 'n' roll, capital of the Continent, as well as Europe's gay capital, thanks again to the centuries-old tradition of tolerance (homosexuality has been legal here for almost 200 years) and a natural bent for commerce. You can smoke small quantities of hash and marijuana, or nibble magic mushrooms, in more than 200 "smoking coffee shops"; prostitution is legal so long as services are performed in registered whorehouses (prostitutes are covered by social security and have their own labor union). The number of cafes—many exquisitely cozy, others wild and woolly—boggles the mind. Experimental music, dance, and theater flourish. Streets are animated and most of them are amazingly safe day and night because people live, work, and play all over town instead of scurrying to the suburbs when darkness falls. The presence of two large universities explains only in part the number of young people living here. In fact, Amsterdam is a talent magnet, drawing ambitious artists and businesspeople from all over Europe. Environmental consciousness is high, too (particularly if the problem is not in Amsterdam's backyard): It's no coincidence that Greenpeace International—a fine-tuned Dutch business with a multimillion-dollar budget—is based here.

Sound like paradise? Well, sort of. The ironic old Dutch saying, "Everything is possible, but you're not supposed to enjoy it," seems hopelessly dated today. Modern Amsterdammers seem untouched by Calvinism (there are more practicing Muslims than practicing Calvinists in the city). The cliché about a Calvinistic obsession with cleanliness is patently false, too: The city's two liveliest squares, Leidseplein and Rembrandtplein, are often pigsties. And don't be surprised if the tabletop at your favorite cafe or restaurant is sticky with spilled beer. Amsterdam's weather is abysmal—consistently rainy and often cold—and prices continue to climb. Toleration of soft drug use may sound enlightened; unfortunately, many smoking coffee shops and magic mushroom stores are dives controlled by organized crime. Environmental consciousness? Yes, car traffic is limited; the air (outside) is clean. But locals smoke like chimneys; most cafes, restaurants, and clubs are blue with pollution, and non-smoking sections are still not respected. Because it is legal here, prostitution is refreshingly unhypocritical as it eliminates pimps and keeps prostitutes off the streets.

But the architecturally stunning Red-Light District is shabby in some parts, and, in the opinion of many conservatives, the whole place is pretty squalid—a contemporary Sodom and Gomorrah.... Imagine a place that's wall to wall with barely clad prostitutes cavorting behind red-fringed windows, many of them (the hookers, that is) hailing from Eastern Europe and Third World nations, and who just conceivably might not be doing this as their preferred career choice; where brain-dead junkies and sad-looking heroin whores flop around, gazing out on what's left of their world through vacant eyes; where what constitutes a night out at the theater is crowds of fired-up drunk guys ogling stage artists inserting bananas into their vaginas or going at it doggy-style in "live shows"; where pimps, dope dealers, pickpockets, muggers, and all kinds of weird folks are legion; where leather is the apparel fabric of choice; where the titles in the local bookstores cover the gamut of sexual obsessions and fetishes—sex with minors, sex with animals, gang bangs, rape, and more; where sex-appliance stores stock everything from the mildly titillating to the physically dubious, to the positively anxiety-inducing; where "You want a blow job?" is on its way to becoming a traditional greeting. While it's not necessarily somewhere you'd want to take your maiden aunt—though, who knows, maybe she'd be keen to go along—the astonishing thing is that this isn't the whole story: Real people live here, walk the dog, buy their groceries, take the kids to school, visit bookstores, drink in decent bars, and eat in decent restaurants. And most of the tourists are just strolling around in search of a laugh and a giggle.

The local strain of tolerance does not mean loving acceptance, either. While most Amsterdammers are cosmopolitan and curious, plenty are bigots. Citizens of ex-colonial origin—Indonesians, Surinamese, black Africans—sometimes say the Singelgracht is really a moat designed to keep them out. The opposite of "white flight" has happened in Amsterdam: Old-money families and new-money yuppies have stayed in the high-rent, fortresslike old city, while immigrants and the poor are exiled to outlying neighborhoods or suburbs. Central Amsterdam is beautiful, tolerably clean, and pretty safe. But modern suburbs like Amsterdam-Noord and Amstelveen are as dull as ditch water, and the Bijlmermeer housing project—80% immigrant—is a bastion of soulless modern architecture and a haunt of crime.

But let's be fair. Amsterdam remains one of the most alluring and prosperous cities on earth. One breed of visitor can stay in a chain hotel, take canal-boat cruises, tiptoe through tulip fields, buy clogs, and never see a prostitute, nightclub, or smoking coffee shop. A different sort can wear spiky leather to S&M workshops, cruise live-sex shows, and stay stoned day and night in dens of depraved carnality. You can also opt for a world-class hotel, dine in epicurean restaurants, take in classical concerts at the Concertgebouw and jazz and contemporary music at the new Muziekgebouw aan 't IJ, shop for peerless antiques, and spend glorious days with the Dutch masters in the Rijksmuseum. Or combine any of the above.

Amsterdam today is unquestionably the Continent's most compact, sophisticated worldly city. Its inhabitants have created and nurtured a way of life—or more accurately, ways of life—that visitors either love or abhor; few remain indifferent to it. Some people, visiting for the first time, want to throw up everything and live this way forever; others just want to throw up. Amsterdammers are invariably too busy enjoying their place of abode to care much either way. Multilingual, multicultural, rich, and disarmingly tolerant, irreverence fits them to a tee.

YOU PROBABLY DIDN'T KNOW

How to tolerate the Dutch sense of tolerance...
The Dutch in general, and Amsterdammers in particular, are very tolerant people. And they're the first to let you know that. Their extreme tolerance can sometimes be hard to take. The only thing Amsterdammers won't tolerate is intolerance, so rule number one is: Never criticize tolerance. The locals put up with prostitution; sex between (consenting) children ages 12 to 16; soft drugs and the attendant sleaze; millions of tourists; astronomical taxes; overcrowding (the city has one of the highest population densities in the world); huge numbers of immigrants and refugees; heavy smoking everywhere; frightful drivers; spoiled children; and streets all but paved with dog shit. On the international scene, they must put up with big, boorish neighbors like France and Germany, who are always telling them what to do when it comes to drugs, prostitution, immigration, and cooking. Among other things, this means that you too, as a visitor, are fully expected to put up—graciously—with the

aforementioned. This applies particularly when in restaurants, clubs, and cafes where the combined cigarette, cigar, dope, and pipe smoke is as thick as Dutch pea soup (see "When smoke gets in your eyes," below).

Dutch tolerance experienced a trauma akin to a heart attack in 2004, when gadfly filmmaker Theo van Gogh was shot and stabbed to death on an Amsterdam street by an Islamic extremist who objected to a film he had made about Muslim attitudes to women. The brutal slaying and the response to it, which saw both mosques and churches go up in flames, were enough to shake anyone's complacency. But despite this shock, and a new awareness of ethnic, religious, and cultural tensions in the city and the nation at large, there's no real sign that Amsterdam is about to change the ways that have made it famous—or infamous—around the world.

How to swallow a fish like the locals... Some nations love shrimp heads, others tree grubs, others still raw oysters that slither down your throat, and yet others "mountain oysters." The Dutch have a peculiar predilection for herring, raw or pickled, which they gobble in a variety of ways. Go to the zoo to see how the seals do it, or observe the Dutch at one of the countless sidewalk fish stands in practically every city, town, and village in the Netherlands. Outside Amsterdam, herring is held by the tail and swallowed whole (gutted and cleaned already, of course). Little ado is made about bones and fins. Amsterdammers instead chop their herring into three or four pieces and eat them off a napkin or small plate. They can always spot out-of-towners by the way they eat fish; pointing their faces at the sky, opening their mouths, and lowering the entire fish in for a bite. More than a few Amsterdammers like to consume them this way, too, surreptitiously—or as surreptitiously as can be given the nature of the activity—in the same way that they might try to avoid being recognized aboard a canal tour boat.

How to avoid becoming a crime statistic... The Red-Light District is in one of the oldest parts of town, roughly from Warmoesstraat east to Nieuwmarkt, and from Zeedijk south to Damstraat (which, within the district, changes its name to Oude Doelenstraat, and changes again to Oude Hoogstraat). Known as De Wallen (The Walls) in Dutch, or if they're feeling particularly sentimental, De Walletjes (The Little Walls), in memory of the city walls that once stood here, this neighborhood is architecturally appealing, historically significant, and seedy as hell. Regulating prostitution is a good idea for many reasons, including lower health risks, but concentrating it in one area has its downside.

Contrary to what you'd expect, the district is pretty much safe by night when tittering tourists pour in for some sordid entertainment, but it can get dicey in the early morning when the Venus business is slow and the shops haven't yet opened. This is the time when druggies and pickpockets lurk in the district's narrow alleys and prey on jet-lagged tourists out for a 7am stroll (a few hours later, by 9 or 10 say, most of the lowlifes and ne'er-do-wells have crashed out for the day and the district takes on a fresh, almost innocent air). Stow away your camera at any time of day or night, and don't take snapshots of the ladies in the picture windows. They don't want their photos taken because, as locals point out, "their daddies don't know" how they earn a living. If you are spotted taking snapshots, you're liable to have your fancy digital unit stomped, along with parts of your anatomy. Business-minded readers will want to know that these painted ladies rent their windows for 8-hour shifts (typically they pay about 75€/$94), during which time they take in 200€ to 400€ ($250–$500). Services begin with the poetically named "suck and fuck" (condom required), for 25€ to 40€ ($31–$50), and proceed from there to your wildest desires. The prostitutes' union is called De Rode Draad (The Red Thread).

The once-infamous (for being a hellhole) Zeedijk street, which curves along the eastern edge of the district, is no longer the dicey shooting gallery and mugger's mile it was, since some upscale hotels opened nearby and the police chased the malefactors out of sight over the rim of the broad Dutch horizon—or at any rate a few blocks away and deeper into the district. But other parts of the district are still the haunts of drug dealers and addicts, purse snatchers, and other charming fauna. In general, use common sense: Don't stagger around the district when you're high; keep close track of your wallet or purse; don't flash your cash; and avoid the local dope peddlers, who sell low-quality wares and sometimes operate in cahoots with muggers. (Smoking coffee shops, described below, are much safer bets if you just want to enjoy some hash or marijuana.) At night especially, however, stick to the crowded streets and be wary of pickpockets at all times. Don't even stop for the sob story from some strapping youth—who could easily manage to do a decent day's work—but who needs a euro for a cup of coffee: While you're relieving his distress, someone else will likely relieve you of your wallet, or at least your iPod. There can be a sinister air to the bunches of often weird-looking men who gather on the canal bridges—I don't know, they *might* be waiting for the Museum Boat. Amsterdammers call the bridge that crosses Oudezijds Achterburgwal canal at Oude Hoogstraat (not far from Zeedijk, in the Red-Light District) the "Pillenbrug" (Pill Bridge) because so many druggies still hang out there, despite police efforts to move them on. And there is a sad aura around the "heroin-whores" who wander the darker streets.

What those pesky suffixes mean… In Dutch, *-straat* means "street," *-gracht* means "canal," *-plein* means "square," *-markt* means "market" or "market square," *-dijk* means "dike," and *-laan* means "avenue," all of which are used as suffixes attached directly to the name of the thoroughfare (for example, Princes' Canal becomes Prinsengracht).

How to define the indefinable gezellig… The Dutch make a cult of *gezellig*. *Gezellig*-ness (or *gezelligheid*) is the opposite of the other Dutch cult, that of efficiently run businesses and anything-goes commerce. The word is unpronounceable, and there's no English equivalent—cozy, homey, friendly, snuggly, cute, and swell all come close but don't quite get it. If you take something *gezellig* and stuff it into *gezellig* surroundings, *gezellig* becomes both form and function, medium and message. A well-worn brown cafe, a local restaurant, a living room with fireplace and friendly hound, even a good people-person, or a wonderful experience can be *gezellig*. Got that?

How to enjoy your hash and grass without getting arrested… Tolerance may be a byword in Amsterdam, but so is ambiguity. For example, it's currently illegal to possess, use, or sell drugs, hard or soft. But if you have 5 grams (.18 oz.) of hash (or marijuana) or less, and a "small amount" of magic mushrooms, strictly for personal use, and you are 18 or older, you probably won't be hassled. However, you aren't allowed to buy or sell the stuff or smoke it outside so-called smoking coffee shops (which may stock no more than 500g/18 oz.). If the police want to, they can confiscate anything you have and fine you, but they seem to do this only when dope users behave obnoxiously. The authorities crack down indeed on hard-drug dealers and anyone causing a public nuisance. Currently there are some 200 smoking coffee shops in town (see the Nightlife & Cafes chapter), down from 450 in 1995, which must follow certain "guidelines"—i.e., no hard drugs, no public nuisances, no sales to minors, and no transactions involving more than 5 grams. If a place breaks these rules, it will be shut down, and its license to operate as a coffee shop revoked forever (more than 200 licenses have been pulled in the last 5 years).

Magic mushrooms and so-called "smart drugs," the trend since the late '90s, are natural or synthetic hallucinogenics sold in specialized shops with names like "Conscious Dreams"; as long as users do not make trouble for others, they are ignored by the authorities. You can find out everything you ever wanted to know about dope and evolving legal issues at the Hash Marihuana Hemp Museum (p. 113). To speak to an official about drug use (and abuse), call city hall at 020/552-9111; the operator will direct you to the info office. You can also call the Dutch Ministry of Justice (Tel 070/370-7911; www.min just.nl). *Beware:* A lot of Amsterdammers are fed up with pot smokers and the scruffy image they've given the city. You should not light up on the street, in cafes, or on trams and trains (though enough dopey people do). Smoking weed in nonsmoking establishments—many now display a NO DRUGS sign, in English—will make you very unpopular, and you'll probably be asked to leave.

What the Jamaican flag really stands for... For one thing, the term "coffee shop" is never used nowadays by a normal cafe—often, though, the coffee sold in a "coffee shop" is surprisingly good, considering it's only an excuse for selling something else. You quickly figure out what that "something else" is and where to find it. Sometimes it's the smell. Sometimes it's the name (Homegrown Fantasy, Smokey, Mellow Yellow, Grasshopper, etc.). Or the clientele—bleary-eyed, touristy, and/or trendy. Sometimes it's the use of palm trees or fronds (marijuana leaves cannot be shown) or the Jamaican flag on the shop front. Most often it's the decor—modern, slick, the opposite of *gezellig* brown cafes—and the music—grunge, funk, whatever is currently in fashion—played very loud. Bear in mind when you light up that organized crime has bought into most smoking coffee shops—an estimated 90% of them—which are ideal for money laundering.

When smoke gets in your eyes... Tobacco and dope pollution pose a serious challenge in all public places—hotel rooms, restaurants, cafes, lobbies, shops, businesses, and even (though it's illegal) public transportation. It's tough to avoid cigarette addicts, but many big hotels now have nonsmoking rooms (or entire floors); at others, call ahead and request management to air the room and bring in clean blankets. Fast-food, vegetarian, and luxury and/or hotel restaurants often have nonsmoking sections (though they're not always respected). The only way to survive at cafes is to sit outside (often not an option, given the weather). Cafe de Jaren, one of the few spots with a nonsmoking room, got rid of it because managers were unable to keep smokers at bay. See the Accommodations and Dining chapters for hotels and restaurants with nonsmoking rooms and areas.

How to ride—and not lose—a Dutch bike... There are about 500,000 bicycles in this city of three-quarters of a million. You can rent one cheaply, for about 8€ ($10) a day, and you'll usually be asked to leave an ID card or passport as collateral. But bouncing over the cobbles on a typically rigid Amsterdam bike—known as a *stadfiets* (city bike), and, if it's really old, rigid, and full of character, an *omafiets* (granny bike)—some with back-pedal brakes, in the rain, is no picnic. To begin with, car, bike, and tram traffic is chaotic. Pavements are often slippery, uneven, and furrowed with tram tracks that seem expressly designed to trap tires. Cross them at an angle if you value your life (trams don't like to stop for clumsy bikers). Bikes do not have the right of way in Amsterdam. Never ride two abreast or without reflectors both fore and aft, or you'll risk getting a ticket (though the police have better things to do than go chasing pedal-bikers). Keep a plastic bag handy to cover your seat when you park your bike: It rains a lot in these parts.

Bike thieves are legion... Witness the cheap deals at flea markets and on the so-called "Fietsenbrug" or "Bridge of

PICKPOCKETING

Violent crime is rare in Amsterdam, but pickpocketing continues to be big business here, with thousands of cases reported annually. The police declare the last 3 months of each year as open season on foreign pickpockets, implementing special sting operations all over town that routinely net hundreds of professionals, all of them foreigners: South Americans, Africans, and East Europeans. The police warn known local pickpockets to stay home during such raids. Why? To break several international crime rings operating in Amsterdam and other European cities. (Local criminals are only too happy to oblige.) The prime locations for pickpocketing are the Dam, Damrak, Centraal Station, Schiphol Airport, and the Red-Light District. The techniques are varied: In one, the pickpocket slips his hand into your back pocket and pushes you violently forward behind the shoulders. Your wallet is swiped as you fall. Sometimes the culprits work in teams: One distracts you as the other removes your valuables. The police often set up information booths on the Dam to inform visitors of risks. Take note.

Stolen Bikes" (its real name is the Sleutelbrug, next to Amsterdam University on the edge of the Red-Light District), where you can pick up a stolen two-wheeler for as little as 10€ ($13). Locals readily admit that "after you've had your bike stolen five times, you too become a bike thief." They always use two locks, usually lug their bikes indoors, and offer up prayers to ward off their fellow thieves. Some hang their bikes off upper-story balconies, anti-black-bear style, others from the mooring cables of their houseboats. Avoid chaining your bike to a tree—you might harm the tree, and the Dutch, like most right-thinking folk, prefer not to harm trees. Under no circumstances should you use a finely tooled bike of the kind that would be perfect for riding through the Dutch country; that crowd of people around you has come not to admire your bike, but to steal it. If you rent from one of the dozens of bike-hire agencies in town, ask about their theft policy. All of them supply at least one lock; most supply two. Generally, if the bike is stolen it's your responsibility, and it'll cost you 100€ to 200€ ($125–$250). Only a few agencies offer theft insurance. Most hotels do not have a guarded bike-parking area.

On the other hand, there are plenty of bike lanes (marked with an obvious symbol or the word *fietspad*), and cycling is a wonderful way to see the city—just ask Queen Beatrix, an avid cyclist. Though she lives near The Hague, she sometimes pedals through Amsterdam. You can spot her by her beautiful, classic Dutch bike and discreet police escort (a posse of about 20, also on bikes).

How to whiz around town... Forget the Amsterdam Metro—it serves dreary suburbs you'll likely never see (unless you're heading to the ballpark, i.e., the Ajax soccer stadium, or the new Amsterdam Poort entertainment and shopping complex nearby). Most visitors don't realize, however, that trams (streetcars) provide a fun, fast, and cheap way to roller coaster around town, which makes them very popular with locals. Those in the know buy either a *strippenkaart* (punch as-you-go "strip tickets," which contain varying numbers of horizontal divisions, called strips, that are time-stamped when used), or a day, week, or month pass, all valid for any city transportation. (But note that the new national OV-chipkaart (chip card) is due to take over, beginning in 2006, with a transition period that runs until 2008 during which time both types of ticket will be valid.) Strip cards are sold at the GVB transit authority office—GVB Tickets & Info—in front of the main train station, at tobacco shops, post offices, VVV tourist info offices, and some train station ticket windows. The per-unit cost declines the more units you buy, so work out how many days you'll be in town and the distances (zones) you think you'll want to cover. A rough rule of thumb would be that if you're in town for just a few days, a 15-strip ticket should suffice; beyond that you should consider purchasing a 45-strip ticket (the maximum size possible). Of course, how often you use public transportation determines how fast you'll use up the strips. Tickets are also sold onboard the trams, but cost more per strip. There are 11 zones in greater Amsterdam; knowing exactly how many strips to punch is an art not easily mastered. A typical central-city ride (in Zone 5700 Centrum) is one zone, for which you punch two strips; two zones require three strips, and so forth (always one strip more than the total number of zones). Once stamped, the ticket is valid for at least 1 hour on trams, buses, and Metro lines.

If you have any doubts about the number of strips needed for your trip—even locals sometimes do—ask the driver or conductor to stamp your ticket for you and to tell you when you've reached your desired stop. Keep in mind that there are two types of trams in town: On those with conductors, drivers can't sell or stamp tickets, and they're trained to bark at you if you ask them to. A small sticker at the front of the tram will tell you to board at the rear if a conductor is present. But the best way to know where to jump on is simply to watch where the locals are lining up. Most trams have conductors, and on these the only available access door opens automatically; you board toward the rear (in the case of the oldest trams, at the rear) following arrowed indicators that point the way to the door. To board a tram that has no such arrowed indicators (and no conductor), push the button on the outside of the car beside any door. Getting off, you may need to push a button with an "open-door" graphic or the words *deur open*. Tram doors close automatically and they do it quite quickly, so don't hang around; you can place either a bag, or more riskily, a foot, in the opening so that the doors bounce back, or on older trams, tread on the bottom step to prevent the door from closing.

The system simply can be confusing. Even trams that do have conductors sometimes don't have them—God knows why—and intending passengers mill around in a state of confusion until somebody figures out what to do. It's made even more complicated by the fact that there are now several different models of tram, each model with a different layout of doors and conductor's station. If you read the previous advice carefully, you'll see it makes sense. But if it doesn't, just remember to go where the locals go to get on (and off). Don't sweat it: You'll get on—people manage it all the time.

How to avoid being eaten alive by mosquitoes in summer... Canals hold water. Mosquitoes breed in water. Amsterdam has a lot of canals. Therefore Amsterdam has a lot of...mosquito nets (*muskietennet*, in Dutch). In fact, mosquitoes can make a summer visit miserable. How to beat the bugs? Stay in a hotel with screens (ask before reserving), bring a net with you to drape around your bed, or buy one, if you need it, once you've arrived. Or launch a search-and-destroy mission before turning out the lights at night.

How to ice-skate like the locals... As Rembrandt might say if he were alive today, if you skate on thin ice, you can expect to sink through into dirty, cold canal water. You'll know when the time is right to strap on your gear and venture onto the icy waterways: When the locals migrate from easy pond skating in parks (Vondelpark and Oosterpark), squares (the Museum District), and at the Jaap Edenbaan outdoor skating rink, and begin zipping up and down the solid sections of the canals. They stay away from the edges and the areas around bridges, and so should you. If you're a serious skater, you're best off bringing your blades from home, or buying some new, since most Amsterdammers own their own—long-bladed *Noren* skates are favored—and skates are difficult to rent (see the Getting Outside chapter).

How to order and drink Dutch jenever (gin)...

Jenever Dutch gin—is a potentially lethal concoction made from molasses and juniper berries. This is the national spirit, in the widest sense of the term, and comes in three basic varieties: *jong* (young), *oud* (old), and *zeer oud* (senile). Sometimes it has delightful flavorings—*bittertje* (with angostura bitters), *citroenjenever* (lemony), or *bessenjenever* (sweetened with black-currant syrup). Belly up to the bar of a brown cafe or *proeflokaal* tap house (see the Nightlife & Cafes chapter for details), lean over your brimming, tulip-shaped glass, and slurp. When the glass is properly overflowing, it's called a *kamelenrug* (the one that broke the camel's back), or an *over het IJ-kijkertje* (view over the IJ channel, the narrow channel of water behind Centraal Station that, among other things, separates central Amsterdam from Amsterdam-Noord). The hip, if generic, way to ask for one is a *borrel* (a shot). There's a whole vocabulary to accompany *jenever: recht op neer* (straight up), *pikketenussie* (something akin to "cheers"), and half a dozen other unpronounceable (and probably obscene) terms. Many locals knock back their booze with a beer chaser, called a *kopstoot,* literally "a blow to the head." Fitting. When it comes to *jenever,* as with many other products— beer, cheese, mineral water, chocolates—many Dutch people sneakingly prefer artisanal Belgian brands to their own mass-produced champs.

How to navigate the gay capital of Europe...

Admittedly, "Gay Amsterdam" doesn't ring quite as poetically as "Gai Paris," but this is where the action is. Homosexuality has been legal here since 1811, and the age of consent (since 1971) is a low 16. In 1987 the city erected the world's first memorial to gays and lesbians persecuted by the Nazis, the so-called Homomonument, three rose-colored granite triangles spilling across the small square behind Westerkerk church and into the waters of the Keizersgracht canal. It has since become a rallying point for the gay community. Scores of clubs, bars, restaurants, and hotels all over town cater to every imaginable taste and tendency (though most are more oriented toward gay men, as opposed to lesbians). Gays are thoroughly integrated into business, journalism, politics, and the arts in Amsterdam; nonetheless, four largely gay districts exist.

> ### The Lost Art of Beer Drinking
> Today's Amsterdammers are no more than a pale shadow of their esteemed ancestors when it comes to quaffing beer. In 1613 there were 518 taverns in the city, one for every 200 or so inhabitants. Today the ratio has slipped to one per 725. It seems that the 17th century was a golden age in more senses than one.

Reguliersdwarsstraat, between Rembrandtplein and Koningsplein, and Amstel, on the south riverbank between Vijzelstraat and the Blauwbrug (the Blue Bridge, over the Amstel), attract a young, hip crowd. Warmoesstraat, which traverses the Red-Light District on its western edge, draws more of a leather, S&M, and cling-wrap-jeans bunch. Kerkstraat, between Leidsegracht and Vijzelstraat, is tame, and appeals to quieter, older gays.

A lot of gay venues welcome straights, and some are among the city's liveliest. Local lesbians have a limited club scene; mostly, they hang out in cafes and at ad hoc all-night parties listed in local magazines (Amsterdam *Day by Day* and *Gay & Night Magazine* are published in English). Lesbian (and gay/lesbian) bars, cafes, and discos like **Café Saarein II** (Elandsstraat 119; Tel 020/623-4901), **You II** (Amstel 178; Tel 020/421-0900), and **GETTO** (Warmoesstraat 51; Tel 020/421-5151), or bookshops like **Xantippe** (Prinsengracht 290; Tel 020/623-5854) and **Vrolijk** (Paleisstraat 135; Tel 020/623-5142; www.vrolijk.nl) also provide fliers advertising these parties. All the latest gay info is available at www.gayamsterdam.com or www.switch board.nl. (See the Accommodations, Nightlife & Cafes, and Hotlines & Other Basics chapters for more on gay Amsterdam.)

What passes for an age of consent... Tolerance and ambiguity blend in the question of the age of consent for both heterosexual and homosexual intercourse. Legally, it is 16. However, a difficult-to-interpret law, passed in December 1991, makes nonviolent sexual acts among persons ages 12 to 16 an affair to be dealt with by parents. If complaints are made by either the children or parents, the case can be referred to the Council of Youth Protection or to the police. Such complaints can be filed for up to 12 years after the alleged act. The law was intended to allow cases of sex among teenagers of about the same age to be resolved outside the legal system and was in no way intended to encourage sex between adults and children. Nonetheless, the result has been that child prostitutes and "rent-a-boy" agencies continue to do business.

How to greet (or take leave of) an Amsterdammer...

When you meet locals for the first time and are introduced, you shake hands. Thereafter no more handshaking is expected until you meet up again after a considerable period of separation. With their constant clasps and kisses, the French and (especially) Italians seem to embarrass the Dutch. Ditto Americans with their countless hearty handshakes. In Amsterdam, once you've made friends, you exchange three pecks (really just a smacking of the lips) on the cheeks. The proper order is left-right-left. Three times. Never two or four. Men do this with women; women with men; women with women; but not often men with men, unless they are very good friends, or gay (or Italian).

> **Don't Say "Go"**
> Gogh is not pronounced Go, as many Americans incorrectly say it, but like Khokh (the "kh" sound is like "ch" in the Scottish pronunciation of "loch"—not "lock"). If you can pronounce van Gogh (Fan Khokh) correctly, you should have no problem with Schiphol (Skhip-ol), Scheveningen (Skheveningen), and 's-Gravenhage (ss-Khraven-hakhe), the correct full name for Den Haag/The Hague.

ACCOMM

Do Not
Disturb

ODATIONS

Basic Stuff

Parts of Amsterdam may be renewing, modernizing, trendifying, and gentrifying, but many of its hotels retain the character of earlier epochs. In Amsterdam hotels, don't mind the labyrinthine corridors and the lace-draped window that looks onto a wall. Call it *gezellig*, i.e., cozy. The Dutch obsession with coziness applies doubly to hotels in Amsterdam. Ask Amsterdammers what counts in a hotel and you're likely to hear them say "atmosphere" or "character," rather than "luxury," "comfort," or "convenience." A location on one of the Golden Age canal sides doesn't hurt either, and in that case, atmosphere and character are just about guaranteed. What locals might consider a great room can be cramped, cluttered, nearly inaccessible, and impregnated with the smell of stale tobacco, so long as it affords a taste of the two primarily desirable attributes noted above and doesn't disappoint when it comes to value. Happily, the Dutch are also a nation of neatniks, and, like the Swiss, worship efficiency. So, many Amsterdam hotels are homey, squeaky clean, and professionally run.

The city has a startling capacity to accommodate all tastes; you'll be delighted to discover hotels sleazy and sublime, catering to backpackers, gays, philosophers, musicians, S&M aficionados, dope smokers, and cyclists. If Dutch "charm" doesn't come high on your list, most international chain hotels are also here, as well as the home-grown AMS and what survives locally of the Golden Tulip group (most of its hotels were transferred to the Spanish-based NH Hotels chain, which seems to have somehow taken some of the class out of many of the hotels they took over). Amsterdam has two super-luxury hotels—the **Amstel Inter-Continental Amsterdam** and the **Grand Sofitel Demeure Amsterdam**—that rank among Europe's best, plus a constellation of bona fide charmers like the **Ambassade, Dylan,** and the **Hotel de l'Europe.**

Amsterdam's canal-house hotels—centuries-old, converted private homes facing the capital's 100-plus waterways—are the most sought-after properties. Most are small, *gezellig,* family-run gems. Only a few, such as **Ambassade** and **Estheréa,** have elevators, and the staircases in many are like steep ship gangways, leading to rooms where average Americans bump their heads and sleep with their feet hanging off the beds (they later will surely appreciate Abraham Lincoln's rueful remark, after spending a night in a cramped U.S. Navy ship's bunk, that "You can't put a long blade into a short scabbard"), and larger-than-average Americans may need to breathe in or turn sideways to get through the door. Don't forget that there are dozens of leafy gardens and courtyards in town; often a room overlooking one of these, on the back side of a canal house or other hotel, is preferable to a potentially noisy canal-side room with a view.

Though bed-and-breakfasts are not common in Amsterdam, almost all one-, two-, and three-star hotels include in the room price a copious Dutch buffet breakfast of ham, cheeses, boiled eggs, rolls, butter, jam, croissants, and fruit juices (though in some downscale establishments what you'll actually get are a few sorry-looking, curled-up-at-the-edges slices of cheese, assorted cold cuts of indeterminate provenance, and eggs boiled hard enough to sink an enemy submarine). Some four-star and almost all five-star hotels charge extra—up to 30€ ($35) for continental breakfasts, and more for a Dutch or American breakfast.

Nonsmoking rooms are few and far between in Amsterdam, found primarily in luxury and business establishments, though even these sometimes smell of smoke, since the Dutch simply ignore smoking prohibitions. Be aware that in some Dutch hotels, especially family-run operations, double rooms could have twin beds pushed together. Calvin would approve.

Winning the Reservations Game

Most of the hotels listed here have been inspected and rated by the Benelux Hotel Classification system, which assigns them stars—not according to quality, but simply according to the number of rooms and the facilities provided (such as elevator, garage, and special services).

But Amsterdam is an expensive city, and many of those beds are pricey (around 40% are in four- or five-star establishments). This overabundance at the high-end continues to ramp up competition, bringing prices down for travelers who know to ask for a favorable room rate: No one pays "rack rates" (standard list prices) anymore for upper-end rooms, and because of this continuing price war, you can often get a five-star room for the list price of a four-star room, or a four-star room for the price of a three-star. However, tourist-class and budget hotels are harder to crack, especially those in canal houses, which are very popular.

The best approach is to watch for offers on the hotel's own website; or call, fax, or e-mail several hotels, ask what their standard rates are, then ask for the corporate rate, the weekend rate, the special discount rate, the long-stay rate, the winter (and bad-weather) rate (which ought to be available 9 months of the year), the advance-booking rate, and any other rate you can think of. There's almost always a better rate available (except during the Christmas and New Year's holidays and the last week of April, when the queen's official birthday celebrations occur) than the first one you were quoted. The Dutch are a nation of traders and are used to dickering. Book as far ahead as possible: The prospect of your business can soften up even the toughest managers, and you should also be able to request the kind of room you prefer. The longer your proposed stay, the more leverage you have. Visitors sometimes negotiate a room rate based on a lengthy stay—of a week or more—then switch gears and convince the hotel to apply that rate to their actual (shorter) stay. Dutch hoteliers whine and complain about such underhanded methods, but use them themselves when traveling.

Reserving through a travel agent in your home country will probably get you a good rate, too, since many hotels belong to international reservations systems (Accor, Bilderberg, Carlton, CIGA, Concorde, Golden Tulip International BV, Hilton, Holiday Inn, Mercure, NH Hotels, Swissôtel, Utell International, and so forth). The various branches of the **Amsterdam Tourist Office** (called the VVV—pronounced *fay-fay-fay*) will book rooms for you at the last minute, but you must go in person to one of their offices and pay a fee of about 3€ ($3.75) per person (later deducted from your hotel bill). The main VVV offices are inside Centraal Station and opposite it at Stationsplein 10 (Tel 0900/400-4040; .55€ (69¢) per minute; www. amsterdamtourist.nl, www.visitamsterdam.com, and www. holland.com). Branch offices are at Leidseplein 1 (corner of Leidsestraat), Stadionplein, and the main arrivals hall at Schiphol Airport (marked HOLLAND TOURIST INFORMATION). A further possibility for same-day reservations is the **Holland Tourist Information Office** located at Damrak 35, in central Amsterdam, or **Hotel Bookings,** a private website at www. bookings.nl. Internet bookings on the hotels' own websites usually command a discount.

Is There a Right Address in Amsterdam?

It depends entirely upon what you're looking for. Of the dozen or so distinct neighborhoods within the A10 beltway, which separates Amsterdam from the suburbs, none is bad or dangerous, but not all are desirable, and those that *are* desirable may be so for different reasons.

The city's core, inside the Singelgracht canal, is, unsurprisingly, called the Centrum. Fanning out from it in a wide semicircle are, counterclockwise, the Oud West (Old West), Oud Zuid (Old South) and its multiethnic subdivision De Pijp (The Pipe), and Oost (East); beyond the Old South is Nieuw Zuid (New South). Distances are short: A fast walker can cross from Centraal Station to the New South in an hour and a quarter, a tram or taxi takes 15 to 20 minutes.

The Centrum, the biggest and most interesting district, is really a mosaic of neighborhoods. If you don't mind noisy sex-tourism crowds (both gay and straight), winking red neon lights, and hash or grass smoke wafting from the dozens of smoking coffee shops straight into your room, check out the several top hotels on the edge of the **Red-Light District,** a few hundred yards from the train station, abutting the Dam and the main shopping streets Rokin, Damrak, and Kalverstraat. Despite its reputation for prostitution, drug dealing, and petty crime, this area is perfectly safe if you know how to navigate it (see p. 11 in the You Probably Didn't Know chapter), and in any case, all the upscale hotels here are beyond the carefully contained sleaze zone. And, from these hotels, you can walk in minutes to anywhere in the center of town.

Just west of the Red-Light District, and still in the heart of the Centrum, is a boomerang-shaped neighborhood sometimes referred to as the **Dam** or **Spui.** Stretching from Centraal Station to the flower market at Muntplein, it contains a maze of tiny alleys, several appealing squares, and a handful of the city's best restaurants, spread along Spuistraat. However, the neighborhood's main arteries—Damrak, Rokin, and Nieuwezijds Voorburgwal—are noisy, with heavy tram traffic and crowds of pedestrians. Most of the canals here have been covered over; the exception is the Singel, originally the medieval city's moat, along which you'll see several fine hotels.

Beyond the Singel is the celebrated **Grachtengordel** neighborhood, clustering around three semicircular canals—Herengracht, Keizersgracht, and Prinsengracht—built in Amsterdam's 17th-century Golden Age. "Grachtengordel" in Dutch has also come to mean "chic," "plugged-in," "moneyed," etc., and here you'll find tony restaurants and cafes, boutiques for the megabucks crowd, and the antiques dealers' quarter on Nieuwe Spiegelstraat (see the Shopping chapter). A location here, in the northern sector of the canal ring, is great for exploring the adjacent quirky Jordaan neighborhood; a place in the middle of the Jordaan puts you within striking distance of the big museums and one of the city's two liveliest squares, Leidseplein. At the southern and eastern ends of the curve, you'll be close to the second of the liveliest squares, Rembrandtplein, and to the Amstel River, the flea market on Waterlooplein, and the adjacent Muziektheater opera and dance venue. You may have to book far in advance to get into Grachtengordel hotels, but it's worth it.

Still within the Centrum, on the district's western edge, is the **Jordaan,** a wonderful part of town with narrow streets and narrower buildings; quiet, shady canals; and scads of one-of-a-kind boutiques, cafes, and neighborhood restaurants. Unfortunately, there are only a few hotels here, but these are moderately priced, decent properties.

The prosperous **Old South** neighborhood, beyond the Singelgracht, is looking better all the time, especially if you want quiet nights. The "big three" museums—the Rijksmuseum, Van Gogh Museum, and the modern art Stedelijk Museum (the Stedelijk has rehoused to a location near Centraal Station until 2008)—are here, as well as the handsome Vondelpark, a great place to bike, jog, rollerblade, or picnic. Here, there are quiet streets and turn-of-the-20th-century architecture, plus great shopping, but it becomes hard to wander the central city neighborhoods' marvelous streets at night—one of the great joys of staying in Amsterdam—because the neighborhood is a bit far away. The same (and more so) applies to the **New South,** an even more prosperous and farther-flung neighborhood dotted with interesting Amsterdam School architecture. The Hilton is here, as well as a few four-star places strung along Apollolaan. If you stay in the New South you'll have to rely on trams and taxis to get around. But if easy access to the airport and countryside are your priorities, then go for it.

The Lowdown

In search of canal-house coziness... Just because a building overlooks a canal doesn't mean it's a canal house, or there would be hundreds in Amsterdam. True canal-house hotels occupy old private residences—usually from the 17th or 18th centuries—and have canal-side rooms with views. A few bare-bones canal houses have steep stairs, no elevators, and no facilities to speak of. Still, these are only-in-Amsterdam hotels, which is why visitors put up with their inconvenience. A beer can's throw from Rembrandtplein, popular **Seven Bridges** is a small, intimate perch with affable owners, overlooking one of Amsterdam's most picturesque waterways. Luxuriate amid the comfy old furnishings, the houseplants, and views (ask for a canal-side room on an upper floor—not in the attic or the basement)—but be prepared for slightly inflated prices. The flower market, a few blocks away, seems to have opened an annex in the lobby of **Agora,** an upscale two-star in a 1735 house decorated with Persian throw rugs, feathery armchairs, and scattered antiques. A pocket-sized back garden adds to the charm. Next door at the **Waterfront,** owner Willem Van der Ham has totally remodeled and upgraded, with mahogany furniture, bay windows, thick carpets, and drapes—but it's still two stars and affordable.

At **Amsterdam Wiechmann,** visitors choose between *gezellig,* antiques-filled canal-side doubles or less expensive and more anonymous modern rooms. This narrow canal house has a memorable lobby, with delftware hanging on the walls and the kind of Oriental carpets you see draped over tables in many of Amsterdam's old-fashioned brown cafes. The breakfast room looks like a greenhouse, and there's a suitably snug bar and lounge. The modest **Hegra's** most distinctive feature may well be its step-gable facade; it sure isn't the dull, though tidy, decor or stern staff. The low price and handy central location, however, may make you very forgiving. Pricier but spanking new and full of Calvinistic minimalist charm is **'t Hotel,** a three-star overlooking lovely Leliegracht.

Higher-end canal houses mix charm with practical touches like elevators, bars, and restaurants, though you still shouldn't expect perks like pools, fully equipped health centers, or convention facilities. Near Westerkerk, the four-star **Toren** has a 17th-century marble entrance hall and a lovely breakfast room with a painted, molded ceiling, and some of its doubles come into the moderately priced category. Canal-side rooms have nice views, but consider instead a room looking onto the attractive garden. There are antiques, fireplaces, and cozy public areas. **Estheréa,** a comfy four-star, has cozy rooms with pastel colors and quirky light fixtures. **Ambassade** has museum-quality antiques, a library of books by author-guests, and a heady location near the famous Golden Bend—locals call this hotel the "Mini Amstel" (see "The grande dames," below) because it offers luxury and character: marble bathrooms, prints and oils by minor Dutch masters, crystal chandeliers, and antique armchairs. The **Sheraton Hotel Pulitzer,** sprawling along Prinsengracht and dotted with hidden gardens and courtyards, is downright opulent, in a predictably plush corporate style that's totally un-*gezellig*.

For tourists who want clogs, windmills, and tulips... If gawking at Amsterdam from a tour bus suits you, book rooms at the **NH Grand Hotel Krasnapolsky.** Commonly known as the "Kras'" (can a nickname tell all?—although it's pronounced *kraz*), this Victorian grande dame saw its heyday 100 years ago; the Polish tailor-turned-hotelier who founded it started out in 1866 with the Wintertuin (Winter Garden) restaurant and went on to build a grand hotel around it. The Krasnapolsky now fills several city blocks, drawing package sightseers and conventioneers to its cavernous interior, which has been remodeled countless times. Visitors on whirlwind tours of windmills and tulip fields will like the comfortable rooms and facilities at the **NH Barbizon Palace**—the rooms are basically decorated in cookie-cutter traditional, though some have exposed oak rafters. The over-the-top faux marble colonnade in the lobby looks like it was lifted from a Cinecittà sandals-and-toga movie set (*Hercules Against Rome*, perhaps). Across the center of town, at the immense Marriott-owned **Renaissance Amsterdam,** there's plenty of space to stow souvenirs in the forgettable rooms and to break in your clogs at the Boston Club, a place business types tend to like.

For enemies of clogs, windmills, and tulips... There's not even room to park tour buses in front of the **Ambassade,** a canal-house hotel that occupies 12 17th-century properties on the handsome Herengracht. The discreet, anonymous owner collects antiques, and it shows in the total lack of kitsch. Each room is different, and that appeals to the literary crowd usually found here (many Dutch publishers and agents book rooms here for their star writers—there's now a charming author-guest library on the ground floor). Crystal chandeliers and enormous rooms make you feel like a pearl in an oyster; a few even have canopy beds. Savvy business travelers and other well-heeled guests stay at the **Estheréa,** an upscale canal-house hotel with a great location overlooking the Singel (and just a few doors along from the platinum-card flophouse Yab Yum described on p. 199). Between gazing from your window at surrounding mansions and chatting up your hosts, a friendly family that counts several generations of owners of this hotel, you'll feel more like an Amsterdam resident here than a tourist. The lobby of **'t Hotel,** a canal-house hotel, doubles as an antiques shop. The **Toren,** a small, luxurious four-star, has antiques, a garden, and an exclusive atmosphere. Lovers of spare luxury—along with chic black decor and dress, and more males with pony tails than you'd find on a Kentucky stud farm—will want to check out the **Dylan** (formerly Blakes), with its garden court and top-rated restaurant. A few steps down the designer-price scale, but still with a reasonable claim to distinction, is the **ArenA,** in a 19th century former orphanage. The interior has been redone by a bunch of up-and-possibly-coming young Dutch designers. At the **Lloyd,** overlooking the old—and redeveloped—steamship docks in the Eastern Harbor, just about every room has a different shape, style, and modern decor. Visit the attic library and the Culturele Ambassade art center, and check out the modern art works scattered around.

The grande dames... Back in 1866, when the **NH Grand Hotel Krasnapolsky** opened for business, things like heated winter terraces, modern plumbing, central heating, and electric lights were unknown. The Kras was the first in Amsterdam in all these departments and was the most fashionable place in town. Time hasn't stood still: Much of the charming decor of old is gone—though the Winter Garden, one of the hotel's restaurants, a classy 19th–century–type place, is still going strong—and the location on the rather tacky Dam isn't what it used to be, even if the Royal Palace is no more than an easy lob of a crown across the way. The Victorian gentry who frequented the Kras would probably go elsewhere today, yet there's a bit of the grande dame left, especially off season, when the Winter Garden is a joy and there are no tulips in bloom to attract the bus crowds. In an earlier incarnation, the **Amstel Inter-Continental Amsterdam** (sans "Inter-Continental") was the Krasnapolsky's direct rival, opening a year later in 1867. The Amstel is in a class all its own, with sky-high prices to match. Liveried doormen flank the marble grand hall, and if you're on a shopping spree, diamonds are available at the hotel's boutique. Dutch royals have staged family celebrations in the opulent *Spiegelzaal* (Mirror Room), and the list of celeb guests is long.

The **Hotel de l'Europe,** built in 1896, was the top hotel in town for most of the 20th century. Haughtily perched over the river and Muntplein, it looks much as it probably did the day it opened. Despite all the usual trappings of luxury—the faux Empire furniture, thick carpets, molded plaster decorations, and doorman with epaulets and striped trousers—it remains behind the Amstel and the **Grand Sofitel Demeure Amsterdam.** Though the Grand itself is new, it boasts a historic site—it started out as the 15th-century convent of St. Cecilia, that was captured as a prize by the Amsterdam Admiralty after the Protestant take-over, and served as city hall until 1992. (Queen Beatrix and the late Prince Claus were married upstairs in 1966.) Planted on two beautiful courtyards just south of the Red-Light District, this newest of the grand hotels offers muted colors and understated luxury.

In search of the indefinable *gezelligheid*... In a city where coziness means floral arrangements, knickknacks, antique furniture, grandfather clocks, and pianos (baby grands are best), a young Irish couple runs the cozy **Canal House,** occupying five old houses on (and behind) one of the city's prettiest canals. It wins hands-down in most *gezelligheid* categories. Quiet, quaint, and cute are the operative words. Guests swoon over the memorable breakfast room with its parquet floors, molded plaster ceilings, and baby grand piano. Luckily, back rooms are just as snug, and even quieter. The **Washington**'s armchairs, polished parquet floors, red runners, and carved banister exude Edwardian comfort. It's the kind of seriously quiet place where you nod and whisper to your fellow guests, as classical music plays softly in the background: The Concertgebouw auditorium (Amsterdam's premier venue for classical music) is nearby and most guests are musicians or music-lovers. The book-lined salon and vaguely colonial terrace of **De Filosoof**—a one-of-a-kind hotel with philosophy as a theme (one of the co-owners, Ida Jongsma, is a former high school philosophy teacher)—are quintessentially cozy, though some of the rooms are anything but (the Heidegger Room is thoroughly black). The Aristotle Room has a classical pediment; the Plato Room is black and white, with *trompe l'oeil* decorations; and so forth. At the **Toren,** red bedspreads and heavy fabrics, the roaring fireplaces, and the twinkling chandeliers provide a taste of cozy-luxe *gezellig*, with class.

Taking care of business... If you're looking for a big, American-style hotel, with big, no-nonsense rooms and all the business facilities you'll need, try the **Renaissance Amsterdam** (a Marriott hotel). In addition to its seven-story atrium lobby and tidy theme-decor rooms (Scandinavian, Oriental, Old Dutch, Art Deco), the **Radisson SAS Hotel Amsterdam** has a business and conference center in its south building. You may not even have to leave your comfortable room at the **NH Barbizon Palace,** right across from Centraal Station: Telephones come with computer interfaces, and more technology is available at the front desk. Then, when working hours are over, you can amble downstairs to the lounge—though a bit starchy, it's not bad at all if you fancy relaxing with a book by a crackling fire in winter. If you don't need the apparatus of a big hotel, look into the practical, family-run **Estheréa,** which draws a mix of discreet businesspeople and tolerably well-heeled families. The hotel overlooks the Singel, between the Dam and the flower market, and offers nice canal views and free Internet access. If you want to venture off the buttoned-down track, stay at **Bilderberg Hotel Jan Luyken,** a quietly confident Museum District four-star in a Dutch Art Nouveau building near the Rijksmuseum, Van Gogh Museum, and modern art museum, the Stedelijk Museum. It's in a corporate "boutique-design" theme, with some rooms that are none too large, and attracts a midlevel business clientele.

For travelers with old money... The owner of the extraordinary three-star **Ambassade** knows that old-money travelers hate to spend more than they have to. For the price of a closet at the five-star competition, you can get a suite with a sitting room and two bedrooms here. Half the museums in town would love to get hold of the china and grandfather clocks in the hotel's common areas. If money's no object, then by all means settle into the **Grand Sofitel Demeure Amsterdam.** Keen to have an instant pedigree, this recently founded hotel quietly and rather disingenuously touts the building's 600-year history (in fact, much of the complex dates to the early 1900s). The desk staff dress and behave like good Dutch ladies and gentlemen, whispering what others shout. Black-and-gray marble floors grace the vaulted lobby, and the rooms feature a subdued palette of salmon, teal, and saffron. Guests take tea (or more interesting drinks) in a leafy inner courtyard and meals at Café Roux, the pricey brainchild of restaurateur Albert Roux of London's famous Le Gavroche. The **Amstel Inter-Continental Amsterdam,** with its 1867 birth date and megabucks pedigree, modestly calls itself "a favorite with cosmopolitan society—from royalty and the aristocracy to luminaries in the arts and international affairs." Indeed—as long as they have fat wallets. If you're worried about denting the old trust fund, instead check out the **Hotel de l'Europe,** little changed since its 1896 birth. Less sumptuous than either the Amstel or the Grand, this remodeled oldster will still be sufficiently coddling (and clean).

For travelers with new money... The **Amstel Inter-Continental Amsterdam** has just enough old-school cachet to attract both Golden Age spenders and the aggressively nouveau. Rock stars and groupies with euros to burn monopolize the palatial health club and pool. Water taxis drop shiploads of crocodile bags on the private dock, and deeply tanned torsos draped in gold chains and diamonds are spotted in midwinter in the magnificent arcaded lobby. Some guests probably wish the pianist in the swank La Rive restaurant would stop with the classical stuff already and play "New York, New York," "Volare," or anything less stiff. The endless roster of glitzy visitors is the talk of the town (Red Hot Chili Peppers, Janet Jackson, Madonna, Jagger, Spielberg...). Naturally, a chauffeured Rolls-Royce and historic saloon boat are at your disposal.

The immense **NH Grand Hotel Krasnapolsky** is especially popular if you want to show the locals that you own (or have rented) a large luxury car and are going to drive through Amsterdam despite traffic restrictions, right into the garage at the Kras, at the center of the universe on the Dam. The landmark Dutch Art Nouveau **Amsterdam American,** on lively Leidseplein, likes to call itself "the entertainment hotel" because minor rock stars and groupies who can't quite manage the Amstel (though still manage to be mildly obnoxious) book spacious rooms here (redone in mock Art Deco, many have views over Leidse-plein or the Singelgracht canal). Guests here pose in the famous Bar Américain (p. 207), feeling wonderful when the bartender remembers their names and favorite drinks. (He remembers everyone's name and favorite drink.) The hip new-rich are fighting over the 20-odd rooms of super-luxe **Dylan,** in a 17th-century former theater/almshouse/lawyers' office converted into a showcase for British designer Anouska Hempel's megabuck Asian-spartan-look rooms (mostly black). And if you've got not very much new money, try the **ArenA.** The exterior of this ex–19th-century orphanage bears a passing resemblance to Dracula's castle, but the interior proves they really knew how to do an orphanage in those days. Monumental marble staircases, cast-iron banisters, stained-glass windows, marble columns, original murals—all have been faithfully restored. The rambling spaces where the dormitories once were now house stylish doubles and twins. Spare modern rooms, some sporting timber roof beams and wooden floors, line long, high-ceilinged corridors on two floors. Or go out on a limb at the **Lloyd Hotel**, which opened in 2004 on the waterfront redevelopment zone of the old steamship docks east of Centraal Station. The Lloyd has returned to the city hotel scene after a long absence and a colorful history. Originally an emigrants' hotel, it opened in 1921 and closed in 1935. You'll stay here in a standout Amsterdam School of Architecture building that from 1940 to 1999 served as a prison, then a house of corrections for young offenders, then a studio space for hard-up artists. Since then it has been thoroughly renovated—you'll scarcely believe you're lodging in a former prison. The two restaurants aim to make it cool to dine in a hotel: Snel is fast, affordable, and open 24/7; Sloom is leisurely and expensive, and you can order whatever you feel like, and the kitchen will aim to cook it.

Dowdy but lovable... Even the name sounds nice and sweet. **Acacia.** It's the kind of place where first-time travelers meet gentle, middle-age folks wearing sandals and white socks. Owners Hans and Marlene van Vliet have kids and like people, and their little, triangle-shaped Jordaan hotel is simple and clean. The staircase is as steep as they come (naturally there's no elevator). The **Amsterdam Wiechmann,** a narrow canal-house hotel, has too much character to be prim, but the lady at the desk will protect you from undesired elements: "No one not registered is allowed in the rooms," she booms. The **Bridge** has a grand lobby but plain-Jane rooms and a mousy-friendly staff. The

Owl, a pleasant, family-run three-star hotel with two-star prices, just one block from Vondelpark on a quiet residential street, is the kind of place where you might run into birdish maiden aunts who've brought their nieces up from the provinces. With a pastel color scheme, the no-nonsense, summery style matches the garden setting. Tidy **Van Onna** is a cheap one-star on peaceful Bloemgracht canal in the Jordaan. All rooms are furnished in a modern but comfortable style; the bathrooms are squeaky-clean but eccentric: The shower heads stick out over the toilets and drain in the middle of the floor. At the **Van Ostade Bicycle Hotel,** a little hotel wedged into a narrow, early-1900s building in the blue-collar De Pijp neighborhood, guests are encouraged to pedal their days away sightseeing. A bike hangs from the facade of the hotel, and its owners, Jos and Clemens, are keen cyclists and will rent you two-wheelers for about 5€ ($5.75) a day (fractionally cheaper than commercial rates). Renovated in 1995, the place is clean both literally and figuratively: A NO DRUGS sign adorns the front door.

For those who hate surprises... If you're used to the plush, overstuffed, thick-carpeted brand of luxury found at the Sheraton hotels worldwide, you'll be delighted by the **Sheraton Hotel Pulitzer.** Occupying 24 old canal houses in the shadow of Westerkerk, this luxury hotel has a warren of inner gardens and courtyards, some with a private entrance on one of the canals. The **Radisson SAS Hotel Amsterdam,** in Old Amsterdam south of the Red-Light District, offers typical SAS theme rooms—choose between faux Scandinavian, old Dutch, Oriental, or Art Deco. There's a pleasant enough restaurant (the De Palmboom Brasserie), a brown cafe (the Pastorie Bar, set in a transplanted 18th-century landmark vicarage), and a glassed-in atrium lobby with a fountain. The **NH Schiller,** a seven-story, turn-of-the-20th-century property overlooking Rembrandtplein, remains a monument to its original owner, Fritz Schiller, a slightly mad amateur painter whose kitschy landscapes adorn the lobby, cafe, and rooms to this day. A certain amount of character remains in the comfy leather armchairs and sofas in the vaulted lobby and in the wood-paneled, crepuscular Cafe Schiller, once a cutting-edge literary hangout but now a comfortable and original hideout for friendly locals.

Luscious love nests... The hushed, antiques-filled salons, library, and canal-view rooms of the **Ambassade,** on the Herengracht's Golden Bend, are ideal for soulful yearnings. Middle-age and older romantics who don't make noise when making love will find a cozy, antique-feathered nest at **Canal House,** overlooking Keizersgracht, almost next door to Westerkerk. If you always wanted to float that romantic proposal but didn't know how, you can rent a cute little houseboat covered with flowers from the **Acacia,** in the supremely romantic Jordaan, and make love afloat on the leafy Lijnbaansgracht. Gays who prefer a mixed clientele, lots of green plants, and comfy old furniture favor **Seven Bridges,** a tiny canal-house hotel near Rembrandtplein. The **Toren,** a plush four-star with red bedspreads, antiques, fireplaces, and crystal chandeliers, also has a pocket-sized garden for sniffing roses and tiptoeing through tulips. Westerkerk is nearby, in case you want to tie the knot before (or after) parting the thick curtains here. The marble entrance hall is nearly 400 years old, and if the breakfast room with the molded, painted ceiling ain't romantic, nothing is ("Hey, aren't those cupids flying around up there?").

Rooms with a view... There are no skyscrapers or tall buildings in central Amsterdam, and the only high-rise hotels are so far out that the scenery isn't worth seeing. This is a flat city of intimate, keyhole views—a tree lined bend in a canal, a stretch of wide river—rather than Empire State Building–style oohs and ahs. The **Amstel Inter-Continental Amsterdam** luxuriates on the east bank of the Amstel River, just south of the old locks that regulate the flow of water through the city's canals, and from the rooms' French windows, guests have a panorama of river traffic, city lights, and drawbridges. The **Hotel de l'Europe** also overlooks the Amstel River and some rooms have loveseat-size riverside balconies—make sure you get one so you can watch the trams slink by and the private boats pull up to the hotel's dock. The **Seven Bridges,** a small canal-house hotel, gets a special mention because it overlooks Reguliersgracht, one of the city's prettiest waterways; you'll actually get 15 bridges at a glimpse, but who's counting? Another upscale canal house, **Estheréa,** has several beautifully redecorated rooms with large windows three-abreast looking out at gorgeous Singel houses and mansions, while the **Ambassade** does much the same over the Herengracht or Singel. The most expensive rooms at the **Lloyd** have views of the Eastern Harbor—which is not exactly to die for but is not bad either—or of a specially designed interior (or both).

Home away from home... You can count the actual B&Bs in town on the fingers of one hand, though simple Dutch hotels practically qualify as B&Bs because breakfast bread, ham, and cheese are generally included in the price of the room. A small guesthouse-residence does, however, fit the bill. The simply named but sumptuous **Nr 40** doesn't call itself a B&B, but functions like one. Affable owner Tony van der Veen converted the 1893 Herenhuis mansion, one block from the northern edge of Vondelpark's panhandle, into four full-service studio apartments, rentable by the day, week, or longer. Each room has a minibar, fax/answering machine, and stereo. Chic designer furniture mixes with antiques. And the number is no longer quite accurate, since an expansion into the next-door house (number 38) added two large, split-level one-bedroom apartments with a shared garden.

Convention hotels with flair... The **NH Barbizon Palace** is a city within a city, including a conference center in the startlingly handsome, 15th-century St. Olof's chapel across the street, reached via a tunnel. Unconventional conventioneers will be delighted to know that the Red-Light District and S&M/gay Warmoesstraat (a kind of sleazyish Red-Light District street with a few establishments that raise the tone) are a block away (more conventional ones will want to steer clear), and though it's sanitized, the hotel's Hudson's Terrace is an improvement on the kind of coffee shop found in most convention hotels. The **Renaissance Amsterdam** also has a former church now used as a convention center (is business a religion around here, or what?): the circular, 17th-century domed Lutheran Koepelkerk, the only wholly round building in town. A Marriott property, this thoroughly American-style complex is shoehorned into a series of converted warehouses and other buildings just off the Singel, near Centraal Station. Saying that it has charm would be stretching it—this is a business hotel, after all, but Marriott has redecorated with coziness (and red) as a theme, and quirky architecture adds interest.

To relive the Golden Age... If you want to know what the canal house of a wealthy Netherlands family probably looked like circa the late 1700s, book a room at **Ambassade,** just off Herengracht's snooty Golden Bend. Antiques dealers' hands tremble when they spot the 1750 grandfather clock by celebrated clockmaker Jan Theo van Kempen in the salon (little ships dance on the waves as the seconds tick by). A china cabinet displays delftware and other valuable pieces that would make handsome souvenirs, if only you could convince the hotel's owner, a collector, to part with them.

In search of the perfect pool... Amsterdam is not a city for hotel-bound sports fanatics. Most buildings are centuries old, and space is at a premium, so most hotels simply don't have room for fitness centers and pools. The pool at the **Amstel Inter-Continental Amsterdam** is arguably the city's best, an admittedly smaller version of the one at Hearst Castle. The hotel also sports a big Jacuzzi, a sauna and Turkish bath, and a rather modest weight room, and employs a small army of muscular masseurs, beauticians, and trainers to pummel and pamper you. The **Hotel de l'Europe** has fallen behind in terms of sheer luxury, but it has a pond-sized colonnaded pool with a coffered ceiling (with some nutty garden statuary scattered around). Sybarites staying at the **Grand Sofitel Demeure** are probably more interested in trying out the Molton Brown aromatherapy bath milk in their two-tone Art Deco marble bathrooms; nonetheless, hidden under the 600-year-old complex's beautiful courtyards in the heart of Old Amsterdam is the grandly named "Spa at The Grand," which offers a smallish pool not intended for swimming laps and a serviceable sauna and steam bath. It's not a bad place to sweat off the pounds you put on by eating at the Café Roux (a determinedly trendy restaurant at the Grand).

The royal treatment... The owners of the multigenerational, family-run **Estheréa** may be sartorial look-alikes for Prince Willem Alexander and his bride Máxima, but sisters Esther and Caroline Esselaar are a mine of info on restaurants and culture in Amsterdam, and brother Jan-Willem and his desk staff remember your name and room number, are authentically friendly, and never seem obsequious. Free coffee and tea are served in the lobby. At the

Acacia, Hans and Marlene van Vliet will draw you up lists of their favorite restaurants, cafes, parks, herring stands, canals, foods, books, hairdressers, and more. Coming from hotelier families, they seem to have hospitality in their blood. Many of their clients are repeat customers who appreciate the laid-back atmosphere of this small, extremely simple hotel with triangular rooms (it's a corner building, shaped like a wedge of cheese). You can also rent one of a pair of houseboats from them. If you're really nice, they might even invite you for a ride on their motorboat. The quiet but efficient staff of the **Bridge** are the kind of folks who seem genuinely honored (and somewhat surprised) to have such nice people like you as guests. This modest property (don't be fooled by the misleadingly grand marble entrance) looks out on the locks on the Amstel River that control the flow of Amsterdam's canal water. A handful of the large, spare, casually decorated rooms and new top-floor apartment offer views of the river or Nieuwe Prinsengracht canal.

For cheap sleeps... Don't bother to take your hiking boots off before tramping up to the **Acacia:** You'll need them to scale the Matterhorn of a staircase. Its superb location—in the Jordaan, overlooking peaceful Lijnbaansgracht—offsets the spartan lodgings. The **Van Onna,** on Bloemgracht, is good and cheap; though rooms are tiny, the staircases are plenty wide to allow for giant tortoise-style packs to get through. On the posh Herengracht, the one-star **Hegra** (no elevator) has supremely simple, plain, sturdy furniture in the rooms, which are small with beamed ceilings. The **Van Ostade Bicycle Hotel** is the quintessential place for penurious students and sandal-shod young bikers. Rooms are spartan but neat as a pin, and there's a no-drugs policy. You can buy your daily picnic at the nearby Albert Cuypstraat street market. Cheapest of all (though you might not sleep) are the dormitory-style **Bulldog Low Budget Hotel** and **Kabul Young Budget Hotel.** Good luck! Former cheap sleepers who've come into some cash could try out the **ArenA,** out in Amsterdam East. You'll still see some kids toting backpacks here, but they're a better class of backpack than those that clog corridors in the city's hostels and cheap hotels.

Lavender lodgings... Amsterdam's hotels are used to welcoming people of myriad sexual persuasions, and many small, charming hotels here are gay-owned or -managed. It's illegal for a proprietor to deny lodging due to sexual orientation; this goes both ways. A dozen or so self-styled gay hotels in town may discourage straights from staying in them (some are hardcore places for S&M aficionados, and others practice or tolerate male prostitution). Most other gay properties are simply hotels that happen to be plugged into the gay circuit, though the atmosphere is such that if you're not one of the guys or girls, you might feel uncomfortable. The **Seven Bridges** is considered particularly gay-friendly, though it's not a gay hotel per se, but rather an unpretentious canal-house hotel, a small one-star charmer down the block from Rembrandtplein and within shouting distance of gay-prominent Reguliersdwarsstraat.

Party scenes... Most Amsterdam party hotels are in the Red-Light District and specialize in beyond-the-pale activities. If you want to book into one, just slip on your leather and chains, pack your condoms, and fill your pockets with joints. Don't worry, you can't miss them. The rest is up to you. Or, you can nibble at the edges of exotica by staying at the **Kabul Young Budget Hotel**, stuffed into an old building on the gay stretch of Warmoesstraat in the Red-Light District. Rooms range from monastic singles to 16-bed dormitories equipped with lockers and not much else. The **Bulldog Low Budget Hotel**, above a smoking coffee shop, is redolent of grass and hash, lit by fluorescent lights, and offers bunk beds with a 24-hour rotation of gamey puffers. Zounds! In either of these hotels, sleep should not be a priority, and anyone squeamish about body or dope odors will want to look elsewhere. Hey, the price is right, though, and you asked for it. A far better bet is the designer-ish **ArenA**, way out east near the Tropenmuseum (p. 114). The hotel's continental cafe-restaurant To Dine looks a bit like an upgraded cafeteria but has a great alfresco terrace in the garden and an attached bar, To Drink. Hotel guests get discounted admission to the in-house nightclub, To Night, which plays music from the 1960s onward in an old orphanage chapel. Rooms are collectively called To Stay and there's a conference section called To Meet—it's enough to make you want To Grimace. The ArenA is a bit removed from the center but isn't too far away, and the traffic is two-way, since youthful revelers head out here from the center to the nightspot and the outdoor cafe.

Family values... You can wheel the rented station wagon right into the garage at the **Renaissance Amsterdam** and feel at home. After all, this is a Marriott hotel, and the kiddies will never know they've left the theme park. They'll also have a blast running through the huge lobby and tripping up all the dazed conventioneers in the round 17th-century Koepel church congress center (a sort of convention center set in the 17th-century domed Lutheran church, Ronde Lutherse Koepelkerk, which now belongs to the hotel). The location, a few hundred yards from Centraal Station, means easy access to trams and trains and buses. For moms and pops with money to burn, the **NH Barbizon Palace** is another sort of theme park—corporate Dutch—with 19 rebuilt old houses kids can explore. The proximity of the Red-Light District, a block or so away, is no problem, since Centraal Station is across the street, with trams, trains, and so forth to all the places you'll want to go, including the zoo. There's a top-flight coffee shop–style restaurant for the well behaved, and don't overlook the souvenir shop in the lobby.

No such attractions are found at the **Estheréa,** but the Esselaar family likes kids, has produced many of late, and has equipped nine beautifully redecorated rooms with spiffy Murphy beds that brats get a kick out of. The big, comfy, practical rooms are furnished with child-resistant wooden built-ins. Extra beds, and children's toys, are also available. The double sinks will come in handy, no doubt, and so will the elevator (only a handful of canal-house hotels have one). Though there's no restaurant, the desk staff can order in food for you if you're too exhausted to go out (or grab takeout from the fab Mykonos-style **Traiterie Grekas** [p. 68] a couple of doors along), and kids will love the croissants that are part of the Dutch breakfast (not included in the room price). Across town at the **Owl,** near Vondelpark, you'll be happy to discover a small backyard in which to turn the children loose. This small, family-run, three-star hotel is in a converted turn-of-the-20th-century mansion, which has been so thoroughly transformed that you might be in a pastel Miami resort hotel. Best of all, it's on a quiet residential street, safe from traffic hazards, with the park one block away (it's minutes from the Museum District, if your youngsters are so inclined).

When everything else is filled... "Bigger is better" must have been the motto of the people who built the **Renaissance Amsterdam,** a sprawling, American-owned property filling several skillfully converted warehouses and other buildings. With 400-plus comfortable, if bland, modern rooms (totaling over 500 beds), they'll almost always be able to find space for you, no matter how many conventioneers they have under their roof. It's only a few hundred yards from Centraal Station and has a garage, which comes in handy if you're driving through town. Faded, sprawling **NH Grand Hotel Krasnapolsky** gets first prize for total number of beds (around 900). Little did the Polish tailor turned-hotelier who founded this landmark property in 1866 know that his name, writ rather large, would now be spread across several city blocks, between the Dam and the Red-Light District. If you're set on canal-house charm, the **Sheraton Hotel Pulitzer** has the most rooms (230) and beds (338) of all the canal-house hotels—it can't hurt to check here for last-minute cancellations.

Map 2: Central Amsterdam Accommodations

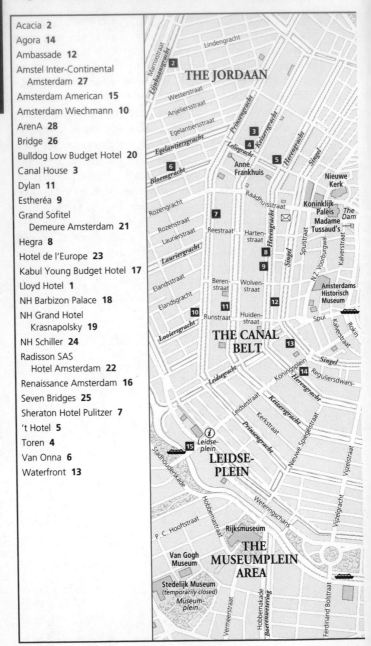

Acacia **2**

Agora **14**

Ambassade **12**

Amstel Inter-Continental
   Amsterdam **27**

Amsterdam American **15**

Amsterdam Wiechmann **10**

ArenA **28**

Bridge **26**

Bulldog Low Budget Hotel **20**

Canal House **3**

Dylan **11**

Estheréa **9**

Grand Sofitel
   Demeure Amsterdam **21**

Hegra **8**

Hotel de l'Europe **23**

Kabul Young Budget Hotel **17**

Lloyd Hotel **1**

NH Barbizon Palace **18**

NH Grand Hotel
   Krasnapolsky **19**

NH Schiller **24**

Radisson SAS
   Hotel Amsterdam **22**

Renaissance Amsterdam **16**

Seven Bridges **25**

Sheraton Hotel Pulitzer **7**

't Hotel **5**

Toren **4**

Van Onna **6**

Waterfront **13**

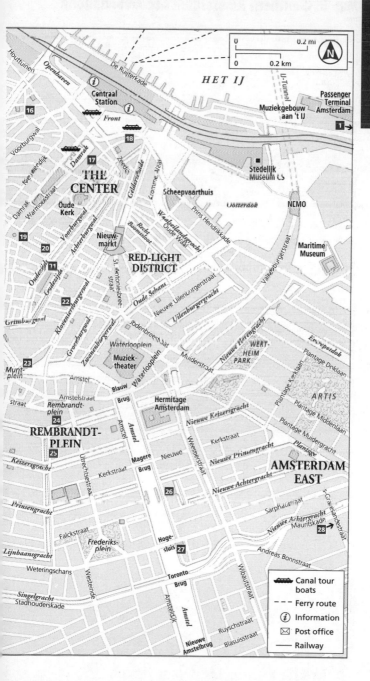

HET IJ

De Ruijterkade

Houttuinen

Openhaven

Front

Passenger
Terminal
Amsterdam

Muziekgebouw
aan 't IJ

IJ-Tunnel

1 →

Centraal
Station

16

Voorburgwal

Nieuwendijk

Damrak

Warmoesstraat

18

Damrak

17

**THE
CENTER**

Stedelijk
Museum CS

Oude
Kerk

Voorburgwal

Achterburgwal

Zeedijk

Geldersekade

Kromme Waal

Scheepvaarthuis

Prins Hendrikkade

Oosterdok

NEMO

Damrak

Nieuw-
markt

Waddenloopgracht

Oude Waal

Recht Boomsloot

19

20

11

Oudezijds

Grimburgwal

22

Kloveniersburgwal

Groenburgwal

Zwanenburgwerwal

**RED-LIGHT
DISTRICT**

St. Antoniebree-
straat

Oude Schans

Nieuwe Uilenburgerstraat

Uilenburgergracht

Valkenburgerstraat

Maritime
Museum

Jodenbreestraat

Waterlooplein

Muziek-
theater

Waterlooplein

Muiderstraat

Nieuwe Herengracht

WERT-
HEIM
PARK

Entrepôtdok

23

Munt-
plein

Amstel

Blauw
Brug

Amstelstraat

Rembrandt-
plein

straat

24

Hermitage
Amsterdam

Nieuwe Keizersgracht

Plantage Kerklaan

ARTIS

Plantage Middenlaan

Plantage Doklaan

**REMBRANDT-
PLEIN**

25

Keizersgracht

Utrechtsestraat

Amstel

Magere
Brug

Kerkstraat

Nieuwe

Weesperstraat

Kerkstraat

Nieuwe Prinsengracht

Nieuwe Achtergracht

Plantage Muidergracht

Plantage

**AMSTERDAM
EAST**

Prinsengracht

Falckstraat

Frederiks-
plein

26

Sarphatistraat

Nieuwe Achtergracht
Mauritskade

28 →

s-Gravesandestraat

Lijnbaansgracht

Weteringschans

Hoge-
sluis

27

Andreas Bonnstraat

Wibautstraat

Singelgracht
Stadhouderskade

Westeinde

Toronto
Brug

Amstellijk

Amstel

Ruyschstraat

Blasiusstraat

Nieuwe
Amstelbrug

Canal tour
boats

- - - Ferry route

(i) Information

⊠ Post office

—— Railway

Map 3: Southern Amsterdam Accommodations

Bilderberg Hotel Jan
 Luyken **4**

De Filosoof **1**

Nr 40 **2**

Owl **3**

Van Ostade Bicycle Hotel **6**

Washington **5**

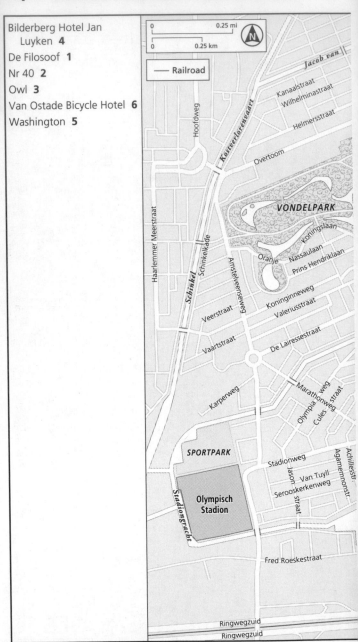

The Index

Note:	1€ = $1.25 U.S.
$$$$$	over 275€/$345
$$$$	180€–275€/$225–$345
$$$	110€–180€/$135–$225
$$	50€–110€/$60–$135
$	under 50€/$60

Price ratings are based on the lowest price quoted for a standard double room in high season, including taxes and charges. Unless otherwise noted, rooms have air-conditioning, phones, private baths, and TVs. Note that four- and five-star hotels in Amsterdam often charge an additional 5% city tax.

The following abbreviations are used for credit cards:

AE	American Express
DC	Diners Club
DISC	Discover
MC	MasterCard
V	Visa

Acacia (p. 40) JORDAAN This flatiron-shaped, family-run hotel has strictly spartan rooms, but a great location overlooking the leafy but by no means stylish Lijnbaansgracht canal. At slightly higher rates, houseboat and studio apartment rentals are also available. No elevator.... *Tel 020/622-1460. Fax 020/638-0748. www.hotelacacia.nl. Lindengracht 251 at Lijnbaansgracht, 1015 KH. Tram 3 or 10 to Marnixplein. 18 rooms, including 2 studios and 2 houseboats (no A/C). MC, V (5% surcharge).* $$

See Map 2 on p. 44.

Agora (p. 29) CANAL BELT A small, comfortable canal-house hotel near the flower market, run by Els Bruijnse and Yvo Muthert. Many rooms have been remodeled and upgraded since 2001. No elevator.... *Tel 020/627-2200. Fax 020/627-2202. www.hotel agora.nl. Singel 462 at Koningsplein, 1017 AW. Trams 1, 2, or 5 to Koningsplein. 16 rooms (15 with bathroom; no A/C). AE, DC, MC, V.* $$

See Map 2 on p. 44.

Ambassade (p. 30) CANAL BELT Twelve gorgeous, 17th-century canal houses on the so-called Golden Bend of Herengracht, the Algonquin of Amsterdam. Rushdie, Boyle, Ford, Seth, and Le Carré are among the literary lights who stay here. No pretentions; discreet class; library. "Float & Massage" spa next door. Elevator to some rooms.... *Tel 020/555-0222. Fax 020/555-0277. www.ambassade-hotel.nl. Herengracht 335–353 between Wolvenstraat and Huidenstraat (across the canal), 1016 AZ. Trams 1, 2, or 5 to Spui. 59 rooms (no A/C). AE, DC, MC, V. $$$*
See Map 2 on p. 44.

Amstel Inter-Continental Amsterdam (p. 31) EAST For many, this is the best hotel in town, with more bang for the buck than the Grand. Though located on the eastern bank of the Amstel River beyond Frederiksplein, in an unanchored and rather uninteresting area, the Amstel is perfectly grachtengordel (see explanation on p. 27).... *Tel 020/622-6060 (800/327-0200). Fax 020/622-5808. www.interconti.com. Professor Tulpplein 1 at Sarphatistraat, 1018 GX. Trams 6, 7, or 10 to Weesperplein. 79 rooms. AE, DC, MC, V. $$$$$*
See Map 2 on p. 44.

Amsterdam American (p. 34) LEIDSEPLEIN Formerly a Crowne Plaza hotel, this magnificent Dutch Art Nouveau landmark hotel was built between 1900 and 1902, overlooking Leidseplein. Unfortunately, the rooms, heavily remodeled and "improved" in the 1980s and 1990s, have lost much of their charm. Fitness center, solarium, and sauna.... *Tel 020/556-3001 (800/227-6963). Fax 020/556-3222. www.amsterdamamerican.com. Leidsekade 97 at Leidseplein, 1017 PN. Trams 1, 2, 5, 6, 7, or 10 to Leidseplein. 174 rooms. AE, DC, MC, V. $$$$$*
See Map 2 on p. 44.

Amsterdam Wiechmann (p. 29) CANAL BELT A narrow canal-house hotel with a charming lobby straight out of a Vermeer painting. Some *gezellig* canal-side double rooms are furnished with antiques. There's also a bar and lounge.... *Tel 020/626 3321. Fax 020/626-8962. www.hotelwiechmann.nl. Prinsengracht 328–332 at Looiersgracht, 1016 HX. Trams 1, 2, or 5 to Prinsengracht. 38 rooms (no A/C). MC, V. $$–$$$*
See Map 2 on p. 44.

ArenA (p. 35) EAST This rambling hotel in a former orphanage has gone upmarket with a bang, marked by designer flair—and far higher room rates. The location may be a tad too far from the center for some tastes, but the ArenA carries its own action with it, in the shape of a hot-rep dance club and bar.... *Tel 020/850-2410. Fax 020/850-2415. www.hotelarena.nl. 's-Gravesandestraat 51 at Mauritskade, 1092 AA Amsterdam. Trams 7 or 10 to Korte 's-Gravesandestraat. 121 rooms (no A/C). AE, DC, MC, V. $$–$$$*
See Map 2 on p. 44.

Bilderberg Hotel Jan Luyken (p. 33) MUSEUM DISTRICT This Dutch Art Nouveau four-star—totally remodeled in 2001—is within striking distance of the designer boutiques on P.C. Hooftstraat. There's a pretty patio garden and a comfortable winebar and lounge. Some rooms are nonsmoking. Spa center.... *Tel 020/573-0730 (800/641-0300). Fax 020/676-3841. www. janluyken.nl. Jan Luijkenstraat 58 at Honthorststraat, 1071 CS. Trams 2 or 5 to Hobbemastraat. 62 rooms. AE, DC, MC, V. $$$–$$$$*

See Map 3 on p. 46.

Bridge (p. 40) EAST This small, friendly hotel overlooks the locks on the Amstel River. Rooms and the top-floor apartments are tidy but spare, with linoleum or carpeted floors, rattan chairs, and blond wood furniture. No elevator.... *Tel 020/623-7068. Fax 020/624-1565. www.thebridgehotel.nl. Amstel 107–111 at Nieuwe Prinsengracht, 1018 EM. Tram 4 to Prinsengracht; Metro and trams 6, 7, or 10 to Weesperplein. 36 rooms (no A/C). AE, DC, MC, V. $$–$$$*

See Map 2 on p. 44.

Bulldog Low Budget Hotel (p. 40) RED-LIGHT DISTRICT Strip fluorescent lights, the smell of hash and grass wafting up from the smoking coffee shop downstairs, spartan rooms, and dormitories stuffed with bunk beds. No elevator. Talk about *gezellig*.... *Tel 020/620-3822. Fax 020/627-1612. www.bulldog.nl. Oudezijds Voorburgwal 220 at Damstraat, 1012 GJ. Trams 4, 9, 14, 16, 24, or 25 to the Dam. 95 beds (no A/C, no phone, no private bathroom, no TV). AE, MC, V. $*

See Map 2 on p. 44.

Canal House (p. 32) CANAL BELT A young Irish couple runs this hybrid Dutch/Victorian inn, on one of the city's prettiest canals, near Westerkerk church. No kids under 12 or pets are allowed. One of few canal-house hotels with an elevator; there's also a cozy bar.... *Tel 020/622-5182. Fax 020/624-1317. www.canal house.nl. Keizersgracht 148 at Leliegracht, 1015 CX. Trams 6, 13, 14, or 17 to Westermarkt. 26 rooms (no A/C). DC, MC, V. $$$*

See Map 2 on p. 44.

De Filosoof (p. 32) MUSEUM DISTRICT As the name implies, the theme of this unusual small three-star hotel, a stone's throw from Vondelpark, and in an annex across the street, is philosophy. The garden, veranda, and book-lined lounge encourage mingling.... *Tel 020/683-3013. Fax 020/685-3750. www.hotel filosoof.nl. Anna van den Vondelstraat 6 at Overtoom, 1054 GZ. Tram 1 to Jan Pieter Heijestraat. 38 rooms (no A/C). AE, MC, V. $$$*

See Map 3 on p. 46.

Dylan (p. 35) CANAL BELT Anouska Hempel's ultrachic, designer hotel (modeled on Blakes and The Hempel in London), where East (Asian furnishings) meets West (English silk and style) in a uniquely neospartan temple to trendiness. Housed in a reconverted 1637 Grachtengordel property (theater, almshouse bakery, then law offices). Garden court, gorgeous public areas haunted by well-heeled, black-clad jet-setters.... *Tel 020/530-2010. Fax 020/530-2030. www.dylanamsterdam.com. Keizersgracht 384 at Runstraat, 1016 GB. Trams 1, 2, or 5 to Spui. 26 rooms. AE, DC, MC, V. $$$$$*

See Map 2 on p. 44.

Estheréa (p. 42) CANAL BELT Family-owned and run for the last 50-odd years, this canal-house hotel on the Singel is a thoroughly professional property, with many tastefully redecorated rooms. One of few canal-house hotels to boast an elevator.... *Tel 020/624-5146 (800/223-9868). Fax 020/623-9001. www. estherea.nl. Singel 303-309 at Oude Spiegelstraat (across the canal), 1012 WJ. Trams 1, 2, or 5 to Spui. 75 rooms (no A/C). AE, DC, MC, V. $$$-$$$$*

See Map 2 on p. 44.

Grand Sofitel Demeure Amsterdam (p. 33) CENTER Possibly Amsterdam's top super-luxury hotel. Exudes confidence, from the marble-paved, vaulted lobby to the immense, tastefully decorated rooms. Pity they've only got 15 nonsmoking rooms.... *Tel 020/555-3111 (800/SOFITEL). Fax 020/555-3222. www. thegrand.nl. Oudezijds Voorburgwal 197 at Oude Doelenstraat, 1012 EX. Trams 4, 9, 14, 16, 24, or 25 to Spui. 182 rooms. AE, DC, MC, V. $$$$$*

See Map 2 on p. 44.

Hegra (p. 29) CANAL BELT Modest is the operative word for this narrow, 17th-century canal-house hotel located on the Herengracht near the Dam, the flower market, and Leidseplein. No elevator.... *Tel 020/623-7877. Fax 020/623-8159. Herengracht 269 at Hartenstraat (across the canal), 1016 BJ. Trams 1, 2, 5, 6, 13, 14, or 17 to the Dam. 11 rooms (6 with bathroom; no A/C, no TV). AE, DC, MC, V. $*

See Map 2 on p. 44.

Hotel de l'Europe (p. 32) CENTER This 1896 grande dame offers an excellent, though noisy, location at Muntplein overlooking the Amstel, plus all the trappings of luxury. The lobby and many rooms have been remodeled and upgraded in the last 5 years.... *Tel 020/531-1777 (800/223-6800). Fax 020/531-1778. www. leurope.nl. Nieuwe Doelenstraat 2-8 at Muntplein, 1012 CP. Trams 4, 9, 16, 24, or 25 to Muntplein. 100 rooms. AE, DC, MC, V. $$$$$*

See Map 2 on p. 44.

Kabul Young Budget Hotel (p. 40) RED-LIGHT DISTRICT An Amsterdam institution. Not for light sleepers. No elevator.... Tel 020/623-7158. Fax 020/620-0869. Warmoesstraat 38–42 at Oude Brugsteeg, 1012 JE. Trams 1, 2, 4, 5, 6, 9, 13, 16, 17, 24, or 25 to Centraal Station. 23 rooms (no A/C, no phone, no private bathroom, no TV). No credit cards. $

See Map 2 on p. 44.

Lloyd Hotel (p. 35) EASTERN DOCKS Upscale hotel with a colorful history.... Tel 020/561-3636. Fax 020/561-3600. www.lloyd hotel.com. Oostelijke Handelskade 34 at IJhaven, 1019 BN. Tram 26 to Rietlandpark. 120 rooms (106 with bathroom). AE, DC, MC, V. $$–$$$$

See Map 2 on p. 44.

NH Barbizon Palace (p. 30) CENTER There's something for everyone in this quintessentially Dutch theme park of a business hotel. The neutrally attired rooms have thick, flowery curtains and old oak rafters. Remodeled in recent years, with about 45 nonsmoking rooms.... Tel 020/556-4564. Fax 020/624-3353. www.nh-hotels.com. Prins Hendrikkade 59–72 at Zeedijk, 1012 AD. Trams 1, 2, 4, 5, 6, 9, 13, 16, 17, 24, or 25 to Centraal Station. 275 rooms. AE, DC, MC, V. $$$$

See Map 2 on p. 44.

NH Grand Hotel Krasnapolsky (p. 30) CENTER The most exclusive place in town, it's now a business, convention, and package-tourism hotel, comfortable if undistinguished. The plant-filled Winter Garden (1879) is still a joy in winter, and the Reflet Brasserie has a striking 1883 decor; otherwise, the hotel's bars and restaurants are forgettable. 100 nonsmoking rooms.... Tel 020/554-9111. Fax 020/622-8607. www.nh-hotels.com. Dam 9 at Damrak, 1012 JS. Trams 4, 9, 14, 16, 24, or 25 to the Dam. 468 rooms. AE, DC, MC, V. $$$$

See Map 2 on p. 44.

NH Schiller (p. 36) REMBRANDTPLEIN Gorgeous turn-of-the-20th-century hotel overlooking Rembrandtplein. Square-side rooms have the best views, but can get noisy.... Tel 020/554-0700. Fax 020/624-0098. www.nh-hotels.com. Rembrandtplein 26–36, 1017 CV. Trams 4, 9, or 14 to Rembrandtplein. 92 rooms. AE, DC, MC, V. $$$$

See Map 2 on p. 44.

Nr 40 (p. 38) MUSEUM DISTRICT This luxury B&B offers four full-service studio apartments, an elegant dining room, wood-paneled lounge, and a small roof garden. (Next door are two split-level, one-bedroom garden apartments with faxes and answering machines, but these are rented long-term and are rarely available.) No elevator.... Tel/fax 020/618-4298. www.number40.scarlet.nl. Roemer Visscherstraat 40 at Eerste Constantijn Huygensstraat, 1054 EZ. Trams 1 or 6 to Eerste Constantijn

Huygensstraat; 3 or 12 to Overtoom. 4 rooms (no A/C). AE, DC, MC, V. $$$

See Map 3 on p. 46.

Owl (p. 42) MUSEUM DISTRICT A converted turn-of-the-20th-century mansion, this family-run, three-star hotel is tidy and pastel, and no nonsense. TV lounge/bar and garden.... *Tel 020/618-9484. Fax 020/618-9441. www.owl-hotel.nl. Roemer Visscherstraat 1 at Tesselschadestraat, 1054 EV. Trams 1 or 6 to Stadhouderskade. 34 rooms (no A/C). AE, DC, MC, V. $$*

See Map 3 on p. 46.

Radisson SAS Hotel Amsterdam (p. 36) CENTER Even though it's just south of the Red-Light District in Old Amsterdam, it looks like it could be anywhere.... *Tel 020/520-8300 (800/333-3333). Fax 020/520-8200. www.radissonsas.com. Rusland 17 at Oudezijds Achterburgwal, 1012 CK. Trams 4, 9, 14, 16, 24, or 25 to Spui. 243 rooms. AE, DC, MC, V. $$$$ $$$$$*

See Map 2 on p. 44.

Renaissance Amsterdam (p. 42) CENTER Owned by Marriott since 1999, this is a huge, sprawling, American business hotel composed of converted warehouses. The round, 17th-century Koepel church is used for conventions, and there's a covered courtyard. The charm factor has been improved with red decor, old prints and paintings, and cozy furniture.... *Tel 020/621 2223 (800/HOTELS-1). Fax 020/623-7742. www.renaissance hotels.com. Kattengat 1 at Spuistraat, 1012 SZ. Trams 1, 2, 5, 6, 13, or 17 to Martelaarsgracht. 405 rooms. AE, DC, MC, V. $$$$–$$$$$*

See Map 2 on p. 44.

Seven Bridges (p. 28) CANAL BELT This *gezellig* canal-house hotel has gone upmarket, with only eight remodeled rooms (inlaid wood, marble, and handmade furniture). No elevator.... *Tel 020/623-1329. Reguliersgracht 31 at Keizersgracht, 1017 LK. Tram 4 to Keizersgracht. 8 rooms (no A/C). AE, MC, V. $$$*

See Map 2 on p. 44.

Sheraton Hotel Pulitzer (p. 36) CANAL BELT The only full-blown luxury hotel in the Grachtengordel neighborhood; the restrained decor is lovely in an opulent, corporate way, though it's still less atmospheric than other canal-house hotels.... *Tel 020/523-5235 (800/325-3589). Fax 020/627-6753. www.luxury collection.com. Prinsengracht 315–331 at Westermarkt, 1016 GZ. Trams 6, 13, 14, or 17 to Westermarkt. 230 rooms. AE, DC, MC, V. $$$$$*

See Map 2 on p. 44.

't Hotel (p. 29) CANAL BELT Opened in 2000, this charming three-star overlooking the leafy Leliegracht canal near the Jordaan has luxury rooms done in a neo-Calvinistic, minimalist style: simple wooden furniture, cream-colored walls, burgundy carpets, and tiled bathrooms. The lobby doubles as an antiques shop. No elevator.... *Tel 020/422-2741. Fax 020/626-7873. www.thotel.nl. Leliegracht 18 at Herengracht, 1015 DE. Trams 6, 13, 14, or 17 to Westermarkt. 8 rooms. AE, MC, V. $$$*

See Map 2 on p. 44.

Toren (p. 29) CANAL BELT This four-star, two-building canal-house hotel with elevator has a marble entrance hall, Old Dutch decor, crystal chandeliers, fireplaces, and an attractive garden.... *Tel 020/622-6352. Fax 020/626-9705. www.toren.nl. Keizersgracht 164 at Leliegracht, 1015 CZ. Trams 6, 13, 14, or 17 to Westermarkt. 40 rooms. AE, DC, MC, V. $$$$*

See Map 2 on p. 44.

Van Onna (p. 36) JORDAAN This unusual one-star, nonsmoking hotel occupies three separate buildings on a lovely side canal. From front rooms you get canal views and glimpses of the Westerkerk over the roofs. Lounge. No elevator.... *Tel 020/626-5801. www.hotelvanonna.com. Bloemgracht 102–104 and 108 at Prinsengracht, 1015 TN. Trams 6, 13, 14, or 17 to Westermarkt. 41 rooms (no A/C, no TV). No credit cards. $$*

See Map 2 on p. 44.

Van Ostade Bicycle Hotel (p. 40) OLD SOUTH Rooms in this narrow, turn-of-the-20th-century building are tidy but spartan. No elevator (and the stairs are steep).... *Tel 020/679-3452. Fax 020/671-5213. www.bicyclehotel.com. Van Ostadestraat 123 at Ferdinand Bolstraat, 1072 SV. Tram 3 to Ferdinand Bolstraat; 12, 16, 24, or 25 to Ceintuurbaan. 16 rooms (8 with bathroom; no A/C). No credit cards. $$*

See Map 3 on p. 46.

Washington (p. 32) MUSEUM DISTRICT Clean and classy, the simple, tasteful rooms here overlook a verdant street or an intimate garden. No elevator.... *Tel 020/679-7453. Fax 020/673-4435. www.hotelwashington.nl. Frans van Mierisstraat 10 at Johannes Vermeerstraat, 1071 RS. Tram 16 to Ruysdaelstraat. 21 rooms (no A/C). AE, DC, MC, V. $$*

See Map 3 on p. 46.

Waterfront (p. 29) CANAL BELT Overlooking the Singel a hundred yards from the flower market, this narrow canal-house hotel has cheerful owners who've remodeled top to bottom.... *Tel/fax 020/421-6621. www.hotelwaterfront.nl. Singel 458 at Koningsplein, 1017 AW. Trams 1, 2, or 5 to Koningsplein. 10 rooms (no A/C). AE, DC, MC, V. $$*

See Map 2 on p. 44.

ING

2

Basic Stuff

Dutch food and Amsterdam restaurants are the butt of a lot of jokes—only some of them deserved. Also true is that a lot of traditional Dutch food is heavy, consisting of meat and vegetable stews, sausages, potatoes and gravy, and plenty of bland cheese. Unlike Italians or French, locals dining out here *avoid* local food, favoring Indonesian, French, Italian, Asian, and other foreign specialties (there are 150 nationalities in town) or fusion mergers thereof. In the last 20 years, though, the once-dreary restaurant scene has become surprisingly dynamic, roller-coastering from the sublime to the ridiculous. You really can get a good meal here at a variety of both international and homegrown restaurants—but you can also spend a lot of money on bad, silly, or contrived food. Still, it's nonsense to claim, as do other Europeans (the French in particular), that there is no such thing as "Dutch cuisine."

Veteran food guru Johannes van Dam (see the "Van Dam vs. Iens" box below) has a collection of centuries-old Dutch cookbooks describing dishes that would send a modern French chef to culinary heaven. Members of the Dutch Regional Cuisine organization (Neerlands Dis) are reviving lost recipes, ingredients, wines, liquors, and cooking techniques from the various regions of the Netherlands. Dozens of flavorful finds include dishes like smoke-dried *nagelhout* beef, braised codfish with mustard sauce, and marrowfat peas with onions, bacon, and pickles. The real dynamism lies, however, with several dozen chefs—Dutch, French, and Indonesian—producing dishes at hip Amsterdam restaurants that would fit right into the foodie scene in New York, Los Angeles, San Francisco, or Sydney. For these chefs, variations on northern Italian, French, and Asian themes—sometimes mixed and matched—are all the rage. Handled by skilled practitioners, these variations can be world-class. Fusion remains the trend of the early 21st century; sometimes the results are more confused than anything else. *And be warned:* Service is almost universally slow and often sloppy. Everyone knows that Amsterdam's restaurants, with few exceptions, are "understaffed with overpaid amateurs."

Only in Amsterdam

Fish, fish, and more fish. The staggering wealth of the 17th-century Dutch Golden Age was based in large part on herrings. The Dutch eat them raw and pickled in a variety of ways. Try them at one of the dozens of establishments called a herring stand *(herringhuis)* scattered around town. Other Atlantic and North Sea fish are on many menus, and they're generally fresh and delicious. Among snack foods, *osseworst* is a delicious smoked beef sausage eaten cold, like salami. The beef or shrimp croquette *(krokette)* is a local obsession. At their worst, these large, gooey dumplings rolled in diamond-hard crumbs, then deep fried, taste like instant gravy mix. They're always served scorching hot; Amsterdammers split them open, place them on a slice of white bread, then add mustard and/or fried parsley. Small, round vegetable-paste croquettes are called *bitterballen* and are a favorite hors d'oeuvre.

Locally you can find dozens of cheeses, including the ubiquitous Edam and Gouda. You can also find delicious aged varieties, and others made with raw milk *(boerenkaas)*, hidden treasures that aren't available abroad. These cheeses, plus various cold cuts, go into the standard Dutch lunch, which consists of small, often round sandwiches—*broodjes*— that would be considered a mere snack or finger food in most other countries.

The most celebrated dish hereabouts is *stamppot*, a vast mound of mashed potatoes and gravy, usually served with endive, sauerkraut, or kale, plus pork ribs and sausages. Don't forget *erwtensoep*, pea soup, that perennial winter favorite; it should be thick enough to hold a spoon

Van Dam vs. Iens

Amsterdam guru of gastronomy **Johannes van Dam** has a mission: to reward talented chefs and encourage others to improve. Improving sometimes means changing jobs. So, while the pneumatic tire man of the Michelin red guide makes chefs tremble in France, it is bearded, Bibendum-like van Dam whose reviews in the daily **Het Parool** can make or break an Amsterdam restaurant. He uses a 10-point system. There is nothing worse than being "van Damned" with a low score. All-time lows have gone to the Reflet Brasserie at the NH Grand Hotel Krasnapolsky (4). Enter **Iens Boswijk**, a rival reviewer whose **"Iens Independent Index"** (www.iens.nl) lists most Amsterdam restaurants worth a damn, rating them with Zagat-style assessments and dividing them conveniently into theme categories. Best of all, this pocket-sized guide is available in English at most Amsterdam bookstores and newsstands. Too bad the "nonsmoking" category remains woefully inaccurate: There are practically no nonsmoking restaurants in town worth your patronage. The verdict? The big man van Dam is still the city's most reliable restaurant barometer. Look for his reviews—often posted prominently—in the windows of Amsterdam restaurants.

upright. A lighter favorite in May and June is white Limburg asparagus, eaten with local boiled ham (and sometimes sprinkled with cinnamon or nutmeg).

Dutch pancakes are the sort of comestible brick that has given Dutch food a bad name. Called *pannekoeken* when pizza-size and *poffertjes* when smaller, they are often gooey and only half-cooked. Toppings include everything under the sun, from curried turkey to pineapple to sweet corn. The less said, the better. Indonesian food from the Netherlands' former colony, the Dutch East Indies, has been thoroughly adopted by the Dutch, who consider it their own. You find chicken *sate* (also spelled *sateh* and *satay*) with peanut sauce everywhere, from ethnic eateries to Dutch steakhouses and sidewalk fry shops. The celebrated Indonesian *rijsttafel* (rice table) is a colonial invention, designed to regale Dutch potentates with a mind-boggling parade of 20 or 30 dishes. Indonesia is a vast country, comprising Java, Borneo, and Sulawesi, with dozens of regional cuisines; what you get in Amsterdam is a pan-Indonesian mix of star dishes, most of them Javanese. Try spicy *babi ketjap* (pork in soya sauce) or mild *gado-gado* (vegetables and bean sprouts in peanut sauce). The true test of an Indonesian chef, however, is *rendang padang*—beef with chile and coconut sauce; it should be very spicy and of a creamy but firm consistency.

• •

STILL HOLLAND'S BEST ICE CREAM

*Back in the 1920s, Silvano Tofani's father, Peppino, emigrated to Amsterdam from Lucca, in Tuscany, with a dream: to open an ice-cream parlor. As of January 2000 you can read about Peppino's ascension at the Amsterdam Historical Museum. You might reasonably ask why Peppino left Lucca for a city where it rains almost 250 days a year and there is a five-month winter. A silly question: Business boomed. Peppino's colorful carts could be seen all over town in spring and summer. The carts are no longer, but Silvano, born in Tuscany, and his wife, Anelide, took over Peppino's modest ice-cream parlor, near the Albert Cuypstraat market, several decades ago and continue the family art. Everything is homemade with fresh produce: strawberries, peaches, zucchinis, rice, and more unexpected ingredients. Silvano has perfected 100 different ice creams, all made with his own recipes. Creamy, light, flavorful—this is possibly the world's best, made with Italian skill and peerless Dutch dairy products. The frothy cappuccinos are unquestionably Amsterdam's most authentic. Best of all, Silvano and Anelide, like their 100 flavors, are as sweet as can be. (**Gelateria Italiana Peppino**; Tel 020/676-4910; Eerste Van Sweelinckstraat 16; daily 11am–11pm, late March to Oct only.)*

• •

Local beers include those inexplicably world-famous brews Heineken and Amstel. There are two good microbreweries in town, Bierbrouwerij 't IJ and Brouwhuis Maximiliaan. Dutch Riesling wine, produced near Maastricht, is good but difficult to find. There is only one local producer of *jenever* (Dutch gin), Cees van Wees; his products are available at De Admiraal (a bar/tasting house).

How to Dress

The Dutch are casual, but not frumpy. As long as you don't have hygiene problems, you can wear just about anything to just about any restaurant. At trendy places people wear casual-chic clothing, but no one will bat an eye if you wear a tie to a diner, or show up in jeans at a schmancy restaurant (exceptions: Vermeer, La Rive, and ultra-starchy L'Excelsior).

When to Eat

Amsterdammers like to eat a hearty breakfast (cheese, ham, bread, and more) and a light lunch (a salad or sandwich) at a cafe, and they prefer to dine early (from 5:30pm on). Local restaurateurs, used to tourists, joke about "national time slots"; the Dutch come first, followed by Americans and Germans (6:30pm), Scandinavians (7pm), French and Italians (8:30pm), and Spanish (9pm). Normal restaurant hours are 5:30 to 10pm; *eethuis* (simple restaurants and diners) serve from about 4 to 10pm; cafe hours vary widely, many open from 10am to 1am. (*Note:* For brown cafes, neobrowns, and white cafes, see the Nightlife & Cafes chapter.)

Getting the Right Table

The trick to snagging a good table is to time your reservation—reserve whenever possible—to suit the kind of restaurant. Go later (8pm on) to an authentic Dutch restaurant; early (7:30pm or so) to a trendy or ethnic spot that fills up late. Once you've got your table, you can stay as long as you like; most restaurants make no attempt to "turn tables." Service is often relaxed, i.e., slow. The Dutch are proud people and are funny about tips (they hate to feel they're being coerced). Slipping the maitre d' a wad might get you a window table at a finer (or ethnic) establishment, but it won't go down well elsewhere.

Celebrity Chefs

Chef-watchers have been stunned in recent years by a series of toque transfers worthy of a quick-change artist: **Robert Kranenborg** left La Rive for a posh new place, Vossius, and since its demise has departed Amsterdam to head up the posh Le Cirque at Scheveningen (The Hague's seacoast resort). His erstwhile second-in-command at La Rive, **Pascal Jalhaij,** became top dog at Vermeer; with watch synchronized, Vermeer's then chef Edwin Kats moved to La Rive to replace Kranenborg. Since then Jalhaij has picked up his toque and walked (figuratively speaking) to the North Sea coast to take over the kitchen at the Palace Hotel's restaurant Chatillon, Noorwijk aan Zee (west of Leiden). Another Michelin-pedigree star chef, **Gertjan Hageman,** came out of mothballs to open the hot spot De Kas in a reconverted hothouse. Meanwhile, at the Dylan's (formerly Blakes) designer restaurant (in a reconverted 18th-century bakery), **Schilo van Coevorden** continues to number among Amsterdam's hottest culinary properties, a proficient practitioner of a number of ethnic cuisines (Thai, Italian, French). Bordewijk, serving French/Italian–inspired seasonal dishes, is the creation of two restaurateur/chefs, **Wil Demandt** and **Hans Mosterd,** but the restaurant's fame derives from the place itself—a chilling, echoing, postmodern designer number, on a trendy Jordaan square. Back to La Rive, at the mega-luxury Amstel Inter-Continental Hotel. It's now under the baton of Michelin-starred chef **Edwin Kats,** who won praise for his classics at another luxury hotel-restaurant, Vermeer, at the NH Barbizon Palace. Frenchman **Jean-Christophe Royer** is Christophe, chic Grachtengordel's perennial haven for reverent epicures. Christophe was among the first chefs in Holland to be awarded a Michelin star, and he isn't likely to let it fall from gourmet heaven. Dutch/French/Thai chef **Jos Boomgaardt** reinvented himself several years ago as the high priest of fusion (at Tom Yam Fusion Cuisine), but is now fighting a rear-guard battle for continued notoriety.

Dining in Cafes

Amsterdam has more than 1,400 brown, white, and designer cafes where people of all ages, looks, and sexual orientations spend a great deal of their time day and night, eating, drinking, smoking and more—some seem to do all but sleep in cafes. And many say the food is better here than in restaurants. See "Best cafe food" below, but the majority of cafe listings are in the Nightlife & Cafes chapter. See "Cafe Society" on p. 196.

The Lowdown

Going Dutch... If you eat only one Dutch meal in Amsterdam, make the award-winning **De Roode Leeuw** the place. It's a fixture on the Neerlands Dis (Dutch Regional Cuisine) circuit. The old-fashioned interior is what you want in a famously stuffy place like this: carved wood, red armchairs, starched white tablecloths, professional service. The raw new herring and shrimp and beef croquettes are about as good as you can get; in spring, the white Limburg asparagus and farmhouse ham are out of this world. Otherwise, unfindable delicacies like dried *nagelhout* beef are a house specialty. There is even surprisingly quaffable Dutch Riesling from the tiny producers around Maastricht in the south on the wine list.

To see office workers, provincials, and package tourists at their happy-hour best, hit magnificently kitschy but cozy **Haesje Claes** near Spui. Mustachioed proprietor André Duyves is a miracle worker: His jovial tourist trap actually serves decent grub (classic mashed potatoes with a pool of gravy, sauerkraut, and pork ribs, plus game in winter). But you haven't seen anything until you've buzzed over to **D'Vijff Vlieghen,** better known as the Five Flies, an Old Dutch theme park of a place founded by flamboyant antiques dealer Nicolaas Kroese (1905–71). Back in the 1950s, he raced out to the airport in a limo every time a celeb came to town, then immortalized their visits with brass plaques on his bentwood chairs. Stuffed with authentic antiques and delft tiles, the labyrinth of dark, cozy rooms spreads through five ramshackle 16th-century buildings near Spui. Through the candlelit gloom, the tourists and conventioneers probably can't see the farm house ham with fresh apple salad on their plates. A pity; it's not bad.

The **Pancake Bakery** is the place to go if you and the kids really must experience the infamous Dutch pancake. You'll soon forget you're in the basement of a converted Prinsengracht warehouse—there are American ice cream parlor–style marble tabletops on old sewing-machine legs, laminated menus, and an old Dutch stove chugging away. Among the 70 kinds of pancakes, stick to the sweet ones. No matter what your constitution, the surreal fantasies topped with turkey in curry sauce, pineapple, apricot, and raisins will stick to you. **Piet de Leeuw** is the kind of joint you feel right at home in. There's a cigarette machine on one wall, and the dark interior was probably last decorated circa 1955. The famous cholesterol-rich killer beefsteaks, pan-fried in margarine with onions, come with a slice of white bread. Central-casting waiters suss you out before bringing you toothpicks with tiny American flags to spear your raw herring, sweet pickles, and triangles of toast.

Dutch on the run... When you've had enough of the potentially lethal french fry stands all over town, and the '50s-style, out-of-the-wall **Febo** automats (Holland's equivalent of McDonald's) selling croquettes, hamburgers, and other dubious-looking quickies on greasy trays, it's time to go fish: Amsterdammers take their herring very seriously. As British ambassador George Downing reported in 1661, the city's Golden Age riches depended on the fact that people were better nourished—on herring—than the rest of Europe. New, young, virginal herring, called *nieuwe haring,* comes on the market late May or early June and is best only for a few weeks, though it's sold well into the summer. There are dozens of *herringhuis* fish stands in the center of town. The best of all is **Van Altena,** a class operation across from the Rijksmuseum. Owner Pieter van Altena has spent a lot of time and money perfecting the raw herring preservation process; connoisseurs travel miles to stock up on his fresh and pickled herring and lunch on delicious salmon or crab salad. No plastic here: You use proper stainless-steel flatware and drink chilled white wine in a stemmed glass. **Van Dobben** has been the spot for the last 55 years to try that famous Amsterdam specialty, the croquette (though these curious lumps are no longer made in-house). Once you've burned your tongue on one and decided croquettes are a quaint curiosity, order a glass of milk at the vintage counter and try an eel or pastrami sandwich instead.

Real *rijsttafel*... Literally, a "rice table"—an Indonesian meal composed of anything from a dozen or more different small dishes. At **Tempo Doeloe,** owner Nagy Ghebrial explains to interested first-time guests how to progress through each course, moving methodically from mild (*risolles*—crepes with beef), to spicy (*soto ajam*—chicken soup), to hot (*ajam roedjak*—chicken with chile and coconut milk), to very hot (*ikan pepesan*—poached mackerel with chile sauce). Take Nagy's advice: Even chile devotees will weep, sweat, and possibly swoon when eating the infernal "very hot" selections. The skillfully contrasting dishes, professional but laid-back service, and pleasant theatrical decor make this the best Indonesian in town. Right next door, Nagy's former business partner Thomas Hart has opened a simpler place with take-out food: **Tujuh Maret.** The food is excellent. Further competition comes from classy **Long Pura,** in the Jordaan. You are handed an orchid blossom and seated under upside-down parasols hung from the ceiling. The *daging mbe* (dried, stewed beef with onions and spices) is divine. **Sahid Jaya** is a luxury restaurant with good food, though the spice has been toned down to please Dutch taste buds. The business and tourist clientele seem most interested in the polished service, the posh decor (apricot drapes, cream tablecloths, and Indonesian shadow puppets), and the alfresco dining in a beautiful Golden Bend backyard. **Sama Sebo** is still among the city's best-known Indonesian restaurants, possibly because it's near the Rijksmuseum and the fashion boutiques of P.C. Hooftstraat. The decor is unobtrusive—traditional dyed fabrics, reed mats—but the tables are small and pushed too close together. The food is no longer the best in town, though the Indonesian signature dish, *rendang padang* (beef with chile and coconut sauce), is excellent. For quick, cheap, and tasty dishes served until the early hours, head for **Bojo,** near Leidseplein. Also, **Kantjil & de Tijger** is chic, modern, and cool, unlike the many Indonesian restaurants in Holland that wear their ethnic origins on their sleeves, literally, with waitstaff decked out in traditional costume. And, brace yourself, the food is actually good.

Mumbai on the Amstel... Amsterdam can't compete with London when it comes to Indian food, but **Memories of India,** a lavish maharajah's palace of a place near Rembrandtplein, is in the running (maybe because it's run by the owners of two distinguished Indian restaurants in London). The kind of place where you'd expect to see an Indian movie star posing under the faux palm trees, it borders on glitzy exotica. The lamb vindaloo is authentically spicy, though, the chapatis and nans fresh and flavorful, and the service polished. **Shiva,** just a few doors down, has been around longer—it's equally upscale, with starched white tablecloths and uniformed waiters, but it's smaller, considerably less showy, and the food is equally excellent. The curries range from mild to scorching, and there is moist tandoori or tikka chicken and nicely spiced madras lamb.

Thai me up... Trendy **Rakang Thai** is the most unusual Thai place in town: originally a tiny designer furniture boutique in the Jordaan, whose owners, seeing that business was slow, mummified the chairs in white canvas, rearranged the furnishings, and hired chef Nathapong Mungkorn in 1995. Seven years later the place is still a hit with trendy media types, artists, models, and foodies. Luckily, the chef is no slouch, and the food, though preciously presented and overpriced, is as spicy and authentic as you'd like it to be.

Asian delights... **Yoichi,** near Frederiksplein, offers plenty of sake, sukiyaki, teriyaki steaks, and other classic Japanese meat dishes on the menu, plus good fish, sushi, and veggies, of course, with bonsai trees and Buddhist calm all around. This was the first Japanese restaurant in town; now there are more luxurious ones in and around the Okura Hotel, way out on the edge of the Old South, but local Japanese still flock to Yoichi. Most non-Japanese are directed to the dreary converted Dutch cafe downstairs—make sure there are no holes in your socks, and reserve a table in the upstairs tatami room instead. New and totally different, **Wagamama** is a new-age noodle restaurant that's so Zen—no smoking, no reservations—you can't help wondering where they're hiding the joy. The ramen and udon noodles are great, though, and the price is right. Local Surinamese swear by **Warung Marlon,** an outwardly unappealing cafe/takeout joint in the far-flung De Pijp neighborhood: great roasted meat and Surinamese Asian melting-pot specialties (everything from banana chips to wonton soup, from *sate* chicken in spicy peanut sauce to Peking duck). It's also cheap, fast, and totally nonsmoking.

Utopian Ethiopian... **Kilimanjaro,** a small, chic East African restaurant not far from the Maritime Museum in eastern central Amsterdam, remains popular after 10 years of favorable reviews. This outpost of exotica serves such authentically good food that, with seating for only 25 or so on the ground floor of a narrow old house, you may not be able to get a table. Persist. The Dutchman who runs the place fell in love with Africa and works with an Ethiopian cook to reproduce a variety of specialties like Senegalese lamb curry, crocodile steak (very snappy), and *doro wat*, spicy Ethiopian chicken sautéed in pepper sauce and served with a spinach salad. And the simple decor—high ceilings, white walls, and colorful tablecloths designed in Africa but made in Holland—smartly manages to avoid the usual colonial jungle-cabana look.

Multi Mediterranean... There are dozens of Italian restaurants in town, most of them more Dutch than Italian, with the usual straw-wrapped flasks and vaguely Neapolitan/Tuscan dishes and pizzas. Open the Yellow Pages and take your pick. Others feature pasta and live opera singing, or people-watching over indifferent food. Pricey **Caruso,** in the Italian-owned Jolly Hotel Carlton overlooking Muntplein, looks like a bordello, with red-velvet armchairs and carpets, huge Venetian chandeliers, and gilt plasterwork. It makes no pretense of offering anything but updated *nuova cucina*—the kind of nouvelle food you'd get in a swank hotel restaurant in Milan or Rome. The chef, brought in from Italy specifically to make this the best *ristorante* in town, hasn't succeeded yet, though he does excel with fish.

Out beyond the Albert Cuypstraat market, in the multiethnic part of central Amsterdam, is one of the city's authentic neighborhood Italian eateries, the kind of place you'd find down a back street in Bari. It's called **L'Angoletto** because it sits on a corner *(un angolo)*, which in terms of decor is its only distinctive feature (other than the fact that you can sit in front of the pizza oven downstairs or on a cramped mezzanine). It's run by young Italians from Taranto, in southern Italy, who serve crisp classic pizzas *(napoletana* and *margherita)*, simple but tasty pasta (spaghetti with tomato sauce and hot pepperoncini), and meat such as Tuscan steaks. Meanwhile, on the Spanish front, the tapas craze—which hit Amsterdam 5 years later than the rest of Europe—is still going strong. So if you thought you could avoid the music, the posturing youngsters, and the endless procession of bite-sized goodies, think again. **Duende** is the quintessential Jordaan tapas bar, where self-conscious 20-somethings lounge around the cool tile-floored interior, or, in summer, hang out on

DINING

the terrace. Try the tasty *calamares* (squid rings), *bacalao* (salt cod), and chorizo. **Tapas Bar Català,** near Spui, probably has better food, and will appeal to middle-age folks looking for empanadas, mushrooms, prawns, and salads of all kinds. **Traiterie Grekas** is a Greek catering and takeout restaurant. Though its few tables are sandwiched between a cold case and the kitchen, it is modern, spotless, plays classical music, and serves perhaps the city's best stuffed bell peppers, *spanakopita* (spinach pie), and stuffed grape leaves, plus daily specials, all at reasonable prices.

The French connection... When in Amsterdam, take the appellation "French" with a truckload of *sel* (salt). Most places serve Dutch variations on French themes, and some of the best restaurants commonly considered French actually serve something more akin to California cuisine than anything you'd find in Paris. A Michelin-star pedigree chef, Gertjan Hageman, has made a comeback with his French restaurant **De Kas,** in a reconverted hothouse in eastern Amsterdam. Hageman grows most of his own (organic) produce and the offering changes daily. There's no menu, but the soups, breads, and simple roasted fish are excellent, so much so that the place gets booked up weeks ahead. At perennial **Bordewijk,** facing Noorderkerk in the Jordaan, the gray-and-black postmodern decor is chilling, the crowd chic. Always inspired, the seasonal menu is at the forefront of the creative pack, with nods to France, northern Italy, and Spain. **Christophe** is chef Jean-Christophe Royer's authentically French yet creative luxury restaurant in the moneyed Grachtengordel neighborhood. It has a comfortable, grayscale postmodern interior, less angular and stark than Bordewijk's. Here, too, the menu changes regularly, offering variations on the theme of southwestern French and Provençal dishes (langoustine *tagine* with broadbeans; turbot with spices and puréed artichokes).

    L'Excelsior, at the Hotel de L'Europe on the Amstel River, is the kind of starchy luxury-hotel restaurant that you might as easily find in London, New York, or Paris. There are faux Louis-something armchairs, thick carpets, and a brigade of uniformed waiters, busboys, and sommeliers to bring you the competently prepared Dover sole with chanterelles, roast lamb with thyme, and mouthwatering desserts. Meanwhile, at the Amstel Inter-Continental

Hotel, **La Rive,** a classic French operation from the name on up, continues to wow locals. There seem to be as many waiters and busboys as diners. Thick carpets tempt you to go barefoot, the baroque flower arrangements are straight out of the Golden Age, and starched cloth drapes elegantly on spacious window-side tables overlooking the Amstel River. Chef Edwin Kats's cuisine has a distinctly Provençal-Med flavor (monkfish with sun-dried tomato wrapped in Jabugo ham, with eggplant purée and creamy caper sauce). **Vermeer,** Kats's former locale (now in the hands of Pascal Jalhaj), remains strait-laced but attracts serious corporate foodies. The pigeon smoked on the bone with roasted pineapple and white-peach and bay leaf *jus* with salsify is ambitious (perhaps too ambitious), but there is a Calvinistic, quintessentially un-fun feel to the place. Housed in two restored buildings, it belongs to the luxury/business NH Barbizon Palace Hotel. The decor features mock–Louis XIII armchairs, delft-blue plates, silver platters, and crystal. **De Silveren Spiegel** is another French/Dutch luxury restaurant, a survivor despite umpteen bad reviews, in two old houses near the Singel, and has yet another interior plucked from a Golden Age canvas: antique black-and-white tile floors, a carved spiral staircase, silver candlesticks, and crisp white tablecloths.

For that special moment... No question, the place to pop corks, people-watch, and applaud when the food arrives is still **Le Garage.** Flamboyant restaurateur Joop Braakhekke is a TV celeb, and at his wildly successful restaurant the smell of garlic hits the socialites and jet-setters smack in the face as they enter. The menu shuttles between a Parisian brasserie and a Tuscan trattoria, with stopovers in Tokyo and Mumbai. The decor would be a hit in Vegas—mirrors, red vinyl banquettes, and black, wraparound wooden chairs. You'll be thankful for the basket of garlic bread because the atmosphere is so festive it can take an hour to get food on the table. At Gertjan Hageman's **De Kas,** you sit in an immense reconverted hothouse with 40-foot ceilings, but the festive mood at dinner (lunch is quiet) fills the space, spilling into the chef's organic plantings and out into the surrounding park. If you dress up in black to celebrate, and I don't mean a tux, then head for the ultra-hip and hyper-pricey **Dylan,** in the hotel of the same name, where the disarmingly affable chef Schilo van Coevorden is cooking up Thai/Italian/French–inspired delicacies (foie gras soup with sweet Thai basil and lime; chicken with gingko-nut curry) in a reconverted landmark bakery decorated by Anouska Hempel (aka Lady Weinberg, if you please).

Forget about the food at the **Café Américain,** and you'll have a grand time drinking, people-watching, and gazing at the gorgeous Art Nouveau–cum–Art Deco landmark interior. The chandeliers are right out of the original *War of the Worlds* set design; ceiling fans create a pleasant haze of smoke that accents the Gatsbyesque atmosphere. This is where locals come for Sunday brunch, before or after the theater, or to celebrate everything from weddings and golden anniversaries to divorces. The French brasserie–style dishes—like smoked rabbit salad with walnut-raspberry dressing or duck breast with caramelized mango sauce and red peppercorns—are perfectly edible, if overly ambitious. **Long Pura** is the place to go for a swanky Indonesian feast amid neocolonial decor, served by costumed waiters. Happily, the food is spicy, authentic, and delicious. **Lucius,** the city's liveliest fish restaurant, is always packed (with locals and tourists), noisy, and fun, and longtime owners George and Marleen Lodewijks do all they can to keep the Parisian brasserie atmosphere frenzied. It's a miracle the fish stay so fresh; it's as if they'd just leapt out of the huge aquarium in the dining room (except that those are tropical fish, in case you're wondering).

Overrated... **De Silveren Spiegel,** a luxurious French/Dutch restaurant near Singel in a gorgeous Old Dutch setting—centuries-old step-gable facade, creaking spiral staircase, antique tables—serves okay food, and the service can be starchy indeed. The clientele is distinctly business- and tourist-oriented, and the staff may think that, what with the antique black-and-white tile floors and the polished silver candlesticks, no extra effort is required. A lot of people used to refer to Tom Yam as the best Thai restaurant in town, confusing luxury with authenticity. Now that it's been reinvented as **Tom Yam Fusion Cuisine,** guess what? The more things change, the more they stay the same. The service is still excellent, the food very good indeed, but let's be honest: Chef Jos Boomgaardt tailors his fusion delicacies to please tame Dutch palates. **Sama Sebo,** near the Rijksmuseum, used to serve some of the best Indonesian food in town, but fatigue has apparently gained the upper hand. The food is okay but nothing more, though visitors continue to flock here, paying premium prices. **Le Pêcheur** has fine-quality fish. The setting is swell—a pleasant dining room or lovely outdoor terrace—but the prices are high, the pretentiousness factor moderate to high, and the fussy herb sauces just possibly unnecessary.

See-and-be-scenes... Amsterdam veteran with a Michelin-star pedigree, Gertjan Hageman, draws a self-consciously sophisticated crowd to his organic, market-menu hot spot, **De Kas,** in a former hothouse reconverted to the tune of $1.5 million. At **Le Garage** you still have to beg to get a reservation. The service is a circus act, and you can wait hours to get fed, but the fusion fare is worth it (cubed tuna tartare with curry and a crisp spinach pancake, and flaming-hot Thai chicken with green chile sauce). **Dylan,** in the ultrachic designer hotel of the same name, is where neomillionaires, jet-setters, and media tycoons go to check out each other's black duds while feeding on skate filet with squid ink sauce or chicken Fabergé with lobster and ginger.

Amsterdam, on the western edge of town in a former water-pumping plant, is where young trendies mix with the middle-age TV and media crowd from the broadcasting studios next door. The menu is eclectic, the food edible (smoked halibut with horseradish; minty lamb stew). **La Rive** is still *the* place to show off your diamonds, Savile Row suit, or designer leather pants. You never know—one of the Amstel Inter-Continental Hotel's dozens of celebrity regulars might stroll in, and chef Edwin Kats is no slouch: He had a star at Vermeer before taking over from Robert Kranenborg. Across town in the Jordaan, land of converted warehouses, you'll find the hip loft set displayed like rough diamonds on **Bordewijk**'s black-and-red tables. You may wonder whether your 30-ish neighbor has come to eat the superb, French/Italian–inspired cuisine or just to see what the competition is up to. Move over a few streets in the Jordaan and shave off a decade from the average age of the clients and you'll find **Rakang Thai,** an exotic design restaurant featured regularly in trendy magazines. This is still *the* place to show off your crazy clubwear and establish your credentials as an eater of hot ethnic food.

Landmarks... Once upon a time, **L'Excelsior,** in the 1896 Hotel de L'Europe, was the top French restaurant in town. The Michelin stars may have departed, but this is still a luxury establishment, its dining room overlooking the Amstel River at Muntplein. Some of the waiters seem like they've been around since the place was built, and the food, though traditional, is rather good. The early 1900s **Café Américain** at Leidseplein is a place architecture students seek out for the landmark Art Nouveau decor, with Art Deco additions. Hanging from the high, vaulted ceiling are huge bronze and stained-glass lamps that look like they might take wing. The wall clock with gold letters and symbolist murals recalls the opulence of West Egg. It's a delight to have a drink or an undemanding French-Dutch meal here and people-watch. **Amsterdam,** a trendy restaurant favored by TV types and wannabes, is in a magnificent 19th-century water-pumping plant, with 100-foot ceilings. Ornamental iron and brickwork, huge pumps, and engines surround the hundreds of wooden tables. **De Roode Leeuw,** in a peculiar turn-of-the-20th-century building, has the city's oldest enclosed (and heated) sidewalk terrace. The old-fashioned paneled dining room is decorated with wonderfully hideous carved wooden wagons hanging from the ceiling on otherworldly sleds. Despite having two strikes against it—it's on neon-lit Damrak and it's Dutch—the place hits a home run for the homey atmosphere and food.

Cheap eats... **Van Dobben** is great for sandwiches and croquettes. Several good bets are near the Albert Cuypstraat market. In the De Pijp neighborhood, **Warung Marlon** is a favorite for cheap, fast, and lip-smacking Surinamese (rice topped with chicken in peanut sauce, wonton soup, Peking duck, and banana chips), and it's totally nonsmoking. One of the cheapest Indonesian restaurants in town is **Bojo,** near Leidseplein. All the usual favorites are served until 4am on Friday and Saturday nights. **Traiterie Grekas,** on Singel near Spui, is more a caterer's shop than a restaurant, but the Greek food—grape leaves, moussaka, and eggplant and chickpea dips—is tops. Nearby **Haesje Claes** has a cheap tourist menu with all the rib-sticking Dutch goodies, including *stamppot.* The **Pancake Bakery,** in the basement of a Prinsengracht warehouse, offers 70 kinds of meal-in-one pancakes, each guaranteed to fill you to bursting for a relative pittance.

Isn't it romantic?... In Amsterdam, you'll pay for romance and atmosphere. **Le Pêcheur** is at its best when the lights are low and the elegant decor—white tablecloths, nautical prints—becomes a mere backdrop. Better still is a table in the flower-filled backyard, tucked between the 17th-century mansions of the Golden Bend; there is no more gorgeous a place to feast on fish—some of the city's best. Try the saffron and fennel soup with sautéed Dutch shrimp, or the thyme-perfumed brill fillet with tagliatelle. When you feel like singing a love duet, **Caruso** may be just the place for you—along with the tasty, updated Italian food, you get a setting worthy of La Scala and a deliciously obsequious staff who will whisper to you in Italian if you like (it's remarkably more romantic-sounding than Dutch).

Tempo Doeloe may have the best Indonesian food in town, but it's also romantic in a spunky, exotic way. The theatrical lighting makes everyone seem to have bedroom eyes. **Long Pura,** the other top Indonesian, has a spiffy neocolonial decor and soft lighting: An orchid blossom greets you at the table, but the rest is up to you. **Wilhelmina-Dok**—still intact after it was rammed by a river cruise ship in 2005 (now there's local color for you!)—can hardly help being romantic, even though on the outside it's a strange-looking place, all by itself beside the water. This cafe-restaurant is on three floors (though the chandeliered top floor Kapiteinskamer/Captain's Cabin is for groups only). Plain wood tables, wood floors, and oak cabinets give the interior an old-fashioned maritime look, and large windows serve up views across the narrow, barge-speckled IJ channel to the cruise-ship Passenger Terminal Amsterdam on the south shore. Candlelight softens the marine decor. The menu favors plain cooking and organic products, and the Continental food—grilled swordfish with saffron rice, grilled veal cutlets with marinated eggplants, flagcolet salad, and pesto—ebbs and flows like the tides in the IJ channel, largely unremarked, as trendy youth stare into each other's mauve makeup, caress each other's designer club-wear labels, and wonder if romance will bloom later on the dance floor of More, Sinners in Heaven, or iT (see the Nightlife & Cafes chapter).

Tourist traps... **D'Vijff Vlieghen,** better known to English speakers as the **Five Flies,** is the mother of all themed tourist traps and a must for anyone interested in the genre.

It was founded after World War II by flamboyant antiques dealer Nicolaas Kroese, whose motto ran, "You haven't been to Amsterdam if you haven't been to the Five Flies." The instant-ancient decor alone is worth a detour. And the French/Dutch fare isn't that bad (lots of updated ham and apple dishes, plus game and fish). **Haesje Claes** has become the Five Flies' direct competitor. Owner André Duyves, too, has an instant-old pedigree: The restaurant has been around since 1970, but he touts the date 1520 prominently because that's when Lady Haesje Claes was born nearby. ("The spirit and period atmosphere linger," Duyves likes to say through his impressive moustache.) The place is marvelously kitsch, with mock everything, except the authentically old buildings (totally rebuilt, of course). Luckily, it's all good fun, and the traditional Dutch food is good enough, as long as you stick to things like *stamppot* or salad with herring and smoked eel. The **Pancake Bakery** is something altogether different, designed especially for Americans, it seems, and for kids who've just gotta have a *pannekoek*. Don't bother to ask your fellow diners what's what—they're not Dutch.

Something fishy... For reasons beyond the ken of a non-Dutch person, all Amsterdam's best fish restaurants are landlocked and about as far from the rivers or canals as possible in this floating city. The Atlantic and North Sea fish at **Albatros Seafoodhouse** have the great virtue of being grilled, poached, and fried in the simplest manner possible, then served in ship-ahoy decor by friendly old-timers in a relaxed Jordaan neighborhood atmosphere (there's even a nonsmoking section). Try the mixed seafood salad, the raw herring, and the sea bass (they make a mean tiramisu, too). No quaint fishermen's nets adorn **Le Pêcheur,** a stylish restaurant on Reguliersdwarsstraat. The canal isn't in view, but you can admire the backsides and gardens of 17th-century mansions as you dine on elaborate fish dishes, skillfully prepared. You'll marvel—or gasp—at the chef's use of herbs and sauces (sea bass with tarragon-mustard sauce; prawns with a garlicky fennel sauce). At lively and fun **Lucius,** the herring, plaice, sole, and bream are equally tasty raw, grilled, poached, or baked. The seafood's so fresh you almost wish you'd ordered it without that delicious, flavorful, but superfluous cayenne or green-pepper sauce.

Can you put that out, please?... Eat out too often in Amsterdam and you could end up sounding like General Grievous on a bad day. The city is a nonsmoker's hell—the opposite of California—so eat outside or pick an uncrowded time and ask the waiter or host to make an effort to seat nonsmokers near you. Call ahead and explain your request in detail—then prepare to be smoked like a local eel. The only totally smoke-free eateries I've found in town are cheap, cheery, and delicious Surinamese **Warung Marlon** and the hip Japanese noodle bar **Wagamama. De Vrolijke Abrikoos,** a vegetarian restaurant, reserves half of its one big room for nonpuffers (weekdays only). The first thing you notice when you enter the vegetarian **Golden Temple** is that you can actually *see* the place—the veil of cigarette smoke that obscures most Amsterdam restaurants has been lifted here by a restaurant-wide no-smoking policy that adds a heavenly touch all by itself. **Café Américain** has a small section in the bar/cafe area (not in the brasserie). **Albatros Seafoodhouse,** a friendly eatery, has a big, bona fide nonsmoking area and a staff that'll defend your air space. The managers of **Haesje Claes** (Dutch classics) and **Memories of India** are sympathetic to the antitobacco crowd, but there's only so much they can do to convince other patrons to stump out those cigs and—ever popular—cigars. Tolerance! And good cough—luck.

When the play's the thing... The Dutch eat dinner very early indeed, and most restaurants stop serving by 11pm, so post-theater meals in restaurants are hard to manage: It's as if Calvin wouldn't approve if you enjoyed two forms of entertainment on a single night. **Café Américain** specializes in feeding the concert and theater crowds of the Stadsschouwburg across the street in Leidseplein and the Lido casino and cabaret around the corner on Singelgracht; it serves dinner until midnight, and light meals and snacks until 1am. So what if the stunning Art Nouveau interior and ambience are more interesting than the French-inspired food? **Le Pêcheur,** a swanky fish restaurant on Reguliersdwarsstraat near Rembrandtplein, is within striking distance of all the city's venues, especially the Muziektheater and Carré, nearby on the Amstel River. The well-heeled international clientele is used to late dining; and if you come in too late for the main menu, after around 11pm, there's a variety of classy snacks served until 1am—caviar, cold lobster, oysters, smoked salmon, and more. One of the wildest, hottest restaurants in town, **Le Garage** is not a late-night place per se, but the kitchen will serve until about midnight, and the tables are still crowded well after the witching hour. At **Amsterdam,** another hip eatery, the kitchen stays open until 11:30pm, and you can get snacks and light meals until 1am (till 2am Fri–Sat). On weekends, you can get a pan-fried steak or a plate of herring until midnight at homey **Piet de Leeuw. Bojo,** a cheap and cheery Indonesian eatery near Leidseplein, serves until 1am (4am Fri–Sat nights). Other after-11 eats are found at: **Lucius** (fish), **Memories of India, Tapas Bar Català, Tempo Doeloe, Van Dobben,** and **D'Vijff Vlieghen.** Beyond these, your best bet for a late-night hangout is a cafe (see brown cafes, neobrowns, and white cafes in the Nightlife & Cafes chapter).

Kid pleasers... The Dutch are very tolerant of rambunctious youngsters. You can take them almost anywhere (at least anywhere not strictly for elitist trendies), as long as you can afford to pay for them. One spot they're sure to love is **Haesje Claes,** a roistering Dutch place with Old Dutch decor. Host André Duyves seems right out of Walt Disney, and his food will remind the kiddies of school lunches—the house specialty, *stamppot,* is none other than mashed potatoes with a ladle of dark gravy, sausages, ribs, sauerkraut, and more. Kids love the croquettes and milk at **Van Dobben.** At the **Pancake Bakery,** you might be back home at a demented IHOP. The kids can splash and spill corn and sugar syrup (no maple syrup in view) without danger, since the tabletops are marble and the menus laminated. They're sure to find something they like among the omelets and 70 kinds of pancakes topped with everything from fried chicken to sweet corn. Since few kids can resist a good pizza, you might also try the straightforward trattoria **L'Angoletto.** Surprisingly, hip **Amsterdam** is very brat-friendly; the eclectic food and industrial decor (an old water-pumping plant) appeal to budding trendies. At **Wilhelmina-Dok**, a free ferry ride across the IJ channel from Centraal Station, kids can sit out on the glassed-in terrace or put their noses up against the big picture windows (to watch the maritime comings and goings on the busy shipping channel). They can also keep an eye open for the rogue river cruiser that nearly sank the restaurant in April 2005.

For a quiet tête-à-tête... **Vermeer,** the NH Barbizon Palace's luxury Dutch/French restaurant, is synonymous with discretion. There's enough room between the tables for rafts of waiters and busboys to glide by, the thick carpets absorb unpleasant sounds, and the mock–Louis XIII armchairs are as upright as the diners in them. Classically French **La Rive** and **L'Excelsior** have some of the highest prices in town, which keeps the number of diners to a minimum. An added plus at La Rive is the pianist, who produces soothing background music **De Roode Leeuw,** a serious Dutch restaurant, has the kind of old-fashioned paneled decor, big tables, and professional waiters that perfectly complement intimate conversations.

Vegging out... The antimeat crowd is well served in Amsterdam, since most menus feature salads and fish. There really is no need to seek out the dozens of joyless, mediocre vegetarian-only eateries where the owners and clients are likely to snarl at anyone wearing leather shoes. However, if that's your bag, and you can stomach the name, try **De Vrolijke Abrikoos,** considered by those in the know the very best veggie eatery in Amsterdam—good for succulent tofu and satisfying salads. Everything is biodynamically grown and respectfully consumed. There's a big nonsmoking section (weekdays), and the walls are a comforting shade of edible apricot. If anything, the limpid atmosphere in the **Golden Temple** is a tad too hallowed, an effect enhanced by a Zen-like absence of decorative flourishes. The menu livens things up, though, with an unlikely roster of Indian, Middle Eastern, and Mexican dishes. This could make for an interesting game of mix-and-match if only the small print didn't all but instruct you to keep them apart. The food is delicately spiced and flavored, and evidently prepared by loving hands. Multiple-choice platters are a good way to go. For the Indian *thali,* you select from constituents like *sag paneer* (spinach and homemade cheese), vegetable *korma,* and *raita* (cucumber and yogurt dip); the Middle Eastern platter has stalwarts like *falafel,* chickpea-and-vegetable stew, and vegetable *dolmas.* Side dishes range across items as varied as guacamole, couscous, and *pakora.*

Described by its owners as a "nondestinational food station," **Wagamama,** a Zen-style Japanese noodle restaurant, has dozens of great veg combos (it's nonsmoking and the food is monosodium glutamate—and humor—free). Most other Asian restaurants, and all the Indonesian places in town, offer a variety of vegetable-only dishes and vegetarian fixed-price menus. **Tempo Doeloe** has two vegetarian menus (plus up to five courses a la carte) that are out of this world, featuring a variety of veggies and bean sprouts with mild or spicy peanut sauce (*gado-gado* and *sajoer lodeh*) and sweet and sour *petjel* sauce, plus saffron-perfumed rice, vegetable pancakes, and fruit desserts.

When the boss is paying... De Silveren Spiegel, which sits across the street from the Amsterdam Renaissance Hotel in two handsome old buildings, is the kind of place food-challenged businesspeople and upscale conventioneers head to when they don't have to spend their own money. The fancy French/Dutch food fits the candlelit, antiques-crammed setting. At **Vermeer,** another architectural gem in two landmark houses, the Golden Age atmosphere accompanies excellent French-inspired cuisine. Across the center of town at **L'Excelsior,** the tables are generously distanced, the wine list is long on three-digit vintages from la belle France, and the punctilious waiters know when to light the candles and stop hovering. Timing the removal of the dishes with amazing grace, they may glide up to your table with a succulent roast lamb or Dover sole with chanterelles. **La Rive**'s comfortable armchairs are never sullied by wallets (they are worn inside suit pockets or carried in diamond-spangled handbags); it's the quintessential place to spend lots of money on classic, Michelin-starred French food. **De Kas,** in a reconverted hothouse, is a hip gold mine: There's no menu, just the chef's picks of the day, and the drinks, dessert, and coffee push the tab through the glass roof. **Bordewijk,** near Noorderkerk in the Jordaan, attracts a similarly chic clientele with its stellar French/Italian food. Nearby **Christophe,** a French restaurant favored by Amsterdam's beau monde, is a great place to squander the company's euros on tempting French regional dishes. At designer-chic **Dylan,** feast on Thai/Italian/French delicacies prepared by celeb chef Schilo van Coevorden; the prices are breathtaking.

Alfresco... Albatros Seafoodhouse, a friendly, simple fish restaurant, has a narrow terrace on the sidewalk where in summer you can watch the seagulls and albatrosses flying overhead. Soak up the atmospheric Jordaan, where there's little traffic and locals chatting on stoops. Trendy **Wilhelmina-Dok** has great riverside views of the IJ from its big windows and a large outdoor terrace across the water from the cruise-liner Passenger Terminal Amsterdam. In summer at **Le Pêcheur,** you can dine on fresh fish in a lovely, flower-filled backyard. A few doors down is **Sahid Jaya,** probably the most luxurious and pricey of Amsterdam's Indonesian restaurants, which also has a pleasant backyard terrace amid Golden Bend mansions.

Take me to the river... For a city built on dozens of canals and two big rivers—the Amstel and the IJ—it's amazing how few restaurants take advantage of the waterfront real estate; you can count them on the claws of one paw. Some of the well-heeled diners at **L'Excelsior** arrive by boat at the Hotel de L'Europe's private dock on the Amstel, ready to dine on classic French food. Down the river a half-mile or so, with its own private dock, is another formal French choice, **La Rive,** the Amstel Inter-Continental's posh and much-touted dining room. When you disembark from your saloon boat and settle into the dining room, which sits almost at water level, you feel like you're on a luxury liner, with canal-boats and yachts cruising past the windows. When those same boats and ships decide to head to sea, they sail down the IJ within view of trendy **Wilhelmina-Dok,** practically the only restaurant in town where you're aware of the sea and port traffic—once Amsterdam's lifeblood.

Best cafe food... Dantzig aan de Amstel, a big, bright white cafe attached to city hall, serves great *bitterballen*, croquettes, egg rolls, *sate* chicken, and daily specials; it's a good place for a pre- or post-theater snack. **Café Luxembourg,** a designer cafe at Spui, gets a lot of its food from top restaurants and has the best croquettes (from Holtkamp; see p. 175), dim sum, chicken *sate*, salads, and sandwiches of all the city's cafes. **De Jaren** is a sunny white cafe on the Amstel with a great salad bar, soups, and good daily quiches; the regular restaurant here features unnecessarily complicated dishes.

Map 4: Amsterdam Dining Orientation

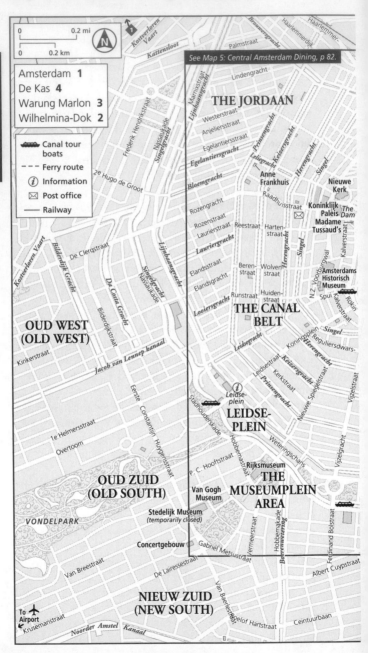

0	0.2 mi	
0	0.2 km	

See Map 5: Central Amsterdam Dining, p 82.

Amsterdam **1**
De Kas **4**
Warung Marlon **3**
Wilhelmina-Dok **2**

🚢 Canal tour boats
- - - Ferry route
ⓘ Information
⊠ Post office
— Railway

THE JORDAAN

Marnixstraat
Lijnbaansgracht
Lindengracht
Westerstraat
Anjeliersstraat
Egelantiersstraat
Egelantiersgracht
Leliegracht
Prinsengracht
Keizersgracht
Herengracht
Singel
Bloemgracht
Anne
Frankhuis
Raadhuisstraat
Nieuwe
Kerk
Koninklijk
Paleis
The
Dam
Madame
Tussaud's
Kalverstraat

Rozengracht
Rozenstraat
Reestraat
Laurierstraat
Hartenstraat
N.Z. Voorburgwal
Amsterdams
Historisch
Museum
Lauriergracht
Berenstraat
Wolvenstraat
Elandsstraat
Elandsgracht
Runstraat
Huidenstraat
Spui
Kalverstraat
Rokin
Looiersgracht

THE CANAL
BELT

Frederik Hendrikstraat
Nassaukade
Singelgracht
2e Hugo de Groot

Kostverloren Vaart
Bilderdijk Gracht
De Clercqstraat
Da Costa Graat
Nassaukade
Singelgracht
Lijnbaansgracht
Bilderdijkstraat

Singel
Leidsegracht
Koningsplein
Herengracht
Reguliersdwars-
straat
Keizersgracht
Leidsestraat
Kerkstraat
Prinsengracht
Nieuwe Spiegelstraat
Vijzelgracht
Vijzelstraat

OUD WEST
(OLD WEST)

Kinkerstraat
Jacob van Lennep kanaal
Eerste Constantijn Huygensstraat

Stadhouderskade
Leidse-
plein

LEIDSE-
PLEIN

Weteringschans

1e Helmersstraat
Overtoom
P. C. Hooftstraat
Hobbemastraat

Rijksmuseum

THE
MUSEUMPLEIN
AREA

OUD ZUID
(OLD SOUTH)

Van Gogh
Museum

VONDELPARK

Stedelijk Museum
(temporarily closed)

Concertgebouw
Gabriel Metsustraat
Vermeerstraat
Hobbemakade
Boerenwetering
Ferdinand Bolstraat

Van Breestraat
De Lairessestraat
Van Baerlestraat
Albert Cuypstraat

NIEUW ZUID
(NEW SOUTH)

To ✈
Airport
Krusemanstraat
Roelof Hartstraat
Ceintuurbaan
Noorder Amstel Kanaal

See Map 5: Central Amsterdam Dining, p 82.

DINING

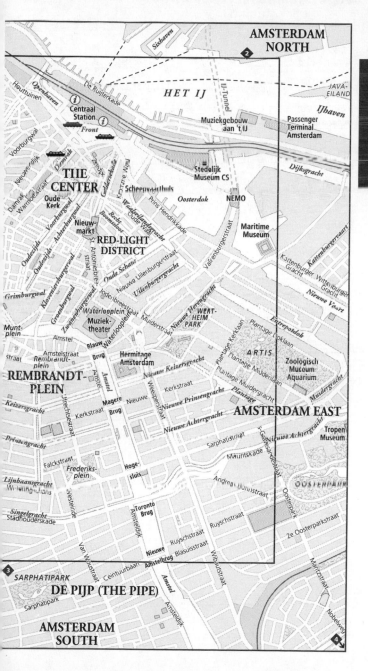

Map 5: Central Amsterdam Dining

DINING

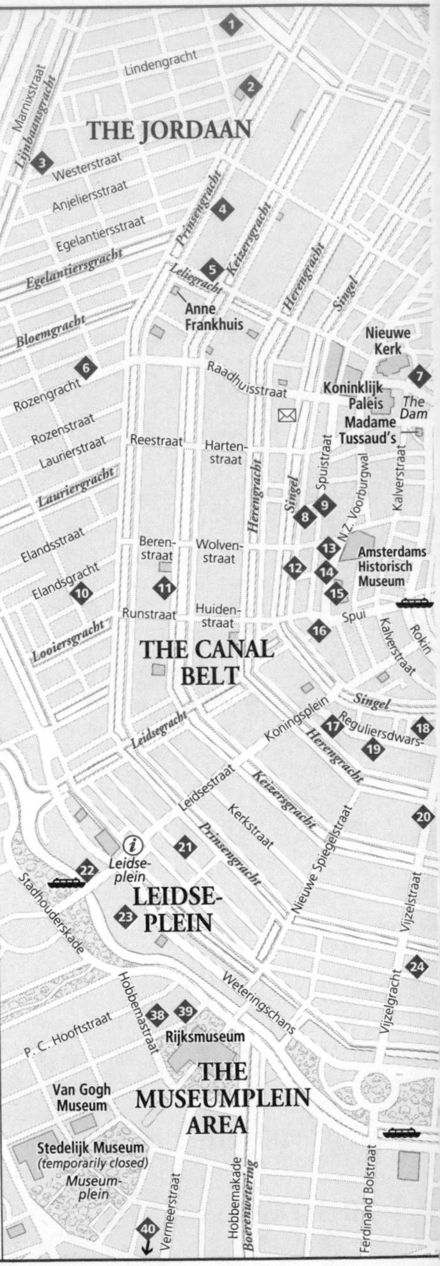

The Index

Note:

	1€ = $1.25 U.S.
$$$$$	over 30€/$38
$$$$	20€–30€/$25–$38
$$$	15€–20€$19–$25
$$	7.50€–15€/$9.40–$19
$	under 7.50€/$9.40

Prices given are per person for entrees only.

The following abbreviations are used for credit cards:

AE	American Express
DC	Diners Club
DISC	Discover
MC	MasterCard
V	Visa

Albatros Seafoodhouse (p. 74) JORDAAN *SEAFOOD* Serving fresh Atlantic and North Sea fish grilled, poached, and fried is the specialty at this neighborhood restaurant.... *Tel 020/627-9932. www.restaurantalbatros.nl. Westerstraat 264 at Lijnbaansgracht. Tram 3 or 10 to Marnixplein. Reservations recommended. AE, DC, MC, V. Thurs–Tues 6–11pm.* $$$$

See Map 5 on p. 82.

Amsterdam (p. 71) WEST *CONTINENTAL* A hip café/restaurant in a reconverted 19th-century water-pumping plant on the western edge of town, with authentic industrial decor and 100-foot ceilings. Try tomato soup, foie gras, calf's brain with sage, minty lamb stew—all of it astoundingly edible.... *Tel 020/682-2666. www.cradam.nl. Watertorenplein 6 at Van Hallstraat. Tram 10 to Van Hallstraat. AE, DC, MC, V. Daily 11am–1am (till 2am Fri–Sat); meals served till 11:30pm.* $$

See Map 4 on p. 80.

Bojo (p. 72) LEIDSEPLEIN *INDONESIAN* Amsterdam's long-established cheap and late-night Indonesian restaurant.... *Tel 020/ 622-7434. www.bojo.nl. Lange Leidsedwarsstraat 49–51 at Leidsestraat. Trams 1, 2, 5, 6, 7, or 10 to Leidseplein. No credit cards. 4pm–1am (till 4am Fri–Sat).* $

See Map 5 on p. 82.

Bordewijk **(p. 68)** JORDAAN *FRENCH/ITALIAN* The French/Ital-
ian–inspired menu is among the city's best, the postmodern setting endlessly hip.... *Tel 020/624-3899. www.bordewijk.nl.
Noordermarkt 7 at Prinsengracht. Trams 1, 2, 5, 6, 13, or 17 to
Martelaarsgracht. Reservations essential. AE, DC, MC, V. Tues–Sun
6:30–10:30pm. $$$$*

See Map 5 on p. 82.

Café Américain **(p. 70)** LEIDSEPLEIN *CONTINENTAL* This landmark cafe's stunning Art Nouveau and Art Deco interior eclipses
the overly ambitious, though perfectly edible, French-inspired
food. Special theater menus, brunch, and high tea available....
*Tel 020/556-3116. www.amsterdamamerican.com. Leidseplein
28 at Leidsekade. Trams 1, 2, 5, 6, 7, or 10 to Leidseplein. AE, DC,
MC, V. Daily 10:30am midnight. $$$*

See Map 5 on p. 82.

Cafe Luxembourg **(p. 79)** CENTER *CAFE* A slick crowd blends into
the designer decor.... *Tel 020/620-6264. www.luxembourg.
nl Spui 22–24 at Spuistraat. Trams 1, 2, 5 to Spui. Sun–Thurs
9am–1am; Fri–Sat 9am–2am. AE, DC, MC, V. $*

See Map 5 on p. 82.

Caruso **(p. 67)** CENTER *MODERN ITALIAN* Italian **nuova cucina**
served in an operatic bordello setting—some of the city's best
Italian (and fish) dishes are here.... *Tel 020/623-8320. www.
ristorantecaruso.com. Singel 550 at Muntplein. Trams 4, 9, 14,
16, 24, or 25 to Muntplein. Reservations recommended. Jacket
and tie recommended. AE, DC, MC, V. Daily 6:30–11pm. $$$$*

See Map 5 on p. 82.

Christophe **(p. 68)** CANAL BELT *FRENCH* Chef Jean-Christophe
Royer's eponymous restaurant—très French and superb. Casual-
chic dress.... *Tel 020/625 0807. www.christophe.nl. Leliegracht
46 at Keizersgracht. Trams 6, 13, 14, or 17 to Westermarkt.
Reservations essential. AE, DC, MC, V. Tues–Sat 6:30–
10:30pm. $$$$*

See Map 5 on p. 82.

Dantzig aan de Amstel **(p. 79)** WATERLOOPLEIN *CAFE* A spacious
white cafe with a river terrace, at city hall; tasty food....
*Tel 020/620-9039. Zwanenburgwal 15 at Waterlooplein. Trams 9
or 14 to Waterlooplein. AE, DC, MC, V. Mon–Thurs 11am–1am,
Fri–Sun 11am–2am. $*

See Map 5 on p. 82.

De Jaren **(p. 79)** CENTER *CAFE* A postmodern, big, and sunny
white cafe overlooking the Amstel near Muntplein, where beau-
tiful young Amsterdammers lounge on the terrace.... *Tel 020/
625-5771. www.cafe-de-jaren.nl. Nieuwe Doelenstraat 20–22 at
Kloveniersburgwal. Trams 4, 9, 14, 16, 24, 25 to Muntplein.
Sun–Thurs 10am–1am; Fri–Sat 10am–2am. V. $*

See Map 5 on p. 82.

DINING

THE INDEX

De Kas (p. 68) SOUTH *CONTINENTAL* Hip new restaurant, owned by celeb chef Gertjan Hageman, in a reconverted hothouse. The French-Dutch specialties change daily. No menu: It's the chef's call.... *Tel 020/462-4562. www.restaurantdekas.nl. Kamerlingh Onneslaan 3 at Middenweg. Tram 9 to Hogeweg. Reservations essential. AE, DC, MC, V. Mon–Fri noon–3pm and 6:30–10pm, Sat 6:30–10pm.* $$$$

See Map 4 on p. 80.

De Roode Leeuw (p. 63) CENTER *DUTCH* Great Dutch regional cuisine served in a cozily kitsch, old-fashioned interior. Try the dried *nagelhout* beef or braised codfish with mustard sauce.... *Tel 020/555-0666. www.hotelamsterdam.nl. Damrak 93–94 at the Dam. Trams 4, 9, 14, 16, 24, or 25 to the Dam. AE, DC, MC, V. Daily 7–10am and noon–10pm.* $$$

See Map 5 on p. 82.

De Silveren Spiegel (p. 70) CENTER *FRENCH/DUTCH* A top-dollar French/Dutch restaurant, with delicious dishes like duck breast on a bed of leeks with tiny corn pancakes or leg and filet of guinea fowl with wild mushrooms.... *Tel 020/624-6589. www. desilverenspiegel.nl. Kattengat 4 at Spuistraat. Trams 1, 2, 5, 6, 13, or 17 to Martelaarsgracht. Reservations required. Jacket and tie recommended. AE, DC, MC, V. Mon–Sat 5:30–10:30pm.* $$$$

See Map 5 on p. 82.

De Vrolijke Abrikoos (p. 77) CENTER *VEGETARIAN* The biodynamically grown veggie goodies taste better than the name sounds. Big nonsmoking section weekdays only.... *Tel 020/624-4672. Weteringschans 76 at Reguliersgracht. Trams 6, 7, 10, 16, 24, or 25 to Weteringcircuit. Reservations recommended. MC, V. Daily 5:30–11pm.* $$

See Map 5 on p. 82.

Duende (p. 67) JORDAAN *SPANISH (TAPAS)* This hip tapas bar in the Jordaan has tile floors, wooden tables, and a summer terrace out front.... *Tel 020/420-6692. www.cafeduende.nl. Lindengracht 62 at Noordermarkt. Trams 1, 2, 5, 6, 13, or 17 to Martelaarsgracht. No credit cards. Daily 5pm–1am.* $

See Map 5 on p. 82.

D'Vijff Vlieghen (p. 73) CENTER *DUTCH* A must for the decor alone: dark wood paneling and a labyrinth of timbered rooms. The Dutch-Continental fare is surprisingly edible.... *Tel 020/530-4060. www.d-vijffvlieghen.com. Spuistraat 294–302 at Spui. Trams 1, 2, or 5 to Spui. Reservations recommended. AE, DC, MC, V. Daily 5:30pm–midnight.* $$$$

See Map 5 on p. 82.

Dylan (p. 69) CANAL BELT *CONTINENTAL/WORLD* Chic-est of all of Amsterdam's new designer restaurants, located in Blakes Hotel. Presided over by affable celeb chef Schilo van Coevorden, master of Thai/Italian/French–inspired wonders.... *Tel 020/ 530-2010. www.dylanamsterdam.com. Keizersgracht 384 at Run straat. Trams 6, 13, 14, or 17 to Westermarkt. Reservations essential. AE, DC, MC, V. Mon–Fri 7–11am, noon–2pm, and 6:30–11pm; Sat 7–11am and 6:30–11pm.* $$$$$

See Map 5 on p. 82.

Golden Temple (p. 77) CENTER *VEGETARIAN* In its fourth decade of tickling meat-shunning palates, this temple of taste is still one of the best vegetarian (and vegan) options in town.... *Tel 020/626-8560. www.goldentemplerestaurant.nl. Utrechtsestraat 126 at Frederiksplein. Tram 4 to Prinsengracht. MC, V. Daily 5–10pm.* $–$$

See Map 5 on p. 82.

Haesje Claes (p. 74) CENTER *DUTCH* This quintessential but ondoor ingly *gezellig* tourist trap actually serves excellent *stamppot* (mashed potatoes with sauerkraut and pork ribs) and salad with herring and smoked eel.... *Tel 020/624-9998. www.haesjeclaes. nl. Spuistraat 273-275 at Spui. Trams 1, 2, or 5 to Spui. Reservations recommended. AE, DC, MC, V. Daily noon–10pm.* $$

See Map 5 on p. 82.

Kantjil & de Tijger (p. 65) CENTER *INDONESIAN* Pretty cool, even though the food can be pretty hot.... *Tel 020/620-0994. www.kantjil.nl. Spuistraat 291-293 at Spui. Trams 1, 2, or 5 to Spui. Reservations recommended on weekends. AE, DC, MC, V. Daily 4:30–11pm.* $$

See Map 5 on p. 82.

Kilimanjaro (p. 66) EASTERN DOCKS *AFRICAN* This chic African restaurant with only seven tables is run by a Dutchman, but the Ethiopian cook makes a variety of East African specialties.... *Tel 020/622-3485. Rapenburgerplein 6 at Prins Hendrikkade. Buses 22 or 32 to Kadijksplein. Reservations essential. AE, DC, MC, V. Tues–Sun 6pm–midnight.* $$

See Map 5 on p. 82.

L'Angoletto (p. 67) OLD SOUTH *ITALIAN* Utterly unpretentious, it's run by young Italians who make good classic pizzas, pasta dishes, and meat.... *Tel 020/676-4182. Hemonystraat 18 at Govert Flinckstraat. Tram 4 to Stadhouderskade. Reservations recommended. No credit cards. Sun–Fri 6–11pm.* $$

See Map 5 on p. 82.

La Rive (p. 69) EAST *DUTCH/FRENCH* Dutch-French food by celeb chef Edwin Kats at ultraluxe restaurant.... *Tel 020/520-3264. www.restaurantlarive.com. Professor Tulpplein 1 at the Amstel. Trams 6, 7, or 10 to Sarphatistraat. Reservations essential. Jacket and tie recommended. AE, DC, MC, V. Mon–Fri noon–2pm, Mon–Sat 6:30–10:30pm.* $$$$$

See Map 5 on p. 82.

DINING

THE INDEX

Le Garage (p. 69) MUSEUM DISTRICT *FUSION* It's a cross between a Parisian brasserie, a Tuscan trattoria, and a noisy Las Vegas nightclub. Nonetheless, the wildly creative food is virtuoso stuff. Chic dress.... *Tel 020/679-7176. www.restaurant legarage.nl. Ruysdaelstraat 54–56 at Van Baerlestraat. Trams 3, 5, 12, or 24 to Roelof Hartplein. Reservations essential. AE, DC, MC, V. Mon–Fri noon–3pm and daily 6–11pm. $$$$*

See Map 5 on p. 82.

Le Pêcheur (p. 74) CENTER *SEAFOOD* This upscale fish restaurant run by Rien van Santen has a flower-filled backyard on the Golden Bend and fresh, highest-quality seafood.... *Tel 020/624-3121. www.lepecheur.nl. Reguliersdwarsstraat 32 at Koningsplein. Trams 1, 2, or 5 to Koningsplein. AE, MC, V. Mon–Fri noon–midnight, Sat 5pm–midnight. $$$$*

See Map 5 on p. 82.

L'Excelsior (p. 68) CENTER *FRENCH* Michelin stars come and go, but this perennial French restaurant at the Hotel de L'Europe stays.... *Tel 020/531-1778. www.leurope.nl. Nieuwe Doelenstraat 2–8 at Muntplein. Trams 4, 9, 14, 16, 24, or 25 to Muntplein. Reservations recommended. Jacket and tie required. AE, DC, MC, V. Mon–Fri 7am–11am, 12:30–2:30pm, and 7–10:30pm; Sat–Sun 7–11am and 7–10:30pm. $$$$$*

See Map 5 on p. 82.

Long Pura (p. 65) JORDAAN *INDONESIAN* Swank Indonesian restaurant, with costumed waiters, neocolonial decor, and some of the best *sambal goreng udang petjel* (shrimp and petjel beans with spicy coconut milk sauce) in town. Steep prices (for Indonesian food) but worth it.... *Tel 020/623-8950. www.restaurant-longpura.com (Website due online in 2006). Rozengracht 46–48 at Prinsengracht. Trams 6, 13, 14, or 17 to Westermarkt. AE, DC, MC, V. Daily 5–11pm. $$$*

See Map 5 on p. 82.

Lucius (p. 70) CENTER *SEAFOOD* Run by friendly George and Marleen Lodewijks, this is among the city's liveliest fish restaurants.... *Tel 020/624-1831. www.lucius.nl. Spuistraat 247 at Spui. Trams 1, 2, or 5 to Spui. AE, DC, MC, V. Daily 5pm–midnight. $$$$*

See Map 5 on p. 82.

Memories of India (p. 65) REMBRANDTPLEIN *INDIAN* Upscale, authentic Indian food. Don't miss the perfumed chapatis and nans, spicy lamb vindaloo, and tender tandoori chicken.... *Tel 020/623-5710. www.memoriesofindia.nl. Reguliersdwarsstraat 88 at Vijzelstraat. Trams 4, 9, 14, 16, 24, or 25 to Muntplein. AE, DC, MC, V. Daily 5–11:30pm. $$$*

See Map 5 on p. 82.

Pancake Bakery (p. 63) CANAL BELT *DUTCH (PANCAKES)* In the basement of a converted Prinsengracht warehouse. Of the 70 pancakes offered, first on the list is the "American Pancake," which boasts fried chicken, sweet corn, paprika, carrots, and spicy Cajun sauce.... *Tel 020/625-1333. www.pancake.nl. Prinsengracht 191 at Prinsenstraat. Trams 6, 13, 14, or 17 to Westermarkt. AE, MC, V. Daily noon–9:30pm. $*

See Map 5 on p. 82.

Piet de Leeuw (p. 64) CANAL BELT *DUTCH (STEAKS)* In the States it would be called "Pete's Place" or "The Lion," with a dark, cozy interior that smells slightly of beer. The famous (and delicious) artery-clogging beefsteak with onions is fantastic.... *Tel 020/623-7181. www.pietdeleeuw.nl. Noorderstraat 11 at Vijzelgracht. Trams 16, 24, or 25 to Prinsengracht. AE, MC, V. Mon–Fri noon–11pm, Sat–Sun 5–11pm. $$*

See Map 5 on p. 82.

Rakang Thai (p. 66) JORDAAN *THAI* A stylish Jordaan restaurant packed with trendies. Try the squid or chicken with lemon grass and coriander, sticky rice, or beef with peppers and basil.... *Tel 020/627-5012. www.rakang.nl. Elandsgracht 29 at Prinsengracht. Trams 6, 7, 10, or 17 to Elandsgracht. AE, DC, MC, V. Daily 6pm–midnight. $$*

See Map 5 on p. 82.

Sahid Jaya (p. 65) CENTER *INDONESIAN* Alfresco dining and the sumptuous, if nonauthentic, rice tables (dozens of dishes, from chicken *sate* in peanut sauce to *rendang padang*—beef with chile and coconut sauce) help alleviate the pain of the bill. Tasteful Indonesian luxury interior, polished service.... *Tel 020/626-3727. Reguliersdwarsstraat 26 at Koningsplein. Trams 1, 2, or 5, to Koningsplein. AE, DC, MC, V. Daily noon–3pm and 6–11pm. $$$$*

See Map 5 on p. 82.

Sama Sebo (p. 65) MUSEUM DISTRICT *INDONESIAN* Among the city's least-undiscovered Indonesian spots, with lots of small tables where you eat increasingly overrated *rijsttafel* elbow-to-elbow with connoisseurs and crowds of bemused tourists.... *Tel 020/662-8146. www.samasebo.nl. Pieter Cornelisz Hooftstraat 27 at Museum District. Trams 2 or 5 to Hobbemastraat. AE, DC, MC, V. Mon–Sat noon 2pm and 5–10pm. $$$*

See Map 5 on p. 82.

Shiva (p. 65) REMBRANDTPLEIN *INDIAN* This small, refined Indian restaurant serves flavorful curries, possibly Amsterdam's best.... *Tel 020/624-8713. Reguliersdwarsstraat 72 at Vijzelstraat. Trams 4, 9, 14, 16, 24, or 25 to Muntplein. AE, DC, MC, V. Daily 5–11pm. $$*

See Map 5 on p. 82.

Tapas Bar Català (p. 68) CENTER *SPANISH (TAPAS)* Belly, shout, and elbow your way through the cocktail-lounge interior to the best tapas bar in town.... *Tel 020/623-1141. Spuistraat 299 at*

Spui. Trams 1, 2, or 5 to Spui. No credit cards. Mon–Fri 4pm–midnight, Sat–Sun 1pm–midnight. $

See Map 5 on p. 82.

Tempo Doeloe (p. 64) CENTER *INDONESIAN* Top-notch Indonesian. Try the succulent *oedang madoera* (prawns in a gentle macadamia-nut sauce).... *Tel 020/625-6718. Utrechtsestraat 75 at Keizersgracht. Tram 4 to Keizersgracht. Reservations recommended. AE, DC, MC, V. Mon–Sat 6–11:30pm. $$$*

See Map 5 on p. 82.

Tom Yam Fusion Cuisine (p. 70) CENTER *DUTCH/THAI* Former Michelin-starred Dutch/French chef Jos Boomgaardt now cooks fusion food in this upscale Dutch/Thai restaurant, where the dishes are beautifully presented but overpriced and under-spiced.... *Tel 020/622-9533. Staalstraat 22 at Groenburgwal. Trams 9 or 14 to Waterlooplein. Reservations required. AE, DC, MC, V. Dinner only Tues–Sat 6–11pm. Closed Sun–Mon. $$$$*

See Map 5 on p. 82.

Traiterie Grekas (p. 68) CANAL BELT *GREEK* This spotlessly clean takeout joint with just a few tables serves the city's tastiest Greek food.... *Tel 020/620-3590. Singel 311 at Oude Spiegelstraat (across the canal). Trams 1, 2, or 5 to Spui. No credit cards. Wed–Sun 5–10pm. $–$$*

See Map 5 on p. 82.

Tujuh Maret (p. 65) CENTER *INDONESIAN* Small, welcoming Indonesian restaurant (eat in or take out) run by veteran restaurateur Thomas Hart.... *Tel 020/427-9865. www.tujuh-maret.nl. Utrechtsestraat 73 at Keizersgracht. Tram 4 to Keizersgracht or Prinsengracht. AE, DC, MC, V. Mon–Sat noon–3:30pm and 4:30–10pm, Sun 4:30–10pm. $$*

See Map 5 on p. 82.

Van Altena (p. 64) MUSEUM DISTRICT *SEAFOOD* The city's premier herring stand. A very serious operation where master fishhandler Pieter van Altena serves raw and pickled herring, salmon or crab salad, and a dozen other fishy delights on warm wholegrain buns.... *Tel 020/676-9139. Stadhouderskade at the Rijksmuseum. Trams 6, 7, or 10 to Spiegelgracht. No credit cards. Tues–Sun 11am–7pm. $*

See Map 5 on p. 82.

Van Dobben (p. 64) REMBRANDTPLEIN *DUTCH (SNACKS/SANDWICHES)* Time has stood still since June 1945, when this wonderful milk-and-soda diner served its first scorching-hot croquette and smoked-eel sandwich. A must.... *Tel 020/624-4200. www.vandobben.nl. Korte Reguliersdwarsstraat 5 at Rembrandtplein. Trams 4, 9, or 14 to Rembrandtplein. No credit cards. Mon–Thurs 9:30am–1am, Fri–Sat 9:30am–2am, Sun 11:30am–8pm. $*

See Map 5 on p. 82.

Vermeer (p. 69) CENTER *FRENCH/DUTCH* The old-fashioned interior is a setting for French-Dutch cuisine (smoked pigeon with roasted pineapple or braised calves' cheeks on sauerkraut).... *Tel 020/556-4885. www.restaurantvermeer.nl. Prins Hendrikkade 59–72 at Zeedijk. Trams 1, 2, 4, 5, 6, 9, 13, 16, 17, 24, or 25 to Centraal Station. Reservations essential. Jacket and tie recommended. AE, DC, MC, V. Mon–Fri noon–3pm and 6–10pm, Sat 6–10pm. $$$$$*

See Map 5 on p. 82

Wagamama (p. 66) LEIDSEPLEIN *NOODLES* New, clean, Zen-style Japanese noodle bar (ramen, kare, gyoza, udon, and other noodle or rice combos). Totally nonsmoking, veg- and kid friendly.... *Tel 020/528-7778, www.wagamama.com. Max Euweplein 10 at Leidseplein. Trams 1, 2, 5, 6, 7, or 10 to Leidseplein. AE, DC, MC, V. Daily noon–11pm. $*

See Map 5 on p. 82.

Warung Marlon (p. 66) OLD SOUTH *SURINAMESE* Amsterdam's most authentic, if spartan, Surinamese eatery. Great roasted meats and rice or banana-based specialties. Nonsmoking.... *Tel 020/671-1526. Eerste Van der Helstraat 55 at Govert Flinckstraat. Trams 16, 24, or 25 to Albert Cuypstraat. No credit cards. Wed–Mon 11am–8pm. $*

See Map 1 on p. 80.

Wilhelmina-Dok (p. 73) NOORD *CONTINENTAL* Waterfront eatery in Amsterdam Noord, worth the short, free ferry-boat ride across the IJ followed by a 5-minute walk.... *Tel 020/632-3701. www.wilhelmina-dok.nl. Nordwal 1 at IJplein. Ferry: IJveer from Pier 8 behind Centraal Station to the dock at IJplein, then go right along the dike-top path. AE, DC, MC, V. Daily 11am–midnight. $$$*

See Map 4 on p. 80.

Yoichi (p. 66) CENTER *JAPANESE* The *sashimi-tako* (octopus), charcoal-grilled teriyaki steak, and sukiyaki beef with veggies rank with the best.... *Tel 020/622-6829. www.yoichi.nl. Weteringschans 128 at Reguliersgracht. Trams 4, 6, 7, or 10 to Frederiksplein. Reservations recommended. AE, DC, MC, V. Daily 6–10:30pm. $$$*

See Map 5 on p. 82.

DINING

THE INDEX

DIVER

SIONS

3

Basic Stuff

Everyone seems to tell the same standard story about a first trip to Amsterdam. First you go to the appropriate cafe to either eat hash brownies or drink *jenever,* then you get lost in the canals, roam the Red-Light District, see a live sex show "by mistake," and finally end up at the Van Gogh Museum.

If you want to come home with more than the same standard story, you have to know how to approach this city. The whole of Amsterdam Centrum (Center), within the semicircular Singelgracht canal, could fit on the tip of Manhattan. Add in the 19th-century Oud West (Old West), Oud Zuid (Old South), and Oost (East) neighborhoods, with the main museums, Vondelpark, and Artis Zoo, and you've got a midsize town. But don't let the size fool you: The number and quality of attractions is very high indeed. It takes time to discover and explore them. So do like the locals and bring clothes in which you can comfortably pedal one of the city's 500,000 old-fashioned *fietsen* (bikes), and most important, a pair of sturdy walking shoes. Amsterdam is not just a stroller's city. It is *the* stroller's city.

Amsterdammers are very proud of their doll's house of a capital, and do their sightseeing and cultural accounts like CPAs. Within this densely populated cosmopolis of 740,000 inhabitants are about 7,000 landmark buildings (from the 16th through the 18th centuries), 2,500 houseboats (probably closer to 5,000, with half docked illegally), and 1,400 cafes and bars. Not to mention the 1,281 bridges (eight of them wooden drawbridges) spanning 165 canals and rivers, or the 28 parks and 42 museums. These numbers are important—everyone knows them. In fact, an obsession with the huge, the minuscule, and all other manner of impressive statistic, is rampant here. For instance, canal tour-boat guides gleefully point out the world's narrowest house (Singel 7)—even though it's something of a cheat, since the house widens out to more sustainable proportions behind its pencil-thin facade—and diamond marketers boast about the world's tiniest diamond (.24mg, cut by Van Moppes). The fact that the Royal Palace sits on exactly 13,659 wooden pilings thrills school kids and tourism officials, as does the knowledge that there are 22 paintings by Rembrandt in town and 206 by Vincent van Gogh—guaranteed tourist draws. I might add that there are probably 1,001 pool tables where you can challenge local sharks. And 9,999 places to sit under one of the city's 220,000 trees and take in the view—of quaint old houses, boats, and tree-lined canals, or of sizzling neon winking meretriciously on Damrak or in the Red-Light District.

You don't have to work hard to enjoy all this. For example, half of the historic buildings have dates engraved on them; exactly 726 of them bear brightly colored antique plaques called "gablestones" that, before street numbering was introduced by Napoléon, explained pictorially who had the house built and what it was used for—a sailing ship for a sea captain, beer barrels for a brewer, fish for a fisherman, and so forth (but watch out for a growing number of brand-new gablestones masquerading as the real thing—usually the new ones look too pristine, but it's not always easy to tell the difference). The past is easy to read here, and Amsterdam is an open book.

Getting Your Bearings

Attractions are spread fairly evenly throughout the center of town, though the big three museums—Rijksmuseum (most of which is currently closed for refurbishing), Van Gogh, and Stedelijk (closed until mid-2008 for refurbishment, but there's a temporary replacement; see below)—are within a few hundred yards of each other in the Museumbuurt (Museum District) in the **Old South** neighborhood, just beyond Singelgracht. So too is the most popular city park, Vondelpark (pronounced "*fon*-dle-park," appropriately, since it's a steamy pickup spot by night). If crowds are what you want, cross Singelgracht and head for **Leidseplein,** a lively square near Vondelpark, or for **Rembrandtplein,** an equally lively (but less cool) square a bit farther east near the Amstel River. Between these lie the three concentric, semicircular 17th-century grand canals of the **Grachtengordel** (Canal Ring)—moving inward, Prinsengracht, Keizersgracht, and Herengracht—where all the canal-house museums are. Cupped within them lies the Singel (not to be confused with Singelgracht), the curving canal that defines the border of the **old city** center—the focal point of which is the tacky, crowded square called the Dam. Between the Dam and Nieuwmarkt, to the east, lies the city's historic Rossebuurt **(Red-Light District),** usually packed with tourists and gawkers at night.

The **former** Jodenbuurt **(Jewish Quarter),** rich with historical and cultural landmarks, lies south of the Red-Light District, just east of Waterlooplein. Though it has few mainstream draws, the **Jordaan** neighborhood, west of Centraal Station and just beyond the Grachtengordel, is an atmospheric part of town for a

King of the Culture Vultures

"My guides are interesting people, not faceless tour operators," says **René Dessing**, *a suave, bespectacled art historian–turned–tour operator. "And please stop calling me a vulture!" If you're finicky about your culture, Dessing is the man to go to for everything from architectural walks to painting classes on canal boats, restaurant or cafe tours, hotel bookings, and private dining in canal mansions. Dessing's multilingual freelance guides—trained art historians—can get you into private collections, the Royal Palace (even when it's closed to the public), and almost anywhere else you want. Trips to clog-makers or tulip fields— though heavily discouraged— are given a highbrow spin. Some clients wind up spending half their day in a cozy brown cafe. "The idea," says Dessing, "is to make new friends." His company,* **Artifex Travel**, *De Erven 2, 1151 AS Broek in Waterland (Tel 020/ 620-8112; www.artifex-travel. nl), can plan your entire trip to Amsterdam, from airfare on.*

stroll, a bike ride, or a game of pool at a brown cafe. Ditto the **Westerdok** and **Western islands,** up-and-coming areas to the west with a Greenwich Village feel. To the east is the **Java-Borneo island development,** with daringly eclectic architecture. The Amstel River cuts across the city's canals from the southeast; a complicated series of locks feeds water from the Amstel into the canals. The **IJ** (pronounced *Ay*) used to be a bay in a sea called the Zuiderzee (just to confuse you, the sea's now a freshwater lake called the IJsselmeer/Lake IJssel), but over the centuries has been dammed, harnessed, dredged, and turned into a wide channel. City street maps rarely seem to indicate street numbers, and if you set out from Centraal Station to, say, Prinsengracht, looking for number 400, you can walk for several miles if you start on the wrong end. Just remember that house numbers always start from the west and run counterclockwise on the concentric, semicircular canals (the Grachtengordel). For example, if you step out of the train station, turn right, and walk to the canal ring, you'll find number 1. On radial arteries, numbers begin at Centraal Station and increase as you move away from the center of town.

The City of the 7,000 Gables

Before Napoléon imposed a rational numbering system on Amsterdam, gablestones indicated who owned the building and what went on there. Walls in the Begijnhof and on Sint-Luciënsteeg at the Amsterdam Historical Museum have some good gablestones, including the oldest known stone, from 1603, showing a milkmaid balancing her buckets. That goes partway to explaining why most of Amsterdam's 7,000 landmark buildings have gables. Gables also hide the pitched roofs (plain, boring, old sloping roofs that the gables ornament like the false fronts of town centers in the American Old West did) and demonstrate the architect's vertical showmanship in a city where tax laws encouraged thin buildings. If you can pick out Amsterdam's various gable styles without developing Sistine Chapel Neck Syndrome, you can date the buildings fairly accurately. The neck gable, for example (about 1660–1790), looks like a headless neck, with curlicues on the shoulders—see the first one at Herengracht 168 (the Netherlands Theater Institute), a 1638 mansion. The earliest is the wooden, triangular gable (circa 1250–1550). Only two remain—Het Houten Huys in the Begijnhof, and 't Aepje at Zeedijk 1.

The Lowdown

Where the tourists go... One of Amsterdam's prime industries is tourism—more than 17 million visitors swim through in a good year, most of them in spring and summer. As in Venice, many stick to well-trod canals and gathering places in the small historic center of town. Unlike many other Europeans, most Amsterdammers actually seem to enjoy their company, which cranks up the energy level of the tourist areas even more. Authentic touristy Amsterdam can be a supremely kitschy experience—don't skip it entirely. Most visitors' first experience of Amsterdam is a stroll from Centraal Station down Damrak, a living Pop Art installation with fast-food eateries, souvenir shops, and bumper-to-bumper traffic. At its end is the **Dam**, the historic heart of town overlooked by the gaudy **Koninklijk Paleis (Royal Palace).** Today the area is noisy, tacky, and a prime spot for pickpockets, so stay alert, but the view from the Dam back up Damrak is an unforgettable 21st-century cityscape (no skyscrapers, but lots of neon, tacky stores, and tacky storefronts).

If you're allergic to crowds and noise, avoid the L-shaped **Leidseplein** and its surroundings on the southwest side of town (not far from the Rijksmuseum). In summer, swarms of trinket hawkers and street musicians besiege Leidseplein's chaotic sidewalk cafes. **Rembrandtplein,** south of the Red-Light District, is a handsome, though frowzy, square ringed by a mix of cafes, touristy restaurants, and sleazy coffee shops frequented by dope smokers and lager louts. While most of Rembrandtplein's cafes cater to the theme-park crowd, a few attract hip locals (De Kroon—see p. 214) or serve as hangout spots for the literati (Cafe Schiller). Other tourist magnets are the dozen or so big diamond factories scattered throughout town, especially **Van Moppes** (sparkling with busloads of gawkers who've seemingly never seen a real gemstone; see p. 191) and the no-longer-brewing-but-still-serving (the beer there is shipped in from its suburban brewery) **Heineken Experience,** where a certain brewing corporation charges for a no-holds-barred marketing presentation.

When the tour buses from Germany roll in, it's Oktoberfest on the Amstel. **Holland Experience** is the kind of "multidimensional film and theater show" (their words) that draws the coach crowds, couch potatoes, tulip-and-clog lovers, and their bawling brats. Here's how the tourist office's monthly newsletter describes the show: "Seated on a moving platform, in the comfort of an aircraft seat, come with us on a trip through the many different faces of Holland. It's all there, the waterland, the agricultural areas, all the tourist-sites, the culture and even the high-tech industry." Gee, maybe we could just buy the video and save on airfare? The **NEMO** science and technology center is a cut above, mobbed by virtual-reality fiends and their nerdy offspring, who want to forget Amsterdam and become a mechanic, doctor, ballet dancer, explorer....

Don't believe the brochures... The must-see sights in Amsterdam are not as advertised—most of them come with disclaimers. The celebrated **"Skinny" Bridge** isn't skinny; the **Heineken Experience "brewery"** stopped brewing beer in 1988; most of the **Bloemenmarkt** "floating" **flower market** doesn't float; Queen Beatrix and Prince Claus doesn't live in the **Royal Palace** (see "Lifestyles of the rich and deceased" on p. 104); and although most of van Gogh's paintings are in Amsterdam, some of his best work is in New York and Paris, not the **Van Gogh Museum** (see "For culture vultures," below). That doesn't mean these sights aren't appealing, though. The Skinny Bridge is broad but handsome; the Heineken Brewery is swell for beer guzzlers; the sidewalk flower market is gorgeous; the Royal Palace is appropriately palatial; and the Van Gogh Museum is heaven for van Gogh fanatics.

The most quintessentially Dutch nonattraction in town is the **Skinny Bridge** (**Magere Brug**—on the Amstel River at Kerkstraat). It's the same kind of white drawbridge van Gogh (and a thousand others) painted as emblematic of Holland. Here's the doubtful tale: Two rich sisters named Mager, living on opposite sides of the Amstel at Kerkstraat, had the bridge built in 1672 so they could visit each other with ease. Well, maybe, but the original bridge—which was authentically narrow—more likely got its name from the Dutch word for skinny *(mager)*. At any rate, it was replaced with this overfed one in the 18th century, but the brochure writers haven't heard about it yet.

The Heineken Brewery brewed its last lager in 1988, but the name hasn't been changed to "museum" yet—instead, welcome to the **Heineken Experience.** If you take a tour and are disappointed to learn that the beer you are offered after visiting the antique vats is brewed in the suburbs, well—let the boozer beware. Don't forget that for centuries Amsterdammers couldn't drink the local water, and brewing it into beer was simply a sanitary precaution. (Tap water is still called *gemeente pils*—"municipal beer.")

How about the "oldest house in Amsterdam"? The brochures say it's in the **Begijnhof,** and indeed there is a wooden house there, Het Houten Huys, dated around 1425, but it was taken down from its original location and moved there and totally rebuilt. So I suppose the accuracy of that one all depends on how you define "old." At **Zeedijk 1** you'll find a similar wooden house, from about 1550. Though heavily remodeled, at least it wasn't moved. As to the "narrowest house in the world," the local misinformation bureau claims it is **Singel 7,** not far from Centraal Station. It looks like it's just over .9m (3 ft.) wide, but actually only the front door is narrow; the house, built on an irregular lot, widens behind it. The house at **Oude Hoogstraat 22** is wider—2m (6.56 ft.)—but it's small all the way back, running only 6m (19.68 ft.) deep. This makes it, according to the Amsterdam tourist office, the narrowest house in Europe, at least—no cheating. And as for the "floating" **flower market (Bloemenmarkt),** well, for the real thing you'll have to go to Bangkok, which has a real floating market, on boats and rafts. Amsterdam's market is on the sidewalk of Singel; some of the shops are built on piers, a few on rusting, permanently moored barges. But at least you can get everything from apricot trees to zinnias here, including marijuana seeds and starter kits, but the only things you'll be able to take home—if you live in America—are phytosanitary-certified bulbs (see the Shopping chapter).

For culture vultures... Culture vultures and coach tourists alike seem to think the **Rijksmuseum** is synonymous with Amsterdam; they simply must see Rembrandt's *The Night Watch.* Luckily, the painting is larger than the Louvre's embattled *Mona Lisa,* so you stand a better chance of seeing it over hundreds of heads. But don't get too close: A security guard hovers nearby. If you're lucky enough to view it in silence, this painting will take possession of you: Irresistibly, one face after another in the Civic Guards company of Captain Frans Banning Cocq and Lieutenant Willem van Ruytenburch draws your eye in. *Note:* Most of the Rijksmuseum is closed for renovation until mid-2008. During this period, key paintings from the 17th-century Dutch Golden Age collection, along with other items, can be viewed in the museum's own Philips Wing, under the heading Rijksmuseum: De Meesterwerken (The Masterpieces). Other elements of the collection are on view at other venues in the city.

No one in Holland would touch van Gogh's wild, tortured paintings when he was alive, but the **Van Gogh Museum** is now a national treasure. The painter's tragic life and times are traced from rural Dutch roots in Nuenen, via Paris, Arles, the asylum of St.-Remy (he'd snipped off part of his ear), to suicide at age 37 in Auvers-sur-Oise. Among the 200 or so van Gogh oils in the permanent collection are *The Potato Eaters, Sunflowers,* and *Wheatfield with Crows.* You can also see letters written between Vincent and his brother Theo; hundreds of sketches, drawings, and watercolors; as well as paintings by van Gogh contemporaries Emile Bernard, Toulouse-Lautrec, Gauguin, Monticelli, and Koning. The collection is housed in a rather aggressively minimalistic, concrete building designed by Gerrit Rietveld in his senescence and opened (after he died) in 1973. The museum's new wing (added in

1999) is a jumble of rounds and rectangles that appears to land on the Museum District, a flying saucer poised on a cracker box. Inside, huge windows catch the city's rarefied light. The building's relentlessly sculptural shapes provide a challenging venue for temporary van Gogh–related exhibitions. Be prepared for crowds in high season.

One of the world's great modern-art collections is at the **Stedelijk Museum (Municipal Museum),** a refreshing break after acres of van Gogh or Dutch masters. So vast are the holdings—works from the sublime (Malevich's *Suprematism*) to the ridiculous (Koons' *Ushering in Banality*)—that you'll never see the museum hung in the same way twice. Post–World War II art is the strongest suit, but thin samplings from 1850 through the present are within the museum's scope, including Manet, Monet, Cézanne, Picasso, and Chagall on the prewar timeline. Abstract and De Stijl practitioners Malevich, Mondrian, and Kandinsky are well represented, as are Expressionists like Kirchner, Polke, and Dix. There are also works you'll never see elsewhere by CoBrA (Copenhagen/Brussels/Amsterdam) group painter Karel Appel—he decorated parts of the museum, including the Appelbar and former cafeteria.

Note that while refurbishment of the museum building continues until about mid-2008, the Stedelijk Museum collection is on display close to Centraal Station, in a building designated **Stedelijk Museum CS** (see The Index, for details).

The Russians are coming... Indeed, they're already here. First it was Peter the Great, Czar of all the Russias, slumming it as a blue-collar worker at nearby Zaandam in 1697 to learn the secrets of Dutch shipbuilding (and in 1716 going on a drunken spree around the canals). Now it's **Hermitage Amsterdam.** Opened in 2004 in the neoclassical Amstelhof building, the Amsterdam branch of Russia's renowned State Hermitage museum of art and fine arts in St. Petersburg recalls links between the two canal-threaded cities that date back centuries. During a visit to Amsterdam in 1697, Peter visited the Amstelhof, which dates from 1681–83 and was a home for seniors (at first only for Protestant women). It is built around a central courtyard and is flanked on two sides by canals, and on a third by the Amstel River. Exhibits change twice a year, at first in six galleries on the two floors of the renovated and modernized Neerlandia Building, which was built next to the Amstelhof in 1888 as a home for indigent married couples. Maybe the Dutch will be getting some of their own cultural patrimony back again, if only on loan, since the Hermitage has 600 paintings by Dutch and Flemish Masters, a collection that is considered by many art experts to be the world's finest. In addition to works from the Russian museum, modern art from New York's U.S. Guggenheim Museum is exhibited here. The full Amstelhof complex is expected to open by 2007, with the Neerlandia section then being re-purposed as a "Children's Hermitage."

Picture perfect... Inaugurated in 1999, **Huis Marseille** is the city's top international photography venue, a nonprofit foundation based in a stunning 1665 canal-house mansion (called Marseille House by the French merchant who built it). Vast display rooms on four floors showcase rotating exhibitions. Even if you're not a shutterbug, the house alone is worth the visit.

Courting privacy... Hidden between center-city blocks, and especially in the Jordaan, are several courtyards housing complexes called *hofjes*. Built as almshouses for pious lay sisters, widows, the elderly, and the disabled, they were the "projects" of their day, underwritten by religious orders or, more commonly, wealthy merchants embarrassed by their riches. Most have become normal apartment complexes now, with a common courtyard and stairwells that you can poke around in, as long as you enter and leave quietly. The biggest, most spectacular, and most visited is the **Begijnhof,** just off Spui (there's no number, but the name is chiseled above the door). Built in the 14th century around an oblong courtyard, this complex of buildings housed devout (sometimes fallen, and often poor) women who couldn't quite convince themselves to take religious vows, but wanted to be left in pious peace. All of the original houses are gone (they were rebuilt in the 17th century and later). Nonetheless, the Begijnhof is marvelous, one of the loveliest spots in the city.

Go at off-hours (the door is open daily 8am–1pm), or out of season, and you'll be able to muse among the lawns and flowers and the horse-chestnut trees towering over humpback buildings. Among several churches in the compound, the De Engelse Kerk (English Reformed Church)—a name that likely wouldn't much please the Scottish Presbyterians for whom it was built—at number 48, has a remarkable wooden-barrel vaulted ceiling with delicate blue decorations. The church was built in 1392 (and doubtless rebuilt since), has been English-speaking since 1607, and offers Sunday worship at 10:30am precisely. An extraordinarily discreet Roman Catholic church, at number 29, has a U-shaped balcony and a series of paintings and stained-glass windows showing the bizarre Amsterdam Miracle of the Host. (It is said that on the Tuesday before Palm Sunday in 1345, a dying man living on Kalverstraat sent for a priest to administer last rites. He was given the Host. Later he vomited and a nurse threw the vomit on the fire. The next day they found the Host, unburnt, amid the embers. The priest was called back and took the Host away, but it miraculously returned itself to the house on Kalverstraat, and did so again after being removed a second time.) The houses lining the grassy courtyard are from the 17th and 18th centuries, including the so-called oldest house in Amsterdam, from the 1400s (it was actually moved here and rebuilt, however).

Ladies with a past... The nuns of the Begijnhof didn't have a monopoly on institutionalized pious living. For further insight into the Dutch mind, keep an eye out for the **Spinhuis** when you're in the neighborhood of the Red-Light District. This 1597 landmark was long used as a women's penitentiary and labor camp, where the unlucky ladies generated considerable income for the managers of the establishment. The women doubled as wool spinners and Scarlet Letter–style performers—upright citizens actually paid an admission price to watch the sinners at work. A plaque over the door reads: "Don't cry, I take no vengeance for wrongdoing, but force you to be good. Stern is my hand, kind is my heart." I'll bet. The building is no longer open to the public, but the nearby neighborhood is full of places where you can pay to engage women plying another trade.

Looking down on it all... Amsterdam is flat as a *pannekoek* (pancake) and has no skyscrapers. The best way to get a perspective is to scale the various church towers in town (call ahead to make sure they're open—admissions policies vary). The highest, and most spectacular, is **Westertoren,** that leaning, 78m (255.84 ft.) Golden Age masterpiece. You'll be panting by the time you reach its imperial crown, the only thing between you and heaven. Below are the roofs, canals, and spreading trees of the Grachtengordel and Jordaan. On a clear day you can see the whole of old Amsterdam. Southeast, just beyond the Red-Light District, is the lower **Zuidertoren,** from which you see the medieval section of town, from the alleys and narrow canals around Oudezijds Voorburgwal to the Amstel River. In the center of the Red-Light District, the onion-domed, 16th-century bell tower of the **Oude Kerk** rears its head. From it, you'll see the twinkle of the neon lights of Sodom and Gomorrah, with particularly detailed, bird's-eye views into the transvestite/prostitutes' area just north of the church. Get another perspective altogether from the top-floor, panoramic cafe of **Metz & Co.,** an upscale department store at the junction of swank Keizersgracht and Leidsestraat, where you can spy on the canal-house mansions of Grachtengordel millionaires. The city's newest tower, in the Kalvertoren shopping mall, rises to a staggering 30m (98.4 ft.) and is located in the center of the tacky Kalverstraat shopping district. Among my favorite views is from the **Beurs van Berlage** tower, a tough climb but worth it for the aerial perspective of the Red-Light District and Damrak. The roof of **NEMO,** in the harbor, offers a great waterfront panorama, as do the showrooms and bug-box cafe-restaurant at **Pakhuis Amsterdam,** a reconverted Eastern Docklands warehouse now used as an interior design center.

Lifestyles of the rich and deceased... Amsterdam, unburnt since the 15th century and largely spared by world wars and real estate speculators, is rich with historic buildings, particularly 17th-century landmarks that express the parvenu tastes of Dutch merchants of the Golden Age. The vast, imposing (and ugly) **Royal Palace** on the Dam is the queen mother of them all. "Piling it on" is the operative phrase: Schoolchildren know it was built in 1648 by Jacob van Campen to replace an earlier city hall and sits on precisely 13,659 wooden pilings (take 365, as in the number of days in a year; add a "1" in front and a "9" afterward...). It's

been the royal palace since 1808, but of course the royal
family no longer lives here. In the 17th century, this was
the zenith of nouveau riche taste—witness the acres of
white-marble floors and staircases and the colossal proportions. Stride across the Citizen's Hall and you cross heaven
and earth: It's paved with inlaid marble and bronze maps
of the hemispheres formerly under Holland's control.

Less ostentatious but far more instrumental in Amsterdam's ascension is the **Oost Indisch Huis (East India
House),** a currently politically incorrect totem of Dutch
colonialism, close to what's now the Red-Light District
(Oude Hoogstraat at Kloveniersburgwal). For centuries,
starting in 1603, it was the headquarters of the Verenigde
Oostindische Compagnie (United East India Company)—
the V.O.C.—a mighty trading company that maintained
its own army and navy and brought to heel Indonesia, Cey-
lon, and other Asian countries. You technically can't enter
this late-1500s landmark (because the University of Amsterdam has offices in it)—actually, though, you can, just by
acting like a student or a professor and doing your sightseeing surreptitiously—but step into its courtyard and you
can almost feel the filthy old lucre holding the bricks
together. Around the corner on Kloveniersburgwal are the
remarkably wide **Trippenhuis** and remarkably narrow
Klein Trippenhuis (the **Trip House** and the **Trip Coachman's House;** the big one isn't open to visitors, but the
small one, which now houses a fashion boutique, is). The
former is one of Amsterdam's most striking statements of
Golden Age taste. It was built in the neoclassical style
between 1660 and 1664 for the Trip brothers, Hendrick
and Louis, fabulously rich arms manufacturers who had
their chimneys sculpted like cannons and their Corinthian
colonnade decorated with a gun. Right across the canal is
the .9m- (3 ft.-) wide servants' house built to shut up the
Trips' upstart coachman—envious of his masters' double-
wide, he said he'd be glad to have a place as wide as the
mansion's front door. (Guess what he got.)

Another significant neoclassical mansion from that era
is **De Pinto House,** now a public library in the former Jewish Quarter. Isaac de Pinto, co-founder of the United East
India Company, was one of the Portuguese Jewish community's leading lights. He bought this house in 1651 and
spent a fortune remodeling it in the Italian Renaissance

style (100 years after it had gone out of fashion in Italy). Only some painted ceilings and paneling have survived, but it's enough to show that ostentation and glitz were not first invented in the late 20th century.

Many of Amsterdam's Golden Age landmarks are the work of Hendrick de Keyser (1565–1621), who, as the city's official architect during the early 1600s, was largely responsible for the design of the Grachtengordel grand canals. **Bartolotti House,** built in 1618 north of the Golden Bend on Herengracht, is one of de Keyser's most ambitious mansions. Wide, tall, ornate, and distinctly red, it was commissioned by a rich brewer and banker, a Mr. Van den Heuvel, who, to satisfy his mother-in-law, changed his name to Bartolotti. You can visit a series of sumptuous rooms via the next-door **Netherlands Theater Institute Museum,** itself a 1638 canal house, built by Philips Vingboons and remarkable for having the city's first "neck gable." Look up to see its ceilings painted with mythological scenes by Jacob de Wit in 1729. The place was restored top to bottom in 1999, and its formal Renaissance gardens are now open to humble visitors. The so-called **House with the Heads** is not a pothead's crash pad—it's a 1624 de Keyser mansion, one canal over at Keizersgracht 121. Its name comes from the row of six huge classical heads across the facade, representing Diana, Bacchus, Athena, Mars, Ceres, and Apollo.

Okay, if you've gotta see windmills... Once upon a time, when Amsterdammers clomped around in clogs, there were hundreds of windmills right in town. Now there are only half a dozen, two of which are worth visiting. The **De Gooyer Windmill,** a former corn mill built in 1725, still towers over the Nieuwevaart canal northeast of Artis Zoo. In it is Bierbrouwerij 't IJ, a terrific microbrewery. A century older, but a total rebuild job, is the thatched **De Rieker Windmill,** moved to a site way out on the banks of the Amstel River at Amstelpark. Now an elegant private house, it was originally built to drain the Rieker polder, a tract of low, reclaimed land a few miles south of Amsterdam. You've doubtless seen this mill in all those Rembrandt paintings and engravings you know by heart; just to make sure you don't miss the connection, there's a statue here of Rembrandt at work.

For history buffs... Spend a few days soaking up the city's atmosphere before exploring the **Amsterdam Historical Museum,** where you can appreciate displays ranging from antique delftware to bits of demolished houses (carved beam consoles, gablestones, etc.), from medieval sculptures to a re-created smoking coffee shop and an entire Amsterdam brown cafe (with a fascinating interview on tape of the cafe's last owner, a piss-and-vinegar dame). The museum building itself is intriguing; it started life as an orphanage in the Middle Ages and was rebuilt around cloistered courtyards in the 17th century. There's a mesmerizing computerized map that shows how the Golden Age boomtown doubled and trebled in size in a matter of decades. Rembrandt's gruesome *The Anatomy Lecture* now hangs here. The immense **Maritime Museum,** housed in the 1655 Admiralty Building in the Eastern Docklands, has rooms so huge that full-sized boats have been lugged into them—dig the dazzlingly kitschy royal barge, so encrusted with gold it's a miracle it ever floated. On the wharf out front bob several historic ships, including the reconstructed *Amsterdam,* a three-master from 1749 where kids can play pirates with costumed performers.

The **Jewish Historical Museum** offers little such light-hearted entertainment. Skillfully set in four former Ashkenazi synagogues from the 17th and 18th centuries, the modern, airy exhibition hall is a serious—though not downbeat—devotion to Jewish history, religion, and culture in the Netherlands, up to and including the Jewish community's near annihilation during the Nazi occupation. Pre–World War II photos of everyday life in the former Jewish district, where the museum sits, are downright mesmerizing. Striking a related note, the nearby **Resistance Museum** takes you back in time to the dark days of World War II in Holland, during the Nazi occupation (1940–45). Using authentic photographs, documents, weapons, communications equipment, spy gadgets, and other materials actually used by the Dutch Resistance, the exhibits show the ingenuity the freedom fighters brought to bear—along with raw courage—on the German occupation forces. The fate of Amsterdam's Jewish community has a prominent place, as do the actions of workers who in 1941 went on strike to protest the first deportation of 400 Jewish Amsterdammers. Yet the museum doesn't shrink from less-palatable aspects of Holland's wartime record cither, like the actions of collaborators, including those who joined Dutch Nazi SS units.

Moments in time… First gorge yourself on the Rembrandts at the Rijksmuseum—or at any rate on as many of them as are on exhibit during most of the Rijksmuseum's long-term closure—then head to the **Rembrandt House Museum,** on the edge of Amsterdam's former Jewish district and lavishly restored and expanded in late 1999. The artist's colorful life and times are captured in the house he owned from 1639 to 1658 (a bon vivant, his extravagance bankrupted him, and he died not in this house but in destitution). Poke around its dark, atmospheric rooms (leaded windows, creaky floors). The Cabinet Room replicates Rembrandt's personal collection of artworks and objects such as Chinese porcelain, bizarre woven baskets, celestial globes, Venetian glass, busts of Roman emperors, weapons, and shells. Some of these turn up in his paintings, making for a highbrow treasure hunt. The glinting high-tech new wing, conceived to display etchings, also hosts temporary exhibitions.

The celebrated **Anne Frank House** is a Prinsengracht canal house with secret back rooms where the gifted Jewish teenager hid from Nazi occupiers with her family from 1942 to 1944. But there's little in the house except a few snapshots of English royalty and movie stars that Anne had cherished—you'd love to stand here and reflect on the unquenchable love of life that made Anne's diary so great, but fuhgettaboutit. Expect long lines, crowded rooms, and an all-too-commercial boutique at the exit, plus a cafe-restaurant in the modern wing.

At the **Van Loon Museum,** an imposing 1671 mansion on Keizersgracht, you are ushered straight into the Golden Age, to wander down the marble halls admiring the stuccowork and the family portraits. One canal away on Herengracht's Golden Bend is the **Willet-Holthuysen Museum,** in an even bigger mansion, this one built in 1687. Its downstairs kitchen has remarkable antique delft tiles, and Jacob de Wit painted the mezzanine room's rococo ceiling. There are also d'Aubusson tapestries, family portraits, and countless intriguing knickknacks. The **Amstelkring Museum,** known in English as "Our Lord in the Attic," was built in 1663 into the upper floors of three canal and back houses in an era when Roman Catholics were forced to worship in secret. Navigate the maze of stairways to stumble onto a startlingly beautiful chapel, and a Golden Age kitchen, bed-nook, and dining room.

Sacred sights... Across the Dam from the Royal Palace is the **Nieuwe Kerk (New Church),** which is in fact one of the oldest churches in town. (It was new when it was built—6 centuries ago—and I guess they just never thought to change the name afterward....) When Golden Age architect Jacob van Campen wasn't gilding the lilies at the Royal Palace, he turned his hand to this Protestant monument to faith, which now works efficiently as both a church and exhibition space. (The Dutch never let sacredness get in the way of a good real estate deal.) The wooden pulpit—about 11m (36.08 ft.) tall—must be the most elaborate outside Italy, with hundreds of figures, and angels sliding down the banister (it took Albert Janszoon Vinckernbrinck 19 years, 1645–1664, to carve it). Beatrix was inaugurated as queen here in 1980; her mother, Juliana, in 1948; and so forth down the centuries. In 2002 Prince Willem Alexander and his bride Máxima tied the knot here. Where there's a New Church that's really old, there must be an old church that's even older. **Oude Kerk (Old Church)** is as old as Amsterdam, and must have been built right after the first dam and the first tavern. We're talking about the early 13th century, though most of the building dates from the 14th to the 16th centuries. Your sense of religious awe may be somewhat spoiled by the ticket booth at the entrance, but no matter. The stained glass and painted wooden ceiling are lovely; the tombstones (Rembrandt's wife Saskia has a memorial stone at number 29K) and choir stalls are masterfully carved; the organ is sonorous and grand. The church is all but surrounded by the tiny red-fringed rooms of the Red-Light District, where the adepts of an entirely different rite keep busy at all hours.

Prominent Golden Age architect Hendrick de Keyser built the **Zuiderkerk** and **Zuidertoren** (**Southern Church** and **Southern Tower**), and when he died in 1621 he was buried here. Built from 1602 to 1611 on the edge of the former Jewish district, it's among the earliest churches erected specifically for a Calvinist congregation and has one of the finest carillons (played each Thurs at noon) in town. Climb the tower for a panorama of Old Amsterdam. Arguably, de Keyser's masterpiece is the **Westerkerk (Western Church)** and its **bell tower,** the **Westertoren,** which he found time to design the year before he died. The 78m (255.84 ft.) tower, topped with Maximilian of Austria's rather obscenely plump imperial crown, leans forward over Prinsengracht, providing see-forever views. Records show that Rembrandt was buried in 1669 in an unmarked rental grave somewhere in or around the church, and the whereabouts of his bones is still hotly debated. In the heart of the former Jewish Quarter, the 1675 **Portuguese Synagogue,** long the world's biggest synagogue, proves how wealthy the Sephardic Jewish community here was, having helped Amsterdam to become Europe's richest city during the Golden Age. Despite savagery during the Nazi occupation, its tall, elegant windows, 12 marble columns, and giant brass chandeliers have survived intact.

Turrets syndrome... Though Golden Age Amsterdam burst outward beyond its medieval boundaries, a handful of landmarks still standing define the old city's outer limits. You can visit two of them, and stroll by others, to reconstruct a view of Old Amsterdam. The Red-Light District's eastern boundary is Nieuwmarkt, an oblong square in whose center stands **In de Waag (The Weigh House),** originally the Sint-Antoniespoort city gate, built in 1487 (now a trendy restaurant and cafe—see p. 216). Bristling with seven mismatched turrets, the fearsome fortress was rebuilt in the early 1600s as a public weighing house, with trade guilds housed on the upper floors. Another tower built in the seaward walls in 1487, on what is now Prins Hendrikkade at Geldersekade, near Centraal Station, is where sailors' wives would come to see their husbands off. That's how it got its name, the Schreierstoren (The Tower of Tears), and a 1569 gablestone shows just such a sobbing wife. In 1609, Henry Hudson embarked from here on a misguided adventure that resulted in the founding of New Amsterdam (New York). This tower, too, now houses a cozy and traditional bar/cafe.

Just down the quay from the Schreierstoren is a relic of a much later era, the 1912–16 Scheepvaarthuis (Shipping Building; Prins Hendrikkade 108). This magnificent,

●●

CATCHING THE MUSEUM BOAT

*Ever resourceful and ever aware of the transportation resource their canals represent, Amsterdammers have introduced the **Museumboot (Museum Boat)**, Stationsplein 8 (Tel 020/530-1090), to carry weary tourists on their pilgrimages from museum to museum. It's an easy way to travel and, for those with limited time, provides some of the advantages of a canal-boat cruise. Boats depart every hour or so (and occasionally half-hourly) daily from 9:55am to 4:45pm from in front of Centraal Station (Stop 1), and stop at key spots around the city, providing access to museums and other sights. These are:*

Stop 1   Centraal Station.

Stop 2   Eastern Dock, for NEMO, Maritime Museum.

Stop 3   Waterlooplein, for Rembrandt House Museum, flea market, Jewish Historical Museum, Muziektheater.

Stop 4   Flower Market.

Stop 5   Leidseplein.

Stop 6   Museum Quarter, for Rijksmuseum Het Meesterwerken, Van Gogh Museum, Stedelijk Museum, Vondelpark.

Stop 7   Prinsengracht, for Anne Frank House, Westerkerk.

Stop 8   Eastern Dock, for NEMO, Maritime Museum.

Stop 9   Centraal Station.

The day ticket for the Museum Boat, which includes a discount on museum admissions of up to 50%, is 14€ ($18) for adults and 9.50€ ($12) for children ages 4 to 12, and free for children under 4. After 1pm, it's 13€ ($16) and 7.25€ ($9.05), respectively.

●●

turreted fantasy (not open to the public), crawling with bas-reliefs recounting the city's naval history, houses Amsterdam's public transportation authority administrative offices. It is the inspired work of Amsterdam School architects Michel de Klerk, Pieter L. Kramer, and J. M. van der Mey and stands as a monument to Amsterdam School architecture. A few hundred yards east, overlooking the Oude Schans canal, is the Montelbaanstoren (Oude Schans at Waals Eilandsgracht; not open to the public), a fortified, tilting tower from 1512 that protected what was the city's main shipyard. By now you'll recognize the tiered crown, added in 1606, as the work of the ubiquitous Hendrick de Keyser. At Muntplein, at the juncture of Singel and Rokin, the Munttoren, another piece (the base of the tower, from 1487, which used to be part of the Reguliers Gate) of the city walls (not open to the public), was transformed by de Keyser in 1620, who topped it with one of his signature crowns. Amsterdam was forced to mint its own money here during a war with France and England in 1672, and the name De Munt has been used ever since for the tower.

Row, row, row your boat... There are more canals here than you'd care to count, and viewing the city from water level shows you a whole different town. The Dutch call pedalos *(waterfiets)* **canal bikes;** no local would be caught dead using one, but who cares? Rent one and splash across the murky brown water to your favorite sights (see the Getting Outside chapter for more details). **Cruises,** in special low and narrow boats built to get under bridges and navigate turns, are the conventional way to go, and make you feel like a bona fide tourist. They run day and night, and even offer lunch, dinner, and wine-and-cheese packages. For the full ultratouristy effect, take one in combination with a diamond workshop or Heineken Brewery tour. The **Museumboot** is a cut above. The tour groups don't usually use it, and the high-tone name puts some people off—after all, not everyone who visits Amsterdam is interested in its museums. You may prefer to just jump on and off of trams instead, but if you don't, this boat can save you a lot of time, and if you think of it as saving you from needing to take and pay for a canal cruise, it's probably a money saver. The Museumboot offers hop-on, hop-off service all day, just like the more generically named **Canal Bus,** except that you also get negligible reductions on museum entry fees. The **De Rederij, Aquadam,** and **Rederij De Nederlanden** companies are the posh way to cruise around—and cost a small fortune. You'll get a gorgeous antique boat with a liquor cabinet, a captain and hostesses in snazzy uniforms, and privacy.

Diamonds in the rough... Diamond-polishing workshops are an Amsterdam specialty, and though the city isn't on a par with Antwerp, New York, or Tel Aviv, it does have a centuries-old tradition in the trade. Paradoxically, the tours (nearly always free, available daily) are better taken in groups; most operators act like it's a bother to explain to individual visitors the process of extracting, studying, cutting, and evaluating these mesmerizing rocks. There are two dozen workshops around town; if you're going to buy a sparkler at the end of the tour—the object of the exercise for your hosts—you should probably stick to the biggies, who have a reputation to uphold. Their tours are pretty much interchangeable, though Gassan, in the old Jewish district, is particularly, well, polished. Van Moppes Diamonds is probably the biggest of them all, and draws the busloads; glitzy Coster Diamonds is also firmly on the package-tour route (the Tourist Tram—see listing later in the chapter—stops there). Stoeltie Diamonds is smaller but reliable, and the tours are particularly informative. The Amsterdam Diamond Center seems like a sales outlet (and Rolex repair shop), but you can still view workers turning roughs into brilliants within striking distance of the cash register. (See the Shopping chapter for details on all five dealers.)

Sex, drugs, and torture museums... Keen on the seamy, steamy side of town? The **Sex Museum,** on suitably sleazy Damrak, and the interchangeable **Erotic Museum** in the heart of the Red-Light District, are favorites for guys and gals—straight and gay—who get off on rental flesh, porn videos, live sex on stage, S&M, and so forth. You might recognize the guy with the raincoat from your local porno cinema. Actually, these titillating museums full of dildos and lewd photos of bumping uglies are both rather harmless; you'll see plenty more shocking stuff in the shops, bars, and neon-lit windows of the Red-Light District itself. That is where **The Hash Marihuana Hemp Museum** is found, within stumbling distance of countless smoking coffee shops, prostitutes, and S&M bars for the skintight-jeans set. Lovers of the pungent weed—and anyone curious about its origins and myriad uses—will be fascinated, I'm sure. Softer-drug addicts will want to wake up and smell the coffee at the **Geels & Co. Coffee and Tea Museum,** also in the Red-Light District. The shop has been around since 1964, sells great stuff, and has a formidable collection of grinders, roasters, tea canisters, and other brewing paraphernalia in its small, upstairs museum, open only Saturday afternoons. You have to be something of a masochist to enjoy the **Torture Museum,** a commercial cabinet of horrors on Singel, near the flower market, where eternal adolescents stare slack-jawed at the centuries-old instruments of torture, from the seat of nails and rack to the guillotine and various charming cages. The

Amnesty International blurb rightly reminds visitors that torture is still going on today, and gives this grotesquerie a patina of respectability.

Museums that won't bore the kids... Watch your sprout become a mechanic, doctor, ballet dancer, or explorer before your boggled eyes in the **NEMO** science and technology center in the harbor, between Centraal Station and the Maritime Museum. Designed by Renzo Piano (aka Mr. Pompidou Center in Paris), the NEMO may look like a beached supertanker, but it manages to ship kiddies into various unknown worlds of virtual reality (real reality just ain't good enough these days). While your young'uns play pirate at the **Maritime Museum** on the three-masted sailing ship from 1749, you can relax in the panoramic cafeteria (with a nonsmoking area that actually lives up to the name, unlike most in town). Kids go hog-wild over all the real boats on the wharf as well as those indoors (including the royal barge, which drips with gold). There are 500 or so antique scale models of ships, too. Across the Nieuwevaart canal is the **Kromhout Shipyard Museum.** Budding mariners and old salts can see historic vessels being repaired in this 19th-century working shipyard. Several leaky old tubs are always on hand, and the warehouse is redolent with the fumes of early internal-combustion marine engines, including the celebrated 12-horsepower Kromhout. The place has seen better days, and that's precisely why it's so charming. The **Houseboat Museum** is in a 1914 former cargo barge, the *Hendrika Maria*, transformed decades ago into a houseboat, and in 1997 into a houseboat museum. Devised to teach kids 6 to 12 about other cultures, the **Kindermuseum TM Junior** (the children's section of the **Tropenmuseum [Tropical Museum]**) is really a fairly adult affair. Youngsters seem perfectly capable of appreciating instead the fascinating, grown-up ethnographic exhibits— reconstructed African, Indian, or East Asian villages and bazaars, complete with rickshaws—in the main museum, whose primary purpose, in less politically correct days, was to glorify Dutch colonialism.

More kidding around... If you're in town with family, the **Artis Zoo** should be on your list. This is the oldest zoo in the country, founded in 1838, and about 6,000 animals from around the world live in it. The park setting is a bonus, and when they've had their eyeful of zebras, pythons, and orangutans and tire of petting them at the animal farm, kids can stargaze in the planetarium. If that doesn't send everyone back to the hotel for a nap, take them to the tiny **Petting Zoo (Kinderboerderij De Dierencapel)** in the Western Islands neighborhood, where exotic-looking piglets, banal chickens, fragrant goats, and woolly sheep nibble, root, and peck along the banks of the Bickersgracht canal. The Punch 'n' Judy show—called "Pantijn"—at the open market at Noordermarkt (in the Jordaan, bordering Prinsengracht) on Saturday mornings may be in Dutch, but kids will love it anyway, since they'll understand the action. The Waterlooplein flea market (on Waterlooplein) is always entertaining, and you can avoid spending your euros by pointing out that most of the junk isn't worth shipping home to the rumpus room.

The **Tram Museum (Elektrische Museumtramlijn)** is in fact a streetcar ride, but all the better: Kids love it. The museum has several old trolleys and trams once used in other European cities, and they rattle down special tracks from Haarlemmermeerstation through the Amsterdamsebos (a wooded park with tons of family amusements; see the Getting Outside chapter) to suburban Amstelveen and back. The same kind of ride is offered by the **Tourist Tram,** a nifty 1920s streetcar that zips from the top of Damrak all over town. They *might* also like the **Historic Ferry,** an old ferry boat that plies the IJ waterway to suburban Nieuwendam and back, an old-fashioned attraction strictly for tourists, as it's not a public transportation service: Skip it unless you like old boats and suburban scenery.

People-watching... Hanging out on cafe terraces is a *major* activity in Amsterdam. There's a great rush for the best places in good weather. Leidseplein is a prime spot to study the fauna, local and imported, and the Café Américain (p. 85) is the best place for it. There's a terrace outside, where you'll see the square's inevitable fire eaters, clowns, and sidewalk musicians. Over in Vondelpark, at the **Netherlands Film Museum,** hardly anyone seems to go into the resource center for cinematographers. They're all looking good on the wide, shaded terraces of the Café Vertigo overlooking the park where people picnic, blade, cycle, and fornicate in plain view. Two postmodern white cafes on the Amstel River, the Café de Jaren (p. 214) and Dantzig (p. 85), have become the ultimate see-and-be-seen venues. Both have riverside terraces; both have big, airy interiors where locals and visitors pose. Over on Damrak—among the winking plastic signs of peep shows and souvenir shops—is the De Roode Leeuw restaurant and cafe (p. 85), with the oldest heated terrace in town, a comfy spot from which to watch dazed tourists and pickpockets in action. Half a mile away, at Spui, the bibliophiles, media types, and fashionable Grachtengordel residents sit on the terrace or crowd onto the sidewalk at Hoppe (p. 216) and Café Luxembourg next door (p. 212), an old brown cafe and a designer newish one, known as Amsterdam's most sophisticated people-watching venues.

Behind the eight ball... About the most action sports locals will go for are beer guzzling and getting snookered at carambole, a devilishly complicated game played on pool tables without pockets. Get them to explain it to you; I can't. Pool-table games are an obsession among the brown cafe contingent, and it's usually easy to pick up a game. Scores of places have tables, but Café Chris (p. 212) in the Jordaan, the oldest brown in town (1624), is a particularly atmospheric, if cramped, spot to chalk a stick with regulars. Ruk & Pluk (p. 217), a crazy joint run by a famous gay couple, is a modern brown cafe east of Oosterpark, with a pocketless table under the Brazilian carnival decor. Serious players should check out the **Bavaria Pool-Snooker-centrum,** out on Van Ostadestraat, south of Singelgracht and not too far from the Heineken Brewery, where sharks bring their own cues and reserve a table on one of four floors. For pickup games, you'd better be good. The rival club, **De Keizer Snooker Club,** on Keizersgracht, near Westerkerk, has individual rooms where titans battle it out on the felt.

Chess cafes... Chess is another local favorite, since chess pieces can be moved with a minimum of effort and allow you to remain within reach of liquid refreshment. Countless cafes have chess sets for their customers, and anyone can play; a handful, called "*schaak* cafes," are frequented almost exclusively by the *schaak*-obsessed. **Gambit** (p. 215) is possibly the most competitive, a Jordaan hangout where you have to cut away at the smoke to see what the queen and king are up to. At **Schaak Café Het Hok** (p. 218), also near Leidseplein, regulars sit in the fog under Ajax soccer posters, sip tea, and reach for the suspended timers.

Where to escape the crowds... There are times when even the most gregarious traveler feels like being alone. You'll find no crowds at the **Trade Union Museum** perusing the yellowed newspaper clippings, warped black-and-white photos, and lengthy documents (in Dutch) recounting the struggle of organized labor in the Netherlands. Sounds like a total yawn—and it is. But lo and behold, the early-1900s Dutch Art Nouveau architecture is stunning stuff, and no one seems to know about it. Hendrik Petrus van Berlage (as in the Beurs van Berlage; see "Art nouveau to go," below) designed the vaulted, tiled building—with stained glass and sculpted bas-reliefs—for the Diamond Workers' Union. Another beautiful building where you'll never be bustled, the quiet **Dijbels Museum,** is a real treat, whether or not you're a religious scholar. It houses rather astounding scale models of biblical archaeology, and the architecture is a revelation: twin 1662 canal houses with an elliptical wooden staircase, and a coffered ceiling with mythological scenes painted in 1717 by Jacob de Wit—so you can even come away with a dose of Sistine Chapel Neck syndrome.

Around the turn of the 20th century, witty Amsterdammers used to quip that if you wanted to meet your mistress in private, the **Willet-Holthuysen Museum** was the place to go. This restored 1687 Golden Bend canal-house museum is still quiet. Polite visitors can peek at the downstairs antique kitchen, the mezzanine room with a rococo, painted ceiling, the d'Aubusson tapestries, and the family portraits of stern ancestors. Probably the quietest museum of them all, though, is dedicated to the memory of 19th-century satirical writer Eduard Douwes-Dekker, aka Multatuli, a legend for the Dutch but largely unknown outside the Netherlands (remember his incomparable *Max Havelaar*, set on a coffee plantation?). Despite international adoption of a "Max Havelaar" logo by fair trade activists (for coffee grown by fairly paid peasants), utter stillness reigns in the **Multatuli Museum,** where a solicitous (and surprised) curator will explain, in English, about the photos, first-edition books, documents, and old furniture in this one-room memorial. Another pure-Dutch treat, of another kind, is the **Pianola Museum,** surely the most *gezellig* museum in town. Player-piano aficionado Kasper Janse has about three dozen old pianolas in his private collection. There's a front-room brown cafe, where local Jordaaners and rare, lost tourists sip coffee and sing along to old tunes.

Art Nouveau to go... Art nouveau aficionados won't want to miss the **Beurs van Berlage,** formerly the Stock Exchange, now a conference center, art exhibition space, museum, and concert hall. Built in 1896 by architect Hendrik Petrus van Berlage, it's a transition between the heavy, eclectic architecture of the late 1800s and the modernity of the Amsterdam School that followed. The complex covers an entire city block—make sure you go inside to see the best of it (the official guides are Artifex Travel; see p. 96). There are tiled arches and columns, ornate ironwork, stained glass, sinuous lights that seem straight out of a jungle, and a stunning cafe with murals. The tower offers breathtaking views—literally (there's no elevator). Another Dutch Art Nouveau landmark, with Art Deco additions, is the **Crowne Plaza Amsterdam American** hotel (p. 49) and its **Café Américain** (p. 85), built in 1900. Its Emerald City–style tower rises over Leidseplein. The cafe's wall clock and the symbolist murals hark back to *Great Gatsby* times. Hanging like bats from the high, vaulted ceiling are huge bronze and stained-glass lamps that look like they might take wing. Another van Berlage treasure is the rarely visited **Trade Union Museum,** near the Artis Zoo in Eastern Central Amsterdam (also see "Where to escape the crowds," above).

When you're down to your last euro... An only-in-Amsterdam musical freebie is provided by the oh-so-quaint jingle-bell carillons strategically distributed around the four corners of the oldest part of town. There are actually nine historic carillons (four date from the 17th century), but only four of them ring out classical tunes (and the occasional pop hit) once a week from the tops of their church towers. Tuesdays, go to the **Westertoren;** Thursdays, the **Zuidertoren;** and Fridays, the **Munttoren,** all at noon. On Saturdays from 4 to 5pm it's the **Oude Kerkstoren**'s turn. Even if you can't manage to get right under the towers, the sweet-and-sour melodies turn each neighborhood into a music box. The **Zuiderkerk** has one of the nicest carillons, and also offers a free, permanent exhibition on Amsterdam's development and planning through the centuries, featuring drawings, photographs, slide shows, and scale models. You can see how the city grew and consult new urban planning schemes to see where it's stumbling next.

From October to June, both the **Muziektheater** and the celebrated **Concertgebouw** (p. 241) offer free lunchtime concerts. Head for the **Boekmanzaal** (part of the Muziektheater) for chamber-music performances by the Choir of the Netherlands Opera, the Netherlands Philharmonic, or the Netherlands Ballet Orchestra (times vary—check at the Muziektheater's info desk). The Royal Concertgebouw Orchestra kicks in on Wednesdays at the same time with public rehearsals of the works they'll be performing that night. Get to both when the doors open at 12:15pm, or you might not find a seat. De Engelse Kerk (English Reformed Church) at the **Begijnhof** offers its own lunchtime classical concerts on Tuesdays at 1:10pm, precisely. The Pulitzer Concert, usually held once a year, on the last Saturday in August, features classical music performed on pontoons built in front of the Pulitzer Hotel (p. 53).

While water taxis and canal buses can be pricey, there is one way to get onto the water without spending a euro. The city operates a free ferry service from the docks immediately behind Centraal Station to the north bank of the IJ River. It takes only about 5 minutes to get across, and isn't exactly thrilling, but you do get a whiff of the sea and a nice view of bustling river traffic. One ferry, the **Buiksloter-wegveer,** operates daily, around the clock. The other, the **IJ-Veer,** is smaller, easier to pronounce, and runs weekdays only, from early morning to dinnertime. Whichever one you take, the ferry is the most pleasant way to get to the dull suburb of Amsterdam Noord (North)—and the outdoorsy pleasures just beyond it. Within 15 minutes on foot or by bike from the ferry terminal, you can explore the centuries-old suburb of Nieuwendam, cycle through the Florapark, or catch the bike and hiking trails leading to nearby villages like Broek in Waterland, Monnickendam, and Zaanse Schans (see the Getting Outside chapter for details). Also leaving from here is a ferry that takes a 20-minute sail to Java Island and its novel architecture, a postmodern mix of Lego and faux Manhattan Beach styles.

Here's a two-in-one: If you don't feel like going into the Amsterdam Historical Museum but are craving some historic art and architecture, stroll through the **Schutters-galerij,** a passageway linking Kalverstraat to Spui, via the Begijnhof, that famously hidden courtyard (p. 140). Under the Schuttersgalerij's glass roof, you'll see 15 bigger-is-bet-ter, 17th-century paintings showing the city's heroic Civic Guards. These paintings are in the same tradition, if not quite the same league, as Rembrandt's *The Night Watch,* but then you don't have to line up and pay to view them, either. And seen in this relaxed context, without crowds, they are well worth the detour. Lovers of romantic ruins should try the **Rijksmuseum's architectural garden,** open and free during museum hours. Scattered among the fountains and flowerbeds are weatherworn garden statuary and a hodge-podge of columns, gables, festoons, and fragments from monuments and houses destroyed over the last century. It provides a sort of whirlwind tour of Dutch architecture since the Middle Ages and even includes 17th-century city gates from the cities of Deventer and Groningen. Despite all of the above, it's invariably empty.

The Red-Light District... To sample the Red-Light Dis-trict's past and prurience, start at Centraal Station and take busy Prins Hendrikkade east a few hundred yards to the Schreierstoren (The Tower of Tears; see p. 110). Oudezijds Kolk alley leads to the Oudezijds Voorburgwal canal and the **Oude Kerk,** the oldest church in Amsterdam. Climb the onion-dome belfry (on pre-arranged group visits only) for views of the Red-Light District; then go inside for the stained glass, carved choir stalls, and painted wooden ceil-ing. There are gables and gablestones galore up and down this canal and surrounding streets and alleys. One canal east, off Oudezijds Achterburgwal, walk down Oude Hoogstraat and you'll see narrow Oude Hoogstraat 22, the alleged narrowest house in Europe, measuring only 2m (6.56 ft.) wide and 6m (19.68 ft.) deep. Cross the Waals

Eilandsgracht canal, go west toward Centraal Station, and you'll run into the immense Scheepvaarthuis (Shipping Building), a turreted, 1912–16 Amsterdam School fantasy with incredible bas-reliefs (p. 137).

The old Jewish Quarter... Start a tour of former Jewish Amsterdam at the **De Pinto House** on Sint-Antoniesbreestraat, once home of Isaac de Pinto, a Portuguese Jew who co-founded the United East India Company. Nearby, just off the same street, is Hendrick de Keyser's **Zuiderkerk** and **Zuidertoren,** built from 1602 to 1611 for a Calvinist congregation. Climb the tower for views of the area. A hundred yards southeast, on Joodenbreestraat, is the **Rembrandt House Museum,** where the artist lived from 1639 to 1658. Follow Zwanenburgwal to the Amstel River and you'll come upon the **Jewish Memorial,** a megalith bearing witness to the Nazi atrocities that claimed 75,000 Jewish Amsterdammer lives and led to the destruction of Amsterdam's Jewish district. Loop around the hideous, modern city hall–cum–**Muziektheater,** also known by the derisive nickname "false teeth." (Look at it from the river and you'll see why.) Behind Mr. Visserplein, a busy traffic circle, is the **Jewish Historical Museum;** next door is the enormous 1675 **Portuguese Synagogue.** A few hundred yards farther east is the **Hortus Botanicus**—a gorgeous 17th-century botanical garden. Follow Plantage Middenlaan to the **Hollandsche Schouwburg,** once a turn-of-the-20th-century comedy theater, now a gutted and roofless wreck. This is probably the most moving of Amsterdam's memorials, a site where an estimated 60,000 to 80,000 Jews crossed the threshold (it was used as a processing center for deportees) awaiting transit to Nazi death camps.

Hofje-**hopping in the Jordaan...** Uncontrolled real estate speculation at the end of the Golden Age gave birth to the Jordaan's eccentric layout, a maze of narrow alleys and canals and tiny, teetering old buildings. Art galleries, hundreds of boutiques, and countless cafes have sprouted up here now. The most atmospheric section is north of Elandsgracht, and the best scenery of all is on the Bloemgracht, Egelantiersgracht, Brouwersgracht, and Prinsengracht canals. There are several open markets around **Noorderkerk,** a landmark 1623 church. *Hofje*-hopping—exploring the hidden courtyards of former Jordaan almshouses—is one way to discover the neighborhood. Start in the north on Palmgracht (28–38) at the tiny **Raepenhofje,** which is filled with flowers and marked with a gablestone showing a beet. Walk south, then right on Lindengracht (147–165) to the **Suykerhofje,** built in 1667 for Protestant women, with steep tile roofs and dormers and a wonderfully overgrown garden. Around the corner to the south is the **Huyszitten Weduwenhof Karthuizerhof,** on Karthuizerstraat (21–131), a large complex whose 80 houses surround a quad and date to 1650; it was built for widows with children. A big old water pump is home to cats, and there's a brightly painted gablestone of a sailing ship. Continue south to narrow Egelantiersdwarsstraat (26–50) and the **Claes Claeszhofje,** a small double courtyard with an unusual wooden tower, wisteria, and hawthorn. Around the corner on Egelantiersgracht (105–141) is the **Sint-Andrieshofje,** twice the size of the Claes Claeszhofje, with a restored garden that's spectacular in spring. A 15-minute walk south takes you to Elandsgracht (104–142) and the **Hofje Venetia** or **Maarloopshofje,** a large courtyard with a gorgeous garden.

The Grachtengordel mansions... To understand why this neighborhood has come to mean "moneyed" in Dutch, stroll along Herengracht's Golden Bend, between Leidsestraat and Vijzelstraat, with shoulder-to-shoulder mansions. Or, if you have a whole afternoon to tackle the Grachtengordel, start at the top of Prinsengracht, west of Centraal Station, walk along it as far as the Amstel River, then double back on Keizersgracht and Herengracht, weaving between them via Reguliersgracht (lots of bridges, plus handsome Amstelveld square), Nieuwe Spiegelstraat (the antiques dealers' quarter), and the small side streets and canals north of Leidsegracht. At Prinsengracht 85–133 is another former almshouse, the beautifully restored and immensely restful **Van Brienen's Hofje,** from 1804 (also known as De Star after the De Star Brewery foundation that took over the site in 1841). Merchant Jan van Brienen supposedly had it built in gratitude for his escape from a vault in which he had accidentally been locked. It has a lovely garden and benches where you can rest. At **Zon's Hofje** (157–171), you'll find an intimate, shaded courtyard. The easily recognizable **Westerkerk,** an imposing 1620–38 Protestant church, and its tall, leaning Westertoren tower, are prime examples of architect Hendrick de Keyser's handiwork, and the tower provides a terrific panorama.

Behind it, on Keizersgracht, is the pink-granite **Homomonument,** a 1987 memorial to persecuted gay men and lesbians. Nearby on Keizersgracht (121) is the celebrated **House with the Heads (Huis met de Hoofden),** a 1624 mansion with large, sculpted heads of Diana, Bacchus, Athena, Mars, Ceres, and Apollo. A few blocks down on the same canal (324) is **Felix Meritis,** an aesthetically challenged neoclassical theater from the 1780s that was long renowned for its acoustics (it's now used for classical musical concerts, lectures, and the like; see p. 242). Five minutes away on the same canal is **Huis Marseille,** a 1665 mansion now housing a photography foundation. A few blocks north on Herengracht (168–170) is the **Netherlands Theater Institute Museum,** a resource center for performance-arts students housed in a remarkable 1638 mansion with the city's first neck gable and ceilings painted by Jacob de Wit. Two ground-floor rooms actually belong to the next-door **Bartolotti House,** a 1618 landmark with an exceptionally ornate redbrick facade.

A Singel-minded stroll... The medieval moat Singel—the outermost ring surrounding the city before the Golden Age boom—starts with what is supposed to be the narrowest house in the world **(Singel 7).** A few bridges down is the Torensluis, a 17th-century bridge with a charming downstairs dungeon that was flooded daily, to the horror of "lazy" prisoners who drowned if they didn't pump the water out fast enough. The canal ends with a flourish at the fragrant **flower market,** between Koningsplein and Muntplein.

Map 6: Amsterdam Diversions Orientation

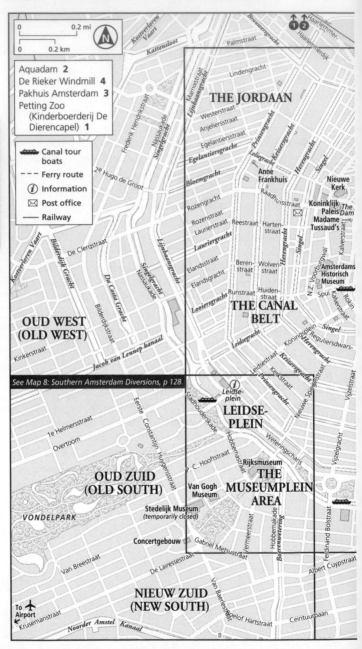

DIVERSIONS

0   0.2 mi
0   0.2 km

Aquadam **2**
De Rieker Windmill **4**
Pakhuis Amsterdam **3**
Petting Zoo
(Kinderboerderij De
Dierencapel) **1**

Canal tour boats
Ferry route
Information
Post office
Railway

THE JORDAAN

Anne Frankhuis

Nieuwe Kerk

Koninklijk Paleis

The Dam

Madame Tussaud's

Amsterdams Historisch Museum

THE CANAL BELT

OUD WEST (OLD WEST)

See Map 8: Southern Amsterdam Diversions, p 128.

Leidseplein

LEIDSEPLEIN

OUD ZUID (OLD SOUTH)

Rijksmuseum

THE MUSEUMPLEIN AREA

Van Gogh Museum

Stedelijk Museum (temporarily closed)

VONDELPARK

Concertgebouw

NIEUW ZUID (NEW SOUTH)

To Airport

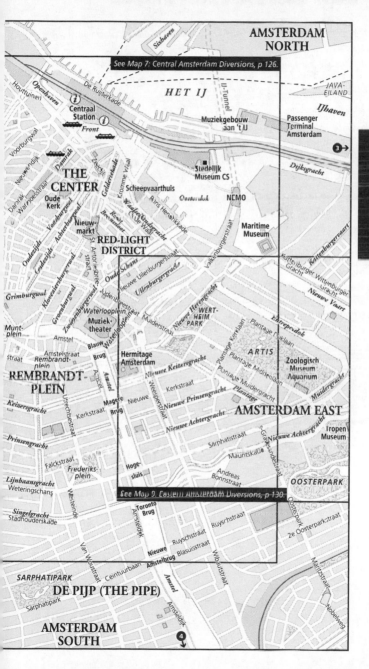

See Map 7: Central Amsterdam Diversions, p 126.

AMSTERDAM
NORTH

Sixhaven

Houttuinen

Oosterwal

De Ruijterkade

HET IJ

IJ-Tunnel

JAVA-
EILAND

IJhaven

Centraal
Station

Front

Muziekgebouw
aan 't IJ

Passenger
Terminal
Amsterdam

➌→

THE
CENTER

Stedelijk
Museum CS

Dijksgracht

Oude
Kerk

Scheepvaarthuis

Oosterdok

NEMO

Nieuw-
markt

RED-LIGHT
DISTRICT

Maritime
Museum

Kattenburgervaart

Grimburgwal

Nieuwe Uilenburgergracht

Ullenburgergracht

Nieuwe Vaart

Nieuwe Herengracht

WERT-
HEIM
PARK

Plantage Kerklaan

Entrepotdok

Munt-
plein

Amstel

Muziek-
theater

Waterlooplein

Muiderstraat

ARTIS

Plantage Middenlaan

Zoologisch
Museum
Aquarium

Amstelstraat
Rembrandt-
plein

Blauw
Brug

Nieuwe Keizersgracht

Hermitage
Amsterdam

Kerkstraat

Plantage Muidergracht

Muidergracht

REMBRANDT-
PLEIN

Keizersgracht

Magere
Brug

Kerkstraat

Nieuwe

Nieuwe Prinsengracht

Plantage

AMSTERDAM EAST

Prinsengracht

Nieuwe Achtergracht

Nieuwe Achtergracht

Tropen
Museum

Sarphatistraat

Mauritskade

Falckstraat

Frederiks-
plein

Hoge-
sluis

Andreas
Bonnstraat

OOSTERPARK

Lijnbaansgracht
Weteringschans

See Map 9: Eastern Amsterdam Diversions, p 130.

Singelgracht
Stadhouderskade

Toronto
Brug

Ruyschstraat

2e Oosterparkstraat

Nieuwe
Amstelbrug

Ruyschstraat
Blasiusstraat

Wibautstraat

SARPHATIPARK

DE PIJP (THE PIPE)

Sarphatipark

Amstel

AMSTERDAM
SOUTH

➍
↓

DIVERSIONS

Map 7: Central Amsterdam Diversions

DIVERSIONS

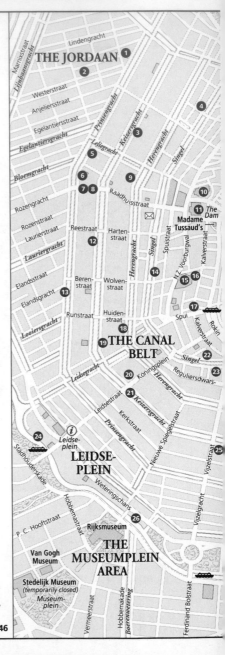

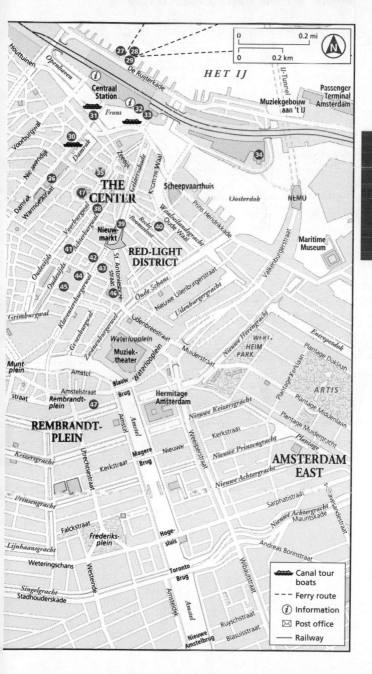

DIVERSIONS

Map 8: Southern Amsterdam Diversions

Bavaria
  Pool-Snookercentrum **6**
Heineken Experience **5**
Netherlands Film Museum **1**
Rijksmuseum **4**
Stedelijk Museum
  (closed at this location
  until 2008) **2**
Tram Museum (Elektrische
  Museumtramlijn) **7**
Van Gogh Museum **3**

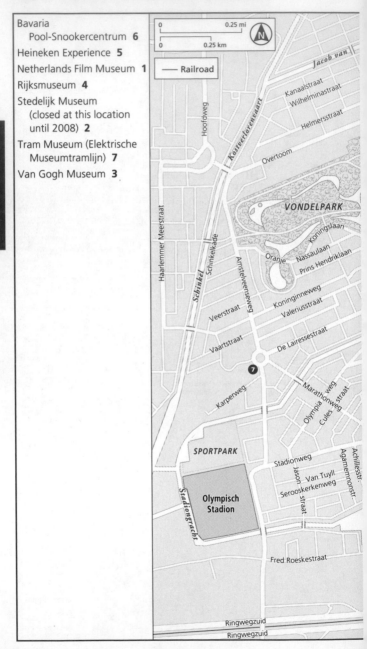

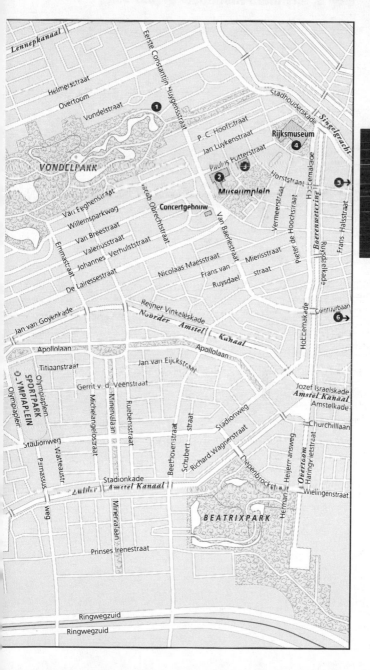

Map 9: Eastern Amsterdam Diversions

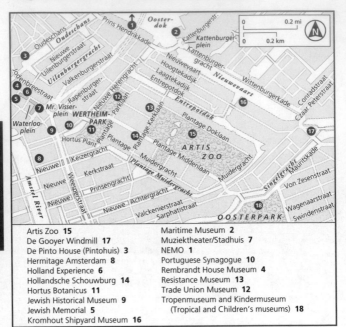

Artis Zoo **15**
De Gooyer Windmill **17**
De Pinto House (Pintohuis) **3**
Hermitage Amsterdam **8**
Holland Experience **6**
Hollandsche Schouwburg **14**
Hortus Botanicus **11**
Jewish Historical Museum **9**
Jewish Memorial **5**
Kromhout Shipyard Museum **16**

Maritime Museum **2**
Muziektheater/Stadhuis **7**
NEMO **1**
Portuguese Synagogue **10**
Rembrandt House Museum **4**
Resistance Museum **13**
Trade Union Museum **12**
Tropenmuseum and Kindermuseum
   (Tropical and Children's museums) **18**

The Index

Amstelkring Museum (Our Lord in the Attic Museum) (p. 108)
CENTER This is the city's finest surviving clandestine or "attic" Roman Catholic church, a baroque bijou built in 1663 into the upper floors of three houses, now on the edge of the Red Light District.... *Tel 020/624-6604. www.museumamstelkring.nl. Oudezijds Voorburgwal 40 at Heintje Hoekssteeg. Trams 1, 2, 4, 5, 6, 9, 13, 16, 17, 24, 25, or 26 to Centraal Station. Mon–Sat 10am–5pm, Sun and holidays 1–5pm (later opening in summer). Closed Jan 1, April 30. Admission charged.*
See Map 7 on p. 126.

Amsterdam Historical Museum (p. 107) CENTER Housed in a medieval era orphanage, this is the repository for jewelry, porcelain, maps, and paintings telling the story of Amsterdam from its birth in the 13th century.... *Tel 020/523-1822. www.ahm.nl. Kalverstraat 92, Nieuwezijds Voorburgwal 359, and Sint-Luciën steeg 27 (3 entrances). Trams 1, 2, 4, 5, 6, 9, 14, 16, 24, or 25 to Spui. Mon–Fri 10am–5pm, weekends and holidays 11am–5pm. Closed Jan 1, April 30, Dec 25. Admission charged.*
See Map 7 on p. 126.

Anne Frank House (p. 108) CANAL BELT Too popular for its own good (it's been called "the Volendam of the Holocaust," i.e., a commercial exploitation of guilt), this little canal house is where Anne Frank wrote her celebrated diary when hiding with her family during the Nazi occupation. It has an annex for exhibitions and a cafe-restaurant to go with the souvenir boutique and bookstore.... *Tel 020/556-7100. www.annefrank.org. Prinsengracht 263 at Westermarkt. Trams 6, 13, 14, or 17 to Westermarkt. April–Aug daily 9am–9pm; Sept–March daily 9am–7pm; Jan 1 and Dec 25 noon–7pm. Closed Yom Kippur. Admission charged.*
See Map 7 on p. 126.

Aquadam (p. 112) WESTERN ISLANDS Luxury saloon boats.... *Tel 020/344-9434. www.aquadam.nl. Rickersgracht 1 at Haarlemmer Houttuinen. Tram 3 to Zoutkeetsgracht; buses 18 or 22 to Haarlemmer Houttuinen. Rental rates range from 175€ ($201) an hour for a 10-passenger launch, to 350€ ($403) an hour for a 40-passenger launch.*
See Map 6 on p. 124.

Artis Zoo (p. 114) EAST Founded in 1838, the oldest zoo in Europe has about 6,000 animals from around the world. And what would a 19th-century temple of the natural sciences be without a planetarium and museums of geology and zoology?.... *Tel 020/523-3400. www.artis.nl. Plantage Kerklaan 38–40 at Plantage Middenlaan. Trams 9 or 14 to Plantage Kerklaan; 6 to Plantage Doklaan. April–Oct daily 9am–6pm, Nov–March daily 9am–5pm. Admission charged.*

See Map 9 on p. 130.

Bartolotti House (p. 106) CANAL BELT Built in 1618, this patrician mansion north of the Golden Bend is an architectural landmark but not open for comprehensive tours.... *Tel 020/551-3300. www.tin.nl. Herengracht 170–172 at Raadhuisstraat. Trams 6, 13, 14, or 17 to Westermarkt. Tues–Fri 11am–5pm, Sat–Sun 1–5pm. Admission charged.*

See Map 7 on p. 126.

Bavaria Pool-Snookercentrum (p. 116) OLD SOUTH Probably the city's hottest spot to chalk a cue, with four floors of tables, including billiards, carambole, snooker, and pool. Call ahead to reserve.... *Tel 020/676-7903. Van Ostadestraat 97 at Ferdinand Bolstraat. Trams 3 to Ferdinand Bolstraat; 12, 16, 24, or 25 to Ceintuurbaan. Daily 11am–1am, Fri–Sat until 2am. Admission charged.*

See Map 8 on p. 128.

Begijnhof (p. 99) CENTER This gorgeous 14th-century **hofje** (almshouse), built around an oblong courtyard, is home to the oldest house in Amsterdam, the English Reformed Church (believed to have been built in 1392), and many other historic treasures.... *No phone. Spui, north side (no number). Trams 1, 2, or 5 to Spui. Daily 8am–1pm. Free admission.*

See Map 7 on p. 126.

Beurs van Berlage (Berlage Stock Exchange) (p. 104) CENTER This large 1896 Dutch Art Nouveau building—the city's former stock exchange—is an intriguing piece of architecture, covering an entire city block; it's now a conference center, museum, and art exhibition and concert hall. It also houses a stunning cafe, open only during exhibitions.... *Tel 020/530-4141. www.beursvanberlage.nl. Beursplein 1. Trams 4, 9, 14, 16, 24, or 25 to the Dam. Tues–Sun 11am–5pm, and at other times for events, concerts, etc. Admission charged. See also the Entertainment chapter.*

See Map 7 on p. 126.

Bijbels Museum (Biblical Museum) (p. 117) CANAL BELT A quiet museum for religious scholars in a fascinating building—twin 1662 canal houses with mythological scenes painted by Jacob de Wit.... *Tel 020/624-2436. www.bijbelsmuseum.nl. Herengracht 366–368 at Huidenstraat. Trams 1, 2, or 5 to Spui. Mon–Sat*

10am–5pm, Sun and holidays 1–5pm. Closed Jan 1, April 30. Admission charged.

See Map 7 on p. 126.

Buiksloterwegveer (p. 119) CENTER One of two free city-operated ferries that crosses the IJ channel from docks directly behind Centraal Station to Amsterdam Noord.... *Tel (use general transit number) 0900/9292. Operates daily around the clock; 6:30am–9pm every 15 minutes, 9pm–6:30am every half-hour.*

See Map 7 on p. 126.

Canal Bike (p. 112) CANAL BELT The Dutch call **pedalos** "canal bikes." Rent them and get splashed with brown water.... **Tel 020/626-5574.** *Available daily 10am–7pm (July–Aug 10am–10pm) at docks at: Rijksmuseum, Leidseplein, Keizersgracht (at Leidsestraat), and the Anne Frank House. Rental is 8€ ($10) per person hourly for 1 or 2 people; 7€ ($8.75) per person hourly for 3 or 4 people; you'll need to leave a deposit of 50€ ($63).*

See Map 7 on p. 126.

Canal Bus (p. 112) CENTER Amsterdam's answer to Venice's vaporetti, though locals don't use it.... *Tel 020/623-9886. Boat-buses stop about every 30–45 minutes at docks at the Rijksmuseum, Leidseplein, Keizersgracht (at Raadhuisstraat), Westerkerk (at the Anne Frank House), Centraal Station, and City Hall. Hop on and off from 10am–6:30pm daily. Tickets required.*

See Map 7 on p. 126.

De Gooyer Windmill (p. 106) EASTERN DOCKS A 1725 former corn mill, northeast of Artis Zoo. It now houses Bierbrouwerij 't IJ, the city's best microbrewery, with a vast summer terrace.... *Tel 020/622-8325. Funenkade 7 at Sarphatistraat. Trams 7 or 10 to Pontanusstraat. Free admission.*

See Map 9 on p. 130.

De Keizer Snooker Club (p. 116) CANAL BELT A classy pool hall for serious players not interested in socializing.... *Tel 020/623-1586. Keizersgracht 256. Trams 6, 13, 14, or 17 to Westermarkt. Daily 1pm–1am, Fri–Sat until 2am. Admission charged.*

See Map 7 on p. 126.

De Pinto House (p. 105) JEWISH QUARTER Bought and remodeled in 1651 by Isaac de Pinto, a Portuguese Jew who fled persecution and co-founded the United East India Company, this early-1600s mansion is now a public library.... *No phone. Sint-Antoniesbreestraat 69. Metro to Nieuwmarkt. Mon–Fri 9:30am–5pm. Free admission.*

See Map 9 on p. 130.

DIVERSIONS

THE INDEX

De Rederij (p. 112) CENTER Vintage saloon-boat rentals include captain, crew, and well-stocked liquor cabinet.... *Tel 020/330-1234. www.derederij.nl. Recht Boomssloot 47C at Geldersekade. Metro to Nieuwmarkt. Rates vary widely.*

See Map 7 on p. 126.

De Rieker Windmill (p. 106) SOUTHERN SUBURBS In the far-flung Amstelpark, detour to the riverbank for this 1636 thatched windmill, now a private home.... *No telephone. Amsteldijk at De Borcht in the Amstelpark. Bus 148 to Kalfjeslaan. Not open to the public.*

See Map 6 on p. 124.

De Waag (p. 110) CENTER An original, and still impressive, turretted city gate—now home to a multimedia center and a trendy cafe-restaurant.... *Tel 020/557-9898. www.waag.org. Nieuwmarkt 4. Metro to Nieuwmarkt. Most of the building is rarely open to the public, but the cafe-restaurant is open Sun–Thurs 10am–1am, Fri–Sat 10am–2am. Admission charged to occasional exhibits in main building.*

East India House (Oost Indisch Huis) (p. 105) CENTER The University of Amsterdam now has offices in what was the nerve center of the Dutch commercial empire from 1603 until recent times.... *No phone. Oude Hoogstraat at Kloveniersburgwal. Trams 4, 9, 14, 16, 24, or 25 to the Dam. Not open to the public; you can visit the courtyard. Free admission.*

See Map 7 on p. 126.

Erotic Museum (p. 113) RED-LIGHT DISTRICT Run by the same charmers who own the Bananenbar and Casa Rosso, this porno haven is filled with books, films, vibrators, S&M accessories, and customers with sweaty palms.... *Tel 020/624-7303. Oudezijds Achterburgwal 54 at Kreupelsteeg. Trams 4, 9, 14, 16, 24, or 25 to the Dam. Daily 11am–1am, Fri–Sat until 2am. Admission charged.*

See Map 7 on p. 126.

Flower Market (Bloemenmarkt) (p. 98) CANAL BELT The famous flower market that "floats" on the sidewalk, piers, and a few old barges anchored to the Singel. Gorgeous plants and cut flowers, plus bulbs and seeds.... *No phone. Singel between Muntplein and Koningsplein. Trams 1, 2, or 5 to Koningsplein; 4, 9, 14, 16, 24, 25 to Muntplein. Mon–Sat 10am–6pm.*

See Map 7 on p. 126.

Geels & Co. (p. 113) RED-LIGHT DISTRICT A coffee-roasting and tea-importing establishment houses a tiny coffee and tea museum.... *Tel 020/624-0683. www.geels.nl. Warmoesstraat 67 at Oude Brugsteeg. Trams 4, 9, 14, 16, 24, or 25 to the Dam. Museum open Sat 2–4:30pm; free admission.*

See Map 10 on p. 178.

The Hash Marihuana Hemp Museum (p. 113) RED-LIGHT DIS-
TRICT Everything you ever wanted to know about the pungent
weed is explained and displayed at this private museum in the
Red-Light District.... *Tel 020/623-5961. www.hashmuseum.com.
Oudezijds Achterburgwal 130 at Stoofsteeg. Trams 4, 9, 14, 16,
24, or 25 to the Dam. Daily 11am–11pm. Admission charged.*
See Map 7 on p. 126.

Heineken Experience (p. 98) OLD SOUTH Actually, the last can
left the brewery in 1988; most of the plant has been demolished
to make way for upscale apartments and shops. You and several
hundred other visitors tour the atmospheric beer museum and
learn about hops and grain and water; then you can drink two
glasses of the stuff, free, and as many more as you have the
cash and the capacity for.... *Tel 020/523-9666. www.heineken
experience.com. Stadhouderskade 78 at Ferdinand Bolstraat.
Trams 16, 24, or 25 to Stadhouderskade. Tues–Sun 10am–
6pm. Closed Jan 1, Dec 25. Visitors under 18 admitted only with
parental supervision. Admission charged.*
See Map 8 on p. 128.

Hermitage Amsterdam (p. 101) EAST Everyone's rushin' to see
what's cookin' at the Amsterdam franchise of the great Russian
museum from St. Petersburg.... *Tel 020/530-8755. www.
hermitage.nl. Trams 9 or 14 to Waterlooplein. Daily 10am–
5pm. Closed Jan 1, Dec 25. Admission charged.*
See Map 9 on p. 130.

Historic Ferry (p. 115) CENTER This old ferry plies the IJ channel
to Nieuwendam.... *Tel 0900/423-1100. Leaves from pier 8
behind Centraal Station. Trams 1, 2, 4, 5, 6, 9, 13, 16, 17, 24, 25,
or 26 to Centraal Station. Operates mid-April to mid-Oct daily, at
noon, 2, and 4pm. Tickets needed.*
See Map 7 on p. 126.

Holland Experience (p. 98) JEWISH QUARTER A multidimensional
film and theater show that gives you something of a nutshell picture of Holland.... *Tel 020/422-2233. www.holland-experience.nl.
Waterlooplein 17. Metro and trams 9 or 14 to Waterlooplein. Daily
11am–7pm; shows on the hour. Admission charged.*
See Map 9 on p. 130.

Hollandsche Schouwburg (p. 121) JEWISH QUARTER An estimated 60,000 to 80,000 Jews crossed the threshold of this
turn-of-the-20th-century comedy theater (now gutted and roofless) for "processing" before being sent by train to Westerbork
concentration camp, and on to the Nazi death camps.... *Tel
020/626-9945. Plantage Middenlaan 24. Trams 9 or 14 to
Plantage Kerklaan. Daily 11am–4pm. Free admission.*
See Map 9 on p. 130.

DIVERSIONS

THE INDEX

Homomonument (p. 123) CANAL BELT Erected in 1987, this unique monument commemorates gay men and lesbians persecuted down the centuries worldwide. It is a rallying point for the gay community.... *No phone. Westermarkt. Trams 6, 13, 14, or 17 to Westermarkt.*

See Map 7 on p. 126.

Hortus Botanicus (p. 121) EAST The lovely 17th-century park and greenhouses of this botanical garden display 6,000 or so specimens in a quiet haven.... *Tel 020/625-9021. www.dehortus.nl. Plantage Middenlaan 2A at Plantage Parklaan. Tram 6 to Plantage Parklaan; 9 or 14 to Plantage Kerklaan. Feb–Nov Mon–Fri 9am–5pm, weekends 10am–5pm (July–Aug to 9pm; Dec–Jan to 4pm). Admission charged.*

See Map 9 on p. 130.

Houseboat Museum (p. 114) CANAL BELT In the 1914 former cargo barge Hendrika Maria, a houseboat for decades, and now a house museum. Discover what life's like on the Amsterdam canals.... *Tel 020/427-0750. www.houseboatmuseum.nl. Prinsengracht, moored opposite number 296, at Elandsgracht. Trams 6, 13, 14, or 17 to Westermarkt. March–Oct Tues–Sun 11am–5pm; Nov–Dec and Feb Fri–Sun 11am–5pm. Closed Jan, April 30, and Dec 25, 26, and 27. Admission charged.*

See Map 7 on p. 126.

House with the Heads (Huis met de Hoofden) (p. 106) CANAL BELT This 1624 mansion, built by Hendrick de Keyser, is celebrated for the six large sculptured heads on the facade.... *No phone. Keizersgracht 121 at Leliegracht. Trams 6, 13, 14, or 17 to Westermarkt. Not open to the public.*

See Map 7 on p. 126.

Huis Marseille (p. 102) CANAL BELT Amsterdam's impressive photography foundation, in a 1665 canal house, has rotating shows of work by international talents.... *Tel 020/531-8989. www.huismarseille.nl. Keizersgracht 401 at Leidsegracht. Trams 1, 2, or 5 to Keizersgracht. Tues–Sun 11am–5pm. Admission charged.*

See Map 7 on p. 126.

IJ-Veer (p. 119) CENTER Free city-run ferry that crosses the IJ Channel from docks directly behind Centraal Station to Amsterdam Noord.... *Tel (use the general transit number) 0900/9292. Leaves pier every 15 minutes, Mon–Fri 6:35am–6:05pm. Trams 1, 2, 4, 5, 6, 9, 13, 16, 17, 24, 25, or 26 to Centraal Station.*

See Map 7 on p. 126.

Jewish Historical Museum (p. 107) JEWISH QUARTER This vast museum, housed in four ancient synagogues, displays photos, paintings, documents, and other objects relating to Jewish culture in the Netherlands. There's also a museum cafe and shop.... *Tel 020/625-4229. www.jhm.nl. Jonas Daniël Meijerplein 2–4 at*

Waterlooplein. Metro and trams 9 or 14 to Waterlooplein. Daily 11am–5pm. Closed Yom Kippur. Admission charged.

See Map 9 on p. 130.

Jewish Memorial (p. 121) JEWISH QUARTER Commemorating the estimated 75,000 Amsterdam Jews killed by Nazi atrocities during World War II.... *No phone. Waterlooplein at Zwanenburgwal. Metro and trams 9 or 14 to Waterlooplein.*

See Map 9 on p. 130.

Kindermuseum (p. 114) See Tropenmuseum.

Kromhout Shipyard Museum (p. 114) EASTERN DOCKS This small working shipyard in eastern Amsterdam, where historic boats are still repaired, has two magnificent ironwork sheds plus a handful of old ships and scores of early ship engines.... *Tel 020/627-6777. Hoogte Kadijk 147 at Kruithuisstraat. Buses 22 or 32 to Wittenburgergracht. Mon–Fri 10am–4pm. Admission charged.*

See Map 9 on p. 130.

Maritime Museum (p. 107) EASTERN DOCKS Everything Dutch relating to the sea.... *Tel 020/523-2222. www.generali.nl/ scheepvaartmuseum. Kattenburgerplein 1 at Prins Hendrikkade. Buses 22 or 28 to Kattenburgergracht. Tues–Sun 10am–5pm (also Mon mid-June to mid-Sept). Admission charged.*

See Map 9 on p. 130.

Metz & Co. (p. 104) CANAL BELT The panoramic, top-floor cafe of this upscale department store at the junction of Keizersgracht and Leidsestraat has lovely views over canal houses and mansions.... *Tel 020/520-7020. Keizersgracht 455 at Leidsestraat. Trams 1, 2, or 5 to Keizersgracht. Mon 11am–6pm, Tues–Wed and Fri 9:30am–6pm, Thurs 9:30am–9pm, Sat 10am–5pm, Sun noon–5pm. Free admission.*

See Map 7 on p. 126.

Multatuli Museum (p. 117) CENTER Photos, first-edition books, and old furniture in this one-room house-museum dedicated to the 19th-century satirical writer Eduard Douwes-Dekker.... *Tel 020/638-1938. Korsjespoortsteeg 20 at Singel. Trams 1, 2, 5, 6, 13, or 17 to Nieuwezijds Kolk. Tues 10am–5pm, Sat noon–5pm, and by appointment. Free admission.*

See Map 7 on p. 126.

Museumboot (p. 112) CANAL BELT Hop-on, hop-off service to 20 museums, with 10% to 15% reductions on museum entry fees. Stops at Centraal Station, Anne Frank House, Rijksmuseum, Leidsegracht (at Herengracht), Muzlektheater Kwartier, and Nautisch Kwartier.... *Tel 020/530-1090. www.lovers.nl. Boats run every 45 minutes 10am–6pm daily. Tickets required.*

See Map 7 on p. 126.

DIVERSIONS

THE INDEX

138

Muziektheater/Stadhuis (p. 119) JEWISH QUARTER This vast, modern complex on the Amstel River at Waterlooplein houses both the city hall *(stadhuis)* and the Muziektheater opera/ concert house.... *Tel 020/625-5455. Waterlooplein 22 or Amstel 1. Metro and trams 9 or 14 to Waterlooplein. Box office open Mon–Sat 10am–6pm, Sun 11:30am–6pm. Free admission Tues at 12:15pm. Other times tickets required.*

See Map 9 on p. 130.

NEMO (p. 98) EASTERN DOCKS This harborside science and tech-nology center features state-of-the-art virtual reality. Designed by Renzo Piano, it looks like a supertanker; great waterfront views from the roof.... *Tel 0900/919-1100. www.e-NEMO.nl. Oosterdok 2 at Prins Hendrikkade. Bus 22 to Kadijksplein. July–Aug daily 10am–5pm; Sept–June Tues–Sun 10am–5pm. Admission charged.*

See Map 9 on p. 130.

Netherlands Film Museum (p. 115) MUSEUM DISTRICT & VON-DELPARK A resource center for cinematographers and film buffs, this movie museum has a two-screen theater that shows Dutch and other films to members.... *Tel 020/589-1400. Vondel-park 3 in Vondelpark. Tram 1 to Eerste Constantijn Huygensstraat; 3 or 12 to Overtoom. Cafe open daily. Library and exhibit: Tues–Fri 10am–5pm, Sat 11am–5pm. Cinema: Mon–Fri from 7pm (and variable later times), Sat–Sun from 1pm (and variable later times). Admission charged for screenings.*

See Map 8 on p. 128.

Netherlands Theater Institute Museum (p. 106) CANAL BELT This rather dry resource center for performance arts students is in a gorgeous, restored 1638 canal house with a Golden Age garden.... *Tel 020/551-3300. www.tin.nl. Herengracht 168 at Leliegracht. Trams 6, 13, 14, or 17 to Westermarkt. Tues–Fri 11am–5pm, weekends 1–5pm. Admission charged.*

See Map 7 on p. 126.

Nieuwe Kerk (New Church) (p. 109) CANAL BELT Venerable (but mostly retired) Protestant church on the Dam, now used to house exhibitions.... *Tel 020/638-6909. www.nieuwekerk.nl. The Dam. Trams 1, 2, 4, 5, 6, 9, 13, 14, 16, 17, 24, or 25 to the Dam. Daily 10am–6pm (Thurs until 10pm during exhibitions). Admission charged during exhibitions; free at other times.*

See Map 7 on p. 126.

Noorderkerk (p. 121) CANAL BELT Another marvel by ubiquitous architect Hendrick de Keyser. Built in 1623, it stands at the edge of the Jordaan and is surrounded several times a week by lively open markets.... *Tel 020/626-6436. Noordermarkt at Prinsengracht. Tram 1, 2, 5, 6, 13, or 17 to Martelaarsgracht; Opstapper minibus to Noordermarkt. Mon 10:30am–12:30pm, Sat 11am–1pm (followed by a 1-hour chamber music concert), Sun (services) 10am and 7pm. Free admission.*

See Map 7 on p. 126.

DIVERSIONS

THE INDEX

Oude Kerk/Oude Kerkstoren (Old Church and Tower) (p. 109)
RED-LIGHT DISTRICT Ancient church (parts of it date to the
early 13th century), in the heart of the Red-Light District.... *Tel
020/625-8284. www.oudekerk.nl. Oudekerksplein at Oudezijds
Voorburgwal. Trams 1, 2, 4, 5, 6, 9, 13, 14, 16, 17, 24, or 25 to
the Dam. Mon–Sat 11am–5pm, Sun 1–5pm. Tower—only for
groups reserved in advance (Tel 020/689-2565); 40† ($50) per
group per hour. Admission charged.*

See Map 7 on p. 126.

Pakhuis Amsterdam (p. 104) EASTERN DOCKS International interior design center in a reconverted warehouse east of Centraal
Station; great views of city and harbor.... *Tel 020/421-1033.
Oostelijke Handelskade 14–17 at Piet Heinkade. Buses 32 or 39
to Piet Heinkade. Open Mon–Sat 10am–5pm.*

See Map 6 on p. 124.

Petting Zoo (Kinderboerderij De Dierencapel) (p. 115) WEST-
ERN ISLANDS Piglets, chickens, goats, sheep, and various
other animals roam along the banks of a canal, near houseboats and shipyards, in the atmospheric Western Islands....
*Tel 020/420-6855. Bickersgracht 207 at Haarlemmer Hout-
tuinen. Buses 18 or 22 to Binnen Oranjestraat. Tues–Sun
9:30am–4pm. Donations accepted.*

See Map 6 on p. 124.

Pianola Museum (p. 118) JORDAAN Player-piano lovers congregate to listen to—and sing along with—vintage tunes played on
35 old pianolas.... *Tel 020/627-9624. www.pianola.nl. Westerstraat 106 at Tweede Boomdwarsstraat. Trams 3 or 10 to Marnixplein. Sun 11:30am–5pm and by appointment. Admission
charged.*

See Map 7 on p. 126.

Portuguese Synagogue (p. 110) JEWISH QUARTER Long the
world's largest synagogue, this 1675 edifice miraculously survived the Nazi occupation.... *Tel 020/624-5351. www.esnoga.
com. Mr. Visserplein 3. Trams 9 or 14 to Mr. Visserplein. April–Oct
Sun–Fri 10am–4pm, Nov–March Sun–Thurs 10am–4pm, Fri
10am–3pm. Closed Jewish holidays. Admission charged.*

See Map 9 on p. 130.

Rederij De Nederlanden (p. 112) CANAL BELT Classy and expensive, with luxury-vintage saloon boats.... *Tel 020/423-3006.
www.denederlanden.com. Singel 309A at Oude Spiegelstraat
(across the canal). Trams 1, 2, or 5 to Spui. Rates vary according
to the boat, the number of passengers, the time of year, and the
time of day.*

See Map 7 on p. 126.

DIVERSIONS

THE INDEX

Rembrandt House Museum (p. 108) JEWISH QUARTER The artist lived and worked here from 1639 to 1658.... *Tel 020/520-0400. www.rembrandthuis.nl. Joodenbreestraat 4–6 at Waterlooplein. Trams 9 or 14 to Waterlooplein. Mon–Sat 10am–5pm, Sun and holidays 1–5pm. Closed Jan 1. Admission charged.*
See Map 9 on p. 130.

Resistance Museum (p. 107) JEWISH QUARTER Housed in the beautiful, neoclassical 1876 Plancius Building, which once housed a Jewish social club, the museum tells the story of Holland's experience of Nazi occupation during World War II.... *Tel 020/620-2535. www.verzetsmuseum.nl. Plantage Kerklaan 61 at Plantage Middenlaan. Trams 9 or 14 to Plantage Kerklaan; 6 to Plantage Doklaan. Tues–Sun 11am–5pm. Closed Jan 1, April 30, Dec 25. Admission charged.*
See Map 9 on p. 130.

Rijksmuseum De Meesterwerken (p. 100) MUSEUM DISTRICT & VONDELPARK Amsterdam's answer to the Louvre (though most of it is closed for renovations until 2008). The architectural garden is open during museum hours.... *Tel 020/674-7047. www.rijksmuseum.nl. Jan Luijkenstraat 1B at Museumplein. Trams 2 or 5 to Hobbemastraat; 6, 7, or 10 to Weteringschans. Daily 9am–6pm. Closed Jan 1. Admission charged.*
See Map 8 on p. 128.

Royal Palace (Koninklijk Paleis) (p. 97) CENTER The quintessential Golden Age architectural statement, designed in the mid–17th century to replace an earlier city hall.... *Tel 020/620-4060. www.koninklijkhuis.nl. The Dam. Trams 4, 9, 14, 16, 24, or 25 to the Dam. Note: The palace is closed for renovations until around Sept 2007.*
See Map 7 on p. 126.

Schuttersgalerij (Civic Guards Gallery) (p. 120) CENTER Difficult to find but worth it, this covered passageway houses 15 large 17th-century paintings showing the city's heroic Civic Guards.... *No phone. Between the Amsterdam Historical Museum and the Begijnhof. Trams 1, 2, 4, 5, 9, 14, 16, 24, or 25 to the Dam. Mon–Fri 10am–5pm, weekends 11am–5pm. Free admission.*
See Map 7 on p. 126.

Sex Museum (p. 113) CENTER A one-stop emporium of carnality. While many of the displays are flaccid, the voyeurs pour in by the thousands.... *Tel 020/622-8376. www.sexmuseumamsterdam.com. Damrak 18 at Prins Hendrikkade. Trams 1, 2, 4, 5, 6, 9, 13, 16, 17, 24, 25, or 26 to Centraal Station. Daily 10am–11:30pm. Admission charged.*
See Map 7 on p. 126.

Spinhuis (p. 103) CENTER A landmark 1597 building in the Red-Light District used for centuries as a correctional facility, i.e., labor camp, for wayward women.... *No phone. Spinhuissteeg at Oudezijds Achterburgwal. Trams 4, 9, 14, 16, 24, or 25 to Spui. Not open to the public.*

See Map 7 on p. 126.

Stedelijk Museum CS (p. 101) CENTER While the home base of the city's world-class modern and contemporary art museum is closed until some time in 2008, this is its temporary home (original building can be seen on map 8 on p. 128).... *Tel 020/573-2737. www.stedelijkmuseum.nl. TPG Building, Oosterdokskade 5 at Centraal Station. Trams 1, 2, 4, 5, 6, 9, 13, 16, 17, 24, 25, or 26 to Centraal Station. Daily 10am–6pm. Closed Jan 1. Admission charged.*

See Map 7 on p. 126.

Torture Museum (p. 113) CANAL BELT This highly commercial "museum" is little more than a cabinet of titillating horrors stuffed with scores of centuries-old instruments of torture.... *Tel 020/320-6642. www.torturemuseum.com. Singel 449 at Koningsplein. Trams 1, 2, or 5 to Koningsplein. Daily 10am–11pm. Closed Dec 25. Admission charged.*

See Map 7 on p. 126.

Tourist Tram (p. 115) CENTER The name says it all: This 1920s streetcar runs from Prins Hendrikkade at the top of Damrak (opposite the Victoria Hotel) around town, with stops at various museums and at Coster Diamonds, on Sundays and on Ascension Day.... *Tel 0900/423-1100. Operates March–Sept Sun and holidays hourly 11am–5pm. Tickets needed.*

See Map 7 on p. 126.

Trade Union Museum (De Burcht Vakbondsmuseum) (p. 117) EAST Exhibits on the struggle of organized labor in the Netherlands; the Art Nouveau building by Hendrik Petrus van Berlage is worth a trip.... *Tel 020/624-1166. www.deburcht-vakbondsmuseum.nl. Henri Polaklaan 9 at Plantage Parklaan. Trams 6, 9, or 14 to Plantage Kerklaan. Tues–Fri 11am–5pm, Sun 1–5pm. Admission charged.*

See Map 9 on p. 130.

Tram Museum (Elektrische Museumtramlijn) (p. 115) AMSTERDAMSEBOS A freewheeling collection of old streetcars, trolleys, and trams rattles from the edge of town through the Amsterdamsebos to suburban Amstelveen in this "moving museum" of antique trams on which you can ride.... *Tel 020/673-7538. www.museumtram.nl. Amstelveenseweg 264 at Cornelis Krusemanstraat. Tram 16 to Haarlemmermeerstation. Easter–Aug Sun and holidays 10:30am–5:20pm. Tickets 3.50† ($4.40), kids under 4 travel free.*

See Map 8 on p. 128.

DIVERSIONS

THE INDEX

DIVERSIONS

THE INDEX

Trippenhuis and Klein Trippenhuis (Trip House and Trip Coachman's House) (p. 105) CENTER A 1660s neoclassical mansion and narrow coachman's house.... *No phone. Kloveniersburgwal 29 and 26, respectively. Metro to Nieuwmarkt. Not open for visits.*

See Map 7 on p. 126.

Tropenmuseum and Kindermuseum (Tropical and Children's museums) (p. 114) EAST Established early this century, the permanent collection here was devised specifically to teach kids ages 6 to 12 about foreign cultures.... *Tel 020/568-8215. www.tropenmuseum.nl. Linnaeusstraat 2 at Mauritskade. Trams 7, 9, 10, 14 to Mauritskade. Daily 10am–5pm (until 3pm Dec 5, 24, 31). Closed Jan 1, April 30, May 5, Dec 25; Kindermuseum: children 6–12 (1 adult per child is allowed), by appointment only (Tel 020/568-8233), Wed, Sat, Sun, national holidays and school holidays. Admission charged.*

See Map 9 on p. 130.

Van Gogh Museum (p. 98) MUSEUM DISTRICT & VONDELPARK Herein discover the tragic life and times of the mad, peripatetic Dutch genius, told in 200 of his oil paintings, hundreds of sketches, drawings, watercolors, and letters. Expanded with an exhibition wing.... *Tel 020/570-5200. www.vangoghmuseum.nl. Paulus Potterstraat 7 at Museum District. Trams 2, 3, 5, or 12 to Van Baerlestraat; 16 to Museum District. Daily 10am–6pm (Fri to 10pm). Admission charged.*

See Map 8 on p. 128.

Van Loon Museum (p. 108) CANAL BELT If you visit only one canal-house museum, make this it. You ring the bell of an imposing 1671 mansion (designed by Adriaen Dortsman) and are admitted to a showcase of life in the Dutch Golden Age.... *Tel 020/624-5255. www.museumvanloon.nl. Keizersgracht 672 at Vijzelstraat. Trams 16, 24, or 25 to Keizersgracht. Fri–Mon (July–Aug daily) 11am–5pm. Admission charged.*

See Map 7 on p. 126.

Westerkerk/Westertoren (Western Church and Tower) (p. 110) CANAL BELT Arguably the masterpiece of the prolific Golden Age architect Hendrick de Keyser, this airy Protestant church is a city landmark.... *Tel 020/624-7766. www.westerkerk.nl. Westermarkt. Trams 6, 13, 14, or 17 to Westermarkt. Church open April–Aug Mon–Fri (July–Aug also Sat) 11am–3pm, open Sun for worship only at 10:30am; tower open April–Sept Mon–Sat 10am–5:30pm. Church free; admission charge to climb tower.*

See Map 7 on p. 126.

Willet-Holthuysen Museum (p. 108) CANAL BELT An atmospheric 1687 Golden Bend canal-house museum, opened in 1889.... *Tel 020/523-1822. www.willetholthuysen.nl. Herengracht 605 at Utrechtsestraat. Trams 4, 9, or 14 to Rembrandtplein. Mon–Fri*

10am–5pm, weekends and holidays 11am–5pm. Closed Jan 1, April 30, Dec 25. Admission charged.

See Map 7 on p. 126.

Zuiderkerk/Zuidertoren (South Church and Tower) (p. 109)
CENTER This 17th-century church has one of the finest carillons in town and houses a free, permanent exhibition on Amsterdam's development and planning down the centuries.... *Tel 020/553-7977. www.zuiderkerk.amsterdam.nl. Zuiderkerkhof 72 at Sint-Antoniesbreestraat. Metro to Nieuwmarkt; trams 9 or 14 to Waterlooplein. Church open Mon–Fri 9am–4pm, Sat noon–4pm; tower open June–Sept, Wed–Sat 2–4pm (at this writing the tower open only to organized groups, for safety reasons, but was due to re-open to individual visitors once certain repairs had been completed). Church free; admission charge to climb tower.*

See Map 7 on p. 126.

DIVERSIONS

THE INDEX

GETTING

OUTSIDE

Basic Stuff

In Amsterdam, drinking beer and socializing at a brown cafe qualify as sports and recreation. Playing pool, snooker, carambole, or chess or picnicking in Vondelpark seem downright active. Like many Europeans, Amsterdammers just aren't sports fanatics. Locals are particularly baffled by joggers; biking is a form of transport, little more; canal bikes (as pedal boats, or pedalos, are known in Amsterdam) are strictly for tourists; rollerblading is for the trendy (and only in good weather, i.e., almost never). Amsterdammers consider golf a game for British snobs, so playing a round here is like ordering champagne at Oktoberfest. As for the seaside, the only readily accessible beach from Amsterdam is Zandvoort, and its scenery (high-rise apartments) and water (seaweed, jellyfish) are about as appetizing as the name. In short, don't come to Amsterdam looking for a resort experience: This is a northern European city—like city.

The Lowdown

Green spaces... Believe it or not, the tourist office has actually counted 28 parks, 220,000 trees, and 600,000 "bulb flowers" (tulips among them) in Amsterdam. Everything is green, including many houses, which often have a patina of moss and lichen. But everyone's favorite city park for picnics, cycling, and musical and carnal improvisation is **Vondelpark** in the Oud Zuid (Old South) neighborhood, just beyond the Singelgracht and near the big museums. Its landscaping is mid-1800s English Romantic, with meandering paths, ponds, and bridges, and it takes its name from Joost van den Vondel, a lighthearted poet of the Golden Age who lived too long for convenience (1587–1679) and died a pauper. His surname, pronounced "fondle," is certainly apropos for this park, given certain activities that go on under its bridges, particularly at night. **Hortus Botanicus** in eastern Amsterdam near Artis Zoo sounds terribly Latin and scientific, but it's a wonderful botanical garden that's been around since the 17th century. Sensitive souls love the quiet old greenhouses, and vegetarian visitors can enjoy a perverse thrill by cheering on the carnivorous botanical specimens (take that, flesh-eaters!).

Houseplant aficionados should ask to see the celebrated potted cycad, a palm that's about 400 years old.

Sarphatipark (near the Heineken Experience and Albert Cuypstraat market), **Beatrixpark** (south of the New South), **Wertheim Park,** and **Oosterpark** (both close to Artis Zoo) are all smallish, landscaped gardens with the usual ponds, paths, and kiddie play areas—but Wertheim, in the old Jewish Quarter, does have a monument to the victims of Auschwitz, and Oosterpark has a relatively new (2002) and spectacular monument to the victims of slavery (the Dutch were big in the African slavery trade). These parks are fine if you're in the neighborhood, but not really worth a detour unless you're visiting during the spectacular tulip season (April–May). You'll need a bike to make the trip to **Amstelpark** worth it, but this vast park on the Amstel River a few miles south of central Amsterdam has a remarkable rose garden and rhododendron dell. On its edge is the thatched 1636 De Rieker windmill that marks one of Rembrandt's favorite bucolic views (p. 106).

When the Great Depression hit in the early 1930s, the city decided to put thousands of folks to work reclaiming land and foresting what is now the 2,200-acre **Amsterdamsebos** (buses 170, 171, or 172 to Bosbaan). It's a wild and woolly place south of the city in suburban Amstelveen. But if you're hankering for seriously long walks, or bike, pony, and horse rides along miles of waterways through deep, dark forests, this is the place. The Bezoekerscentrum (Visitor Center), incorporating the museum, beside the Olympic rowing course, tells the not-exactly-riveting story of the park; pick up a map of the park there or study the one at the main entrance. Just across the way you can rent pedal bikes for 6€ ($7.50) an hour. There's also a goat farm, where you can buy goat's-milk cheese, ice cream, and fresh milk; animal reserves for deer, buffalo, and imported Scottish Highland cattle; a miniature golf course (the Dutch call it "midgetgolf"); and a children's play pool. The jets to and from Schiphol Airport roar just overhead every few minutes, which doesn't do much for the park's tranquillity. Wave at the pilots and passengers and see if they wave back.

Two-wheeling it... Locals bike everywhere to get around, not for recreation. There are probably as many bikes as inhabitants (the official number is 500,000, but tens of thousands are fished from the canals or pried off lampposts every year). Bike lanes abound, so use them because Dutch drivers can be amazingly aggressive. Contrary to what you'd expect, the most awkward and frustrating areas to ride in are the Grachtengordel of grand canals and the Red-Light District. Neither has bike lanes, the streets are cobbled, uneven, and narrow, and there are so many landmark buildings that you'll be constantly stopping for a look. You're better off walking. The same goes for the center of town, between Spui and Centraal Station. The best places to cruise undisturbed include the atmospheric Jordaan district, where there is little traffic; big parks like Vondelpark, Amstelpark, and Amsterdamsebos; the quiet Western Islands and sprawling Eastern Docklands (including the new architecturally astonishing Java and Borneo islands); the residential Old South and New South; and across the IJ channel in Nieuwendam.

Locals snicker at tourists with bikes bearing the rental company's name. If that sort of thing matters to you, rent an unmarked bike from friendly **Fréderic Rentabike** (Brouwersgracht 78; Tel 020/624-5509; www.frederic.nl) or **Bike City** (Bloemgracht 68–70; Tel 020/626-3721); both have good bikes, friendly staff, and rental rates around 10€ ($13) a day. At the biggest operator, **Mac Bike** (Stationsplein 12, at Centraal Station, Mr. Visserplein 2, and Weteringschans 2, at Leidseplein; Tel 020/620-0985; www.macbike.nl), you get a basket with a big name on it, but also the option of taking theft insurance, a rare but valuable benefit; rental rates begin at 4.25€ ($5.30) a day (but 7€/$8.75 is more usual). **Holland Rent A Bike** (Damrak 247; Tel 020/622-3207) has higher rates than most, but offers a choice of hundreds of bikes, including children's models, tandems, and mountain bikes (though mountains aren't too common in the city). Feminists both male and female might want to give their business to **Zijwind Fietsen,** a women's cooperative (Ferdinand Bolstraat 168; Tel 020/673-7026), though it's a bit out from the Center. If your rented bike is stolen, it is usually your responsibility. Always use the locks provided, and always ask about the policy on stolen bikes: If insurance isn't available, how much does it cost to replace a bike?

You're going to look pretty conspicuous taking one of the guided tours offered by **Yellow Bike** (Nieuwezijds Kolk 29, just off Nieuwezijds Voorburgwal; Tel 020/620-6940;

www.yellowbike.nl). Why? Because you'll be one of a dozen or so people bicycling on yellow pedal-bikes, that's why. In partial compensation for sticking out like a sore thumb, you get a close encounter with Amsterdam or the nearby countryside.

Cycling beyond the city limits... Outside Amsterdam, almost every highway and major country road has a bike lane. The land is as flat as the proverbial pancake, so you can cover a lot of ground, but beware that frequent, strong head winds can double or triple traveling times; the inverse may be true if you've got a tail wind. You can either rent a bike in town and cycle out, put your bike on a train (though not during rush hour), or take a train or bus out of Amsterdam and rent a bike where you get off: Bikes are readily available all over Holland. A free ferry ride across the IJ channel from Centraal Station can put you and your bike on the road to several popular villages, including centuries-old Nieuwendam and Durgerdam, exclusive Broek in Waterland, the old fishing ports of Monnickendam and Marken, and the kitschy Volendam and Edam, two tourist-dependent villages that made their names on eels and wax-wrapped cheese, respectively. The ferry crossing to Amsterdam Noord takes minutes on one route (the *Buikersloterwegveer,* operating around the clock from pier 7), and 10 minutes on the other (the *IJ-Veer* from pier 8, running weekdays only and quitting just after 6pm), leaving you a short ride to the atmospheric streets of **Nieuwendam,** one of the city's oldest suburbs. From the ferry terminal, head due north on any of the streets paralleling the right, or east, side of the Noord-Hollandskanaal until you reach Nieuwendammerdijk, which veers east. South, on your right, is the wooded W. H. Vliegenbos park, the IJ, and shipyards. On the north side of the road, your left, are scores of narrow streets lined with centuries-old, two-story brick and timbered buildings. You can stop at the Kleine Haven, the small harbor of the village of Nieuwendam, and sit at a cafe. One-way from Centraal Station to the middle of Nieuwendam, including the ferry, shouldn't take you more than 30 minutes.

To get to the other villages, don't veer east on the Nieuwendammerdijk, but follow the bike lanes along either side of the Noord-Hollandskanaal through the Florapark

● ●

BIKING IN AMSTERDAM

What are the rules of the road for biking in Amsterdam? Apparently, there are none. Bikers can go anywhere they want, whenever they want, however they want, and do whatever they want when they get there. Or so you would think from the antics of Amsterdam's massed legions of pedal-bikers. They're enough to throw a scare into a bunch of Hell's Angels. Biking is one activity where you should disregard the maxim "When in Amsterdam, do as the Amsterdammers do"—you might easily end up dead, which could spoil your entire vacation. It takes a while to get used to moving smoothly and safely through the whirl of trams, cars, buses, trucks, fellow bikers, and pedestrians, particularly if you're on a typically ancient and much-battered stadfiets (city bike), also known as an omafiets (grandmother bike)—the only kind that makes economic sense here, since anything fancier will attract a crowd of people wanting to steal it. It's better to develop your street smarts slowly. I know this sounds like wimpish advice—you might have mountain-biked from one end of the Rockies to another for all I know—but remember that not everyone on the straat is as sensible as you are. The first rule of biking in Amsterdam: Don't argue with trams—they bite back, hard. The second rule: Cross tram lines perpendicularly so your wheels don't get caught in the grooves, which could pitch you out of the saddle. And the third rule: Don't crash into civilians (pedestrians). That's about it. Like everyone else, you'll likely end up making up the rest of the rules as you go along.

● ●

and Volewijkspark. Bike lanes fan out once you reach the picturesque Buikslotermeerdijk and Noord-Hollandschkanaaldijk, dikes with clearly marked routes to the next closest stops: Broek in Waterland and Monnickendam. **Broek in Waterland** (12km/7.44 miles from the ferry terminal, also reachable on bus 111) sits at the end of a route that follows canals, overlooks polders, and traverses pastureland. A picture-book village with old wooden houses, many of them white, it's a suburb where Amsterdam millionaires live, and is known as one of the tidiest—and most conservative—spots on earth. It has a 1628 Protestant church with gorgeous carved pews and painted woodwork; an unbelievably cute central pond (the Havenrak) with a white pagoda gazebo from 1656 (Napoléon was received here by the mayor); and scores of winding lanes with big houses and flower-filled gardens.

About 6.5km (4.03 miles) north, through the same pleasant but never-dramatic scenery, is **Monnickendam** (reachable via bus 111), a former fishing port on the IJsselmeer noted for its smoked herring, and now a favorite on tourist itineraries (the clogs and costumes start to spring up). Among the countless old buildings on winding streets are De Waag, a weigh house similar to the one on Amsterdam's Nieuwmarkt; the hulking, gothic Grote Sint-Nicolaaskerk; the ornate, 18th-century city hall; and the tall Speeltoren, a brick tower from the 1500s with a tuneful carillon.

A few miles east is **Marken,** once a fishing village on an island, but since 1957 linked to the mainland by a causeway, and now totally dependent on tourism. Here is high kitsch: The traditional Dutch costumes are occasionally in full bloom (wide, striped dresses and skirts, long dark smocks, and white caps), though more and more rarely these days. Clogs are carved to order. The old wooden houses—matte green with horizontal white stripes—stand in clumps on pilings because once upon a time, the tides of the Zuiderzee, closed off in the 1930s, reached them.

Volendam, a few miles due north of Monnickendam, was an eel-fishing port but has suffered the same economic fate as most of the other villages around the old Zuiderzee. This is the quintessence of package-tour Holland, and the place to see costumes (winged cotton-and-lace caps), clogs, and wall-to-wall boutiques. Cheese making and Amsterdam commuters lend nearby **Edam** (a few miles northeast) a bit of dignity, though most of the famous, bland curd is made elsewhere. The Kaasmarkt (cheese market, 10am–noon Wed

BIKING ON THE WATER

A suggested tour by water bike: Start at the Canal Bikes mooring on Prinsengracht (at Westermarkt). Pedal south along Prinsengracht, past Lauriergracht, Looiersgracht, and Passeerdersgracht, maybe diverting into one or more of these quiet side canals if you fancy. At Leidsegracht, go straight ahead under the Leidsestraat bridge until you come to Spiegelgracht, where you turn right. Continue to the end, then left under the bridge into Lijnbaansgracht.

Turn right at the first corner into a narrow connecting canal that merges with Singelgracht in front of the Rijksmuseum. Go right along this canal, which is bordered by overhanging trees and the back gardens of waterside villas. You pass the Holland Casino Amsterdam, Leidseplein, and the American Hotel.

Keep going, past the Bellevue Theater and the De la Mar Theater, and turn right into Leidsegracht, which brings you back to Prinsengracht and the long home stretch back to Westermarkt.

July–Aug) is purely for tourists—an exquisitely cheesey theme-park adventure, featuring canal boats and wagons and men in silly costumes. The town itself is crammed with picture-postcard Golden Age houses and the Grote Sint-Nicolaaskerk, whose stained glass is remarkable. The landmark bell tower has a 16th-century carillon. (See "Tiptoeing through the tulips" and "The windmills of your mind," later in this chapter, for other recommended cycling destinations.)

Island hopping... Eastern Amsterdam is booming: From the rehabbed **Pakhuis Amsterdam** warehouse (a building in the redeveloping Eastern Dock area; see p. 104) to the artificial islands called **Java** and **Borneo,** the city has added thousands of new, wacky buildings to its repertoire. You pedal from Centraal Station due east past the new ferry terminal, turn left after Pakhuis, and cross a wild bridge that looks like a giant grasshopper to reach Java island. A broad road rings the island, with views of the IJ. The buildings here and on the adjacent Borneo island are a crazy postmodern hodgepodge evoking your kids' Lego creations and wavy Manhattan Beach houses, with mock Venetian bridges over tiny canals and grassy inner courtyards. This is great biking or walking territory: quiet, clean, and fascinating for its unsettling futuristic qualities. The ferry *IJ-Veer 35* (p. 119) links Java island to Centraal Station's pier 8, with views en route.

Pedaling and paddling on the water... Bike-obsessed Amsterdammers call pedal boats *waterfiets* or *grachtenfiets,* which they have charmingly translated as "canal bikes." Of course they never use them, but who cares? You can pick 'em up and drop 'em off all day, any day at four **Canal Bike** docks in the city: Rijksmuseum, Leidseplein, Keizersgracht (at Leidsestraat), and Prinsengracht (at the Anne Frank House; Tel 020/626-5574 for all locations; rates are 8€/$10 hourly per person for one or two people, 7€/$8.75 hourly per person for three or four people; 50€/$63 deposit required). Farther afield, **Duikelaar,** at the western suburban Sloterpark (Noordzijde 41; Tel 020/613-8855; deposit and passport required), rents canoes for about half the price of a water bike, but you're limited to the park's fairly dull waterways. The boathouse at the **Amsterdamsebos** south of town (no Tel; March–Sept only; rates about 6€/$7.50 per hour; deposit and ID required) has pedalos (another word for water bikes) and canoes, and the park's Roeibaan rowing lake alone is well over a mile long.

Horsing around... The Amsterdamsebos in Amstelveen is the best place to saddle up for outdoor riding, but you won't find many Western saddles, except on ponies. You can mount there at **Amsterdamse Manege** (Nieuwe Kalfjeslaan 25; Tel 020/643-1342; 22€/$28 per hour; reservations essential; bring your own boots, hat, and crop for dressage), whose stables and indoor riding area are used by the serious horsey set, though kids and beginners are welcome and there are plenty of ponies. Monitors will lead you out into the 2,200-acre wooded park. Closer into town, and housed in a gorgeous 19th-century building, is the **Hollandse Manege** (Vondelstraat 140; Tel 020/618-0942; 21€/$26 per hour; experienced riders only—otherwise you need to take a 5-lesson beginner's course for 85€/$106; reservations essential), great for a visit even if you don't ride.

The squash and tennis racket... Amsterdam encourages fans of racquet sports to do most of their swinging indoors, but there are a few tennis courts where you can expose your backhand to the elements. Thrifty, unpretentious types wait outside for hours to play on one of **Vondelpark**'s four free courts. In the Amsterdamsebos is **Amstelpark Sportcentrum** (Koenenkade 8; Tel 020/301-0700; about 20€/$25 per hour outdoors, 27€/$34 indoors, racquets free; reservations essential), Holland's biggest tennis school, with 26 outdoor courts and 16 indoor courts (as well as 12 squash courts and a tanning and fitness center). In the suburb of Buitenveldert, south, near the Amstelpark, is a string of indoor and outdoor tennis courts at clubs that stand practically next door to each other. The best of these is **Gold Star Tennis** (Gustav Mahlerlaan 20; Tel 020/644-5483; www.goldstar.nl; 19€–23€/$24–$29 per hour, racquets 3€/$3.50 and up per hour; reservations essential), with 24 outdoor and 12 indoor courts.

The hippest thing in high-strung sports these days is whacking a hard rubber ball around a tiny white court (indoors, of course) at see-and-be-seen **Squash City**

(Ketelmakerstraat 6; Tel 020/626-7883; 7€–9.50€/$8.75–
$12 per 45 minutes, racquet rental 2.50€/$3.15 and up;
reserve ahead; 14 courts). Of course, squash isn't the only—
or perhaps even the main—thing at this hip fitness club in
the Western Islands neighborhood. It has a cafe and *gezellig* bar, a sauna, a Turkish bath, a health-food restaurant,
and plenty of gorgeous male and female trainers eager to
teach you fat-burning step and funk aerobics. Serious,
humorless squash fanatics hone their skills next door to
Gold Star Tennis at **Dicky Squash** (Gustav Mahlerlaan
16; Tel 020/646-2266; about 12€/$15 per hour; racquets
available; reserve ahead). **Frans Otten Stadion** (Stadion-
straat 10; Tel 020/662-8767; squash 15€–18€/$19–$23
per half-hour slot, tennis about 15€–18€/$19–$22 per
hour, racquet rental 3€/$3.75 and up; reserve ahead), in
the distinctly unhip, far-flung southwest area of town near
the Olympic Stadium, is a place where serious players
compete on 20 squash courts and half a dozen indoor tennis courts (plus fitness center).

Jogging and pickup sports... Basketball isn't big here,
but try Vondelpark if you're looking to get in on a pickup
game. **Soccer** (*voetball*, football) is taken very seriously in
Amsterdam, and you might be able to pick up a game on
the cobbled, exquisitely unforgiving Amstelveld on Prinsengracht (just off Reguliersgracht) or in Vondelpark,
Amstelpark, or Amsterdamsebos. The best **jogging** territory is not in the city at all (too many cobbled streets and
too much traffic). Again, head out to the Amstelpark and
Amsterdamsebos (where you'll find marked hiking paths
and fitness circuits). Vondelpark gets too crowded with pic-
nickers, cyclists, and strollers to be ideal for jogging,
though if you stick to the (often muddy) perimeter trail
you'll be all right. **Roller skaters** and **'bladers** meet at 8pm
at the Café Vertigo in Vondelpark every Friday night, year-
round, and skate in a jolly group around the city. You'd better be good enough to stop at red lights, and avoid
speeding bikes and trams, though!

On ice... As romantic as it may sound, canal skating in Amsterdam has become all but obsolete; only thrice in the last
decade has the ice been thick enough for skating. Try pond
or rink skating in the parks—**Vondelpark** and **Oosterpark**

are favorites—or squares: **Museumplein** has a pond. From roughly early November through February, depending on temperatures. Try the recently restored, world-class indoor-outdoor rink in suburban Watergraafsmeer, the **Jaap Edenbaan** (Radioweg 64; Tel 020/694-9652; 4€/$5 to enter, 5€/$6.25 to rent skates).

In the swim... To swim and enjoy Amsterdam School architecture at a single plunge, go to the hip, handsome **Zuiderbad** (Hobbemastraat 26; Tel 020/679-2217; about 5€/$5.75 admission), a recently renovated indoor pool built just before World War I, with glistening tiles and mosaics, arches, and relief sculptures. Nude swimming is always Sunday afternoons. **De Mirandabad** (De Mirandalaan 9; Tel 020/546-4444; 3.30€–3.65€/$4.15–$4.55) is a mock beach resort on the southeast edge of town, with an indoor mock lake complete with sandy beach, wave machine, slides, and in addition, an outdoor pool (May 15–Sept 15). On the opposite side of town, at the suburban Sloterpark, **Duikelaar** watersports center (Noordzijde 41; Tel 020/613-8855; pools May–Oct only; about 5€/$5.75 to swim) has both indoor and outdoor pools; you can also rent sailboards, canoes, and tiny sailboats for use on the park's waterways.

Tiptoeing through the tulips... How many Netherlanders does it take to screw in the bulbs at **Keukenhof Garden** (Stationsweg 166A, Lisse; Tel 0252/465-555; tickets required)? Several thousand, probably, since there are more than 7 million hyacinths, lilies, crocuses, narcissi, and daffodils, 600 kinds of tulips, and myriad other bulb plants blooming from late March to late May at this, the world's biggest bulb garden. The sight is seriously spectacular; you won't even notice the other million visitors tiptoeing alongside you through the 80 acres of romantic gardens, with a pond and canals, meandering paths, and a centuries-old hunting lodge that belonged to a Bavarian countess. Regular commuter trains run about every 15 minutes daily until midnight from Centraal Station to Haarlem or Leiden stations; the local bus ride on to Lisse through miles of bulb fields is kaleidoscopic. The 8m to 24m (4.96- to 14.88-mile) ride to Keukenhof is even more spectacular on a bike, which you could bring with you on the train from central Amsterdam.

Nothing could be more Dutch than the **Aalsmeer Bloemenveiling** (**Aalsmeer Flower Auction;** Legmeerdijk 313; Tel 0297/392-185; bus 172 from Centraal Station; weekdays 7:30–11am; admission 5€/$6.25), where scents of *bloemen* and euros blend intoxicatingly. Several billion cut flowers and nearly half a billion green plants are auctioned here weekdays year-round, in a vast indoor and outdoor sales area practically the size of old Amsterdam. Visitors cannot participate in the auction. The Dutch countdown method is used, whereby a starting price is given and progressively drops as time passes, marked on a huge timer that clicks nervously from 100 down to 1. Hundreds of buyers must guess when colleagues will hit their buzzers. From a viewing platform you see thousands of specimens being shunted around. It's all very exciting; deals are done in seconds, but the spectacle is strictly for early birds since the best bits are over by 9:30am.

The windmills of your mind... Hidden among the smokestacks of heavy industry is the unusual but handsome mock-village of **Zaanse Schans,** 16km (9.92 miles) north of Amsterdam (Tel 075/616-8218; trains to Koog-Zaandijk, then a 10-minute walk across the river; daily March–Oct 10am–5 or 6pm; Sat–Sun 11am–4pm Oct–March; admission charged to individual attractions). Since about 1950, the Dutch government has been moving old buildings and windmills here from blighted areas around the country to create a habitat that simulates Dutch life of about 200 years ago. A few souls do inhabit the place—after all, someone has to run the souvenir boutiques, restaurants, and workshops. The village draws about 800,000 visitors a year, the big attraction being the working windmills that grind oil seeds, grain for flour, paint pigments, and mustard seeds. From April to October you and the mob can visit the mills and some of the historic buildings. Off season, the sights close, and you can stroll around alone at no charge and soak up the ghostly atmosphere. A new bonus is the **Zaans Museum,** an ultramodern cultural-history vessel dedicated to the life and times of the Zaan River region. There are multimedia displays (wonderful 1920s and '30s black-and-white movies about wind, mills, water, and industry), plus a grab bag of tools, objects, paintings, furniture, sleighs, sailboats, and more. Funny to find a fully fledged museum like this on the edge of such a quintessentially Dutch theme park (Schansend 7; Tel 075/616-2862; www.zaansmuseum.nl; Tues–Sat 10am–5pm; admission charged). Across the Zaan River at the village of Koog aan de Zaan is the **Molenmuseum (Mill Museum),** where you can learn how Holland's 9,000 windmills of 150 years ago have been reduced to a mere 900 today. Grist for the mill.

Haarlem days... It's no coincidence that the distance from Centraal Station to Haarlem (19km/11.78 miles, or 15 minutes on the train, running from dawn to midnight) is about the same as the distance from the tip of Manhattan to Harlem (which were known in the 17th century as Nieuw Amsterdam and Nieuw Haarlem). Founded a thousand years ago, the city of Haarlem is older than Amsterdam, and is thoroughly provincial, prosperous, and conservative (meaning there's only a diminutive Red-Light District here). Wander its narrow streets from the **Grote Markt** main square to the 15th-century **Amsterdamse Poort** city gates, and pretend you've stepped into a Dutch master's painting. One of Haarlem's main draws is the **Grote Kerk** or Sint-Bavokerk, right on the main square, a 500-year-old Gothic mountain of stone with a 75m (246 ft.) lantern tower visible from miles away. The nave itself has lofty vaults and remarkable wrought-iron grilles and woodwork. Handel, Mozart, Schubert, and Liszt supposedly tickled the keys of its **5,000-pipe Christian Müller rococo organ** (Tel 023/532-4399; hear it Tues evenings mid-May to mid-Sept, and Thurs afternoons April–Oct), and the Golden Age painter Frans Hals (1580–1666) is buried here. Hals, the most renowned of the School of Haarlem painters, earned his reputation as a portraitist who had a knack for making every figure in his group portraits equally intense (so they would all pay him). He died in the city's 1608 Oudemannenhuis almshouse, now the biggest attraction in town—the **Frans Hals Museum** (Groot Heiligland 62 at Gasthuis Vest; Tel 023/511-5775; www.franshalsmuseum.com; Tues–Sat 11am–5pm, Sun and holidays noon–5pm; admission 7€/$8.75), where his paintings fill the rooms of handsome, gabled cottages arranged around a main courtyard. Also worth a look—if only for the architecture and curious old-fashioned science, technology, and other displays—is the **Teylers Museum** (Spaarne 16 at Bakenessergracht; Tel 023/531-9010; www. teylersmuseum.nl; Tues–Sat 10am–5pm, Sun and holidays 1–5pm; admission 2.25€/$2.80), the country's oldest museum, an eclectic collection featuring everything from fossils to Michelangelo.

The zcene at Zandvoort... If you feel like drawing a breath of fresh sea air and you don't have much time for it, do what most Amsterdammers do: Head for Zandvoort. On the North Sea coast just west of Haarlem (on the same rail line from Amsterdam), the resort is brash and brassy in summer, though it often looks fairly forlorn in the off season. Yet even in winter it's an Amsterdam tradition to take the train here, stroll up and down along the shore for an hour or so, then, repair to one of the town's cafes. There is not much more to Zandvoort than its **beach**, but what a beach! In summer, this seemingly endless stretch of smooth sand is lined with dozens of temporary **beach cafe-restaurants**. Besides the mainstream beaches, there are **gay and naturist beaches**, where the shocking sight of a clothed individual can generate considerable moral outrage. **Windsurfing** is popular here, and Zandvoort hosts international competitions in this sport, and in catamaran racing. The water—a soup of suspended sand, jellyfish, seaweed, and whatever's drifted down the coast from the industrial IJmuiden—doesn't look inviting, but the Dutch swim anyway (in summer, that is). Trains depart hourly from Amsterdam Central Station for Zandvoort. Transfer at Haarlem (where the Zandvoort train is usually waiting on the adjacent platform). During summer months extra trains go direct from Centraal Station. Trip time is around 30 minutes. Buses depart every 30 minutes from outside Centraal Station, but they take longer than the train. By car, go via Haarlem, on N5, A5, and N200, but beware of summer traffic.

SHOP

PING 5

Basic Stuff

As a city with a long history of trading, Amsterdam is loaded with tempting wares, at premium prices, from all over the world. But as a small burg with a scant tradition in manufacturing or design, it's a bit short on only-in-Amsterdam bargains on world-class merchandise. There are no local crafts industries to speak of, unless you count clog making or ship repair; the best porcelain comes from nearby Delft, or Makkum in Friesland, but frankly, you can get the same stuff in American department stores at comparable prices. Much ado is made of mock-antique pewter wares and grandfather clocks, but the less said about these the better (unless you're into high kitsch). The Dutch flower and plant industry is a booming business indeed, but foreign visitors can take home only certain certified bulbs. Nonetheless, there are plenty of creative ways to spend your euros, especially on imported, used, or antique goods.

What to Buy

Clogs, windmill souvenirs, and tulip bulbs are swell, but you might also consider things like contemporary art—a vibrant activity in this city of young artists (for art gallery listings on the Internet: www.akka.nl). Antiques—maps, prints, objects, books, furniture, genuine old pewter, porcelain, and jewelry—are a major attraction here. There are hundreds of reputable dealers, and you're sure to find something worth shipping or carrying home. Diamonds are still a big industry, and prices are competitive, but make sure you take your time to decide on a purchase: Many diamond-cutting houses give you a brisk tour, deposit you in the salesroom, and wait for the pressure to build. Porcelain from the royal factories at Delft and Makkum can be wonderful, but again, most of it is available in America. Sex-toy aficionados will find an embarrassment of riches (but be warned that some pornographic materials, especially films, cannot be imported into the States). Some of the world's best cigars and pipe tobacco are also available—smoke them on the spot or take a box home. Other products primarily or exclusively for immediate consumption include Dutch gin (*jenever*) and white wine (yes, it does exist, but not in quantity), dozens of varieties of cheeses (Holland is Europe's number-one dairy products exporter), chocolate and pastries, coffee and tea, and hash and grass (in tiny quantities), if you're so inclined (don't even *think* about smuggling dope out of the country, however; the neighbors aren't at all tolerant, and you know what'll happen back home).

Target Zones

Go to **Damrak, Nieuwendijk,** and **Kalverstraat** in central Amsterdam, south of the station, for tacky gift stuff and mass-market clothes; nearby **Rokin** offers upscale fashion, tobacco, and antiques. The antiques dealers' quarter is on and around **Nieuwe Spiegelstraat,** near the Rijksmuseum, with almost 100 stores. Dozens of antiquarian bookshops are between central Spui and the royal palace on **Spuistraat, Singel,** and **Nieuwezijds Voorburgwal.** Dozens of international and Dutch designer boutiques, plus antique and porcelain dealers, are on **Pieter Cornelisz Hooftstraat** (P.C. Hooft to insiders) and adjoining streets near the Museum District in the south. Nearby, **Cornelis Schuytstraat** has been reborn as an upmarket Greenwich Village, with fashion, food, flowers, and collectibles. Small fashion boutiques and one-of-a-kind stores tend to be on side streets (now nicknamed the Negen Straatjes (Nine Little Streets) between canals in the **Grachtengordel** neighborhood. The entire **Jordaan** quarter, west of central Amsterdam, is a junk-and-oddity-lover's paradise. The VVV tourist bureau distributes a free detailed city map called "Shopping in Amsterdam"—worth getting for rabid shopaholics.

Outdoor Markets

Amsterdam has about as many markets as it does museums, and of the two you can guess which the locals prefer. Markets provide

The Spirit of Amsterdam: Distiller Cees van Wees

Dynamic giant Cees van Wees stands about 7 feet tall, has a boyish haircut, and looks about 50. He's actually in his 70s, and attributes his health, bruising handshake, and booming voice to the regular intake of jenever*—Dutch gin. Van Wees—and his family—is Amsterdam's only jenever, eaux de vie, and liqueur maker, the scion of a spirited dynasty whose distillery, warehouse, and wholesale tasting room have perfumed the Jordaan neighborhood since 1883 (having originally started in The Hague in 1782). He is also reputedly the only distiller in the Netherlands to use only natural, organic, homemade flavors and aromatics. Using old ceramic vats, oak barrels, and alembics, he distills everything from raspberries to apples, cinnamon to chocolate. You can visit the* **De Ooievaar** *Distillery (Driehoekstraat 10; Tel 020/626-7752; www.de-ooievaar.nl; Mon and Wed 9:30am-noon), and you can sip and buy van Wees's extraordinary wares at the family* proeflokaal *(tasting house),* **De Admiraal,** *which is equipped with comfortable sofas and chairs to help you through the dozens of nectarous beverages on offer (Herengracht 319; Tel 020/625-4334).*

alfresco shopping and free entertainment, and no one seems to mind the permanently lousy weather. The immense, mile-long **Albert Cuypmarkt** south of Singelgracht (on Albert Cuypstraat; trams 4, 16, 24, or 25; Mon–Sat 9am–5pm, closed Sun) is the city's biggest outdoor bazaar and is a great place to pick up Dutch and exotic food, cheap clothing, and ordinary household goods (though you'd be insane to buy and ship them home). Fresh veggies and lots of local color make the Jordaan's **Boerenmarkt,** or farmer's market (at Noorderkerkstraat and Westerstraat; trams 3 or 10; Sat 9am–4pm, till 3pm in winter), a nice place to wander on a lazy Saturday, especially since that's the day when organic-food peddlers take over the **Noordermarkt** (the name of a square but not itself a market, despite its name; trams 3 or 10; Sat 10am–4pm); kids will love the Punch 'n' Judy show (called "Pantijn"), and aging hippies will flip over the whole-grain breads (and the occasional space cake). (On Mon 7:30am–1pm, the Noordermarkt is host to antiques and collectibles—mostly old junk, but great fun to sift through.) Saturday's **Lindengrachtmarkt** (Lindengracht; tram 3 to Nieuwe Willemsstraat; Sat 9am–4pm), a 5-minute walk south of the Noordermarkt, spreads out food, clothes, and sundry other goods. Another general market in the Jordaan, **Westermarkt** (Westerstraat; trams 3 or 10; Mon–Sat 9am–5pm, closed Sun), is open 6 days a week.

The tourist office and all other guide writers insist that the famous daily flower market, the **Bloemenmarkt** (Singel at Muntplein/Koningsplein; trams 1, 2, 4, 5, 9, 14, 16, 24, or 25; Mon–Sat 8:30am–6pm, closed Sun), literally floats. In fact, almost all of it occupies a wide sidewalk or spreads across piers—not boats—on the Singel canal. But afloat or not, the flowers and plants are beautiful, the atmosphere jovial, and the prices ridiculously low on the things you can't take out of the country: cut flowers and live plants (see "Budding prospects," below).

You don't have to be a bibliophile to enjoy the **Boekenmarkt,** a book fair where used and antiquarian books, postcards, and prints are sold. There are three locations—near Amsterdam University (Oudemanhuispoort; trams 4, 9, 14, 16, 24, or 25; Mon–Sat 11am–4pm); at Spui (trams 1, 2, or 5; Fri 10am–6pm); and **Nieuwmarkt,** a square on the eastern edge of the Red-Light District (Metro to Nieuwmarkt; June–Sept Wed–Sat 9am–5pm). The collectible coins and stamps at the twice-weekly **Postzegelmarkt,** not far from Spui (Nieuwezijds Voorburgwal 280; trams 1, 2, or 5 to Spui; Wed and Sat 1–4pm), draw pimply teenagers, overweight bachelors, and oldsters with grandkids in tow. The **Artmarkt 't Spui** (Spui; trams 1, 2, or 5; March–Dec Sun 10am–6pm), a spring-through-fall Sunday market, and its counterpart, **Thorbecke Artmarkt,** near Rembrandtplein (Thorbeckeplein; trams 4, 9, or 14; March–Dec Sun 10:30am–6pm), are where local Michelangelos and minor dealers hawk the occasional masterpiece, but mostly the kind of paintings that generally look best in motel lobbies.

Finally, there is something disappointingly orderly, clean, and touristy about the daily **Waterloopleinmarkt** flea market (Waterlooplein; trams 9 or 14; Mon–Sat 9am–5pm), a vast affair occupying hundreds of shantytown stands in hideous Waterlooplein, behind city hall. But bargains—on antiquarian books, for example—can be unearthed among the mass-market rubbish and Third World souvenir elephants, whips, and beads.

Bargain Hunting

Sales, discounts, and wholesale prices to retail customers are an Amsterdam specialty—for locals. A *reklame* is an advertised sale; an *uitverkoop, aktie,* or *aanbieding* is a special sale; *alles moet weg* is a clearance sale. Unfortunately, visitors are not encouraged to participate in such savings—in the hope that they will pay full prices—and you'll hardly ever see advertisements in English. Seasonal discounts are largely the same as in America, with significant post-Christmas savings for all. The best sources for bargains are the Waterlooplein and De Looier flea markets and the outdoor markets of the Jordaan or Albert Cuypstraat (see "Outdoor Markets," above), where you can haggle and dicker like the best of them.

Trading with the Natives

The Dutch are canny shoppers, and will phone and shop around to find the best price. They go in for bargaining, but only with other natives and mostly at specific places, like outdoor markets, flea markets, and clearance sales. For visitors unable to wow natives with fluent Dutch, the price on the tag is what you'll pay. Finding flaws in goods and asking for a discount is a favorite trick among locals, but it probably isn't going to work for you. The salesperson will simply set the merchandise aside and return it to the manufacturer or importer (or call a friend and tell them to hurry over and buy it). Most stores displaying the "Duty-Free Shopping" logo will gladly ship your purchases home; others are less willing to do so, but can be coaxed. Waiting your turn in line is essential, especially in crowded food stores, where you'll often have to take a ticket from a dispenser.

Hours of Business

Many stores and businesses are open 6 days a week, Monday through Saturday (no lunch closing). Galleries, antiques dealers, and one-of-a-kind stores open and shut when they please. Some stores are now also open on Sundays, from noon to 6pm, especially in designated tourist areas around Rembrandtplein, Leidseplein, Damrak and the Dam, the Red-Light District, and main shopping streets. Many stores are closed Monday mornings and are open late on Thursdays (usually until 9pm). The rest of the week, hours are usually 9am until 5pm, or 8pm.

Sales Tax

A 19% VAT, or value-added tax (called BTW in Dutch), is included in prices on most consumer goods. Tax-free shopping for tourists is available at participating stores, but the mail-in refund (of 13.5%) is only available when you spend 137€ ($171) or more in one day at one store (see the Hotlines & Other Basics chapter or visit www.globalrefund.com for more information).

The Lowdown

Budding prospects... Raising its head like a sunflower above the dozen other bloom vendors at the famous floating Bloemenmarkt (see "Outdoor Markets," above) in the Singel is **A.H. Abels en Zoon.** Here the displays are living Dutch miniatures worthy of the Rijksmuseum. You might think that the bulbs you choose are nobody's blooming business, but U.S. and Canadian customs won't let you bring them home if they don't have a "phytosanitary certificate," i.e., a clean bill of health. You can spend a lot of money on bulbs, so make sure the ones you buy are approved for export. You can buy health-certified bulbs at Abels en Zoon, but you'll have to ship them yourself from the post office. Just down the way are **M.M.C. Roozen** and **Aviflora,** equally good and willing to ship your U.S.-approved bulbs (from July–Sept only; the shipping also allows you to dodge the 19% VAT). **Laddrak,** less artful, more mass market (check out the wooden clogs stuffed with tulip bulbs), is well stocked. They also export certified bulbs, which is the main reason to give them your business. Heads with green thumbs can buy marijuana starter kits from Laddrak (and most other flower-market stores); they should produce smokeable plants in 10 days or so. Beware, they're strictly illegal to export. **IVY** on Leidseplein and **Menno Kroon** on Cornelis Schuytstraat are the city's top florists and the places to go if you're itching for floral art. The bouquets and exotic plants are magnificently baroque, and beautiful people meet here lingering among the orchids. Edible flowers are the house specialty at **Jemi Bloemsierkunst,** a florist/floral art store in Amsterdam's oldest house, in the Red-Light District. Expect gorgeous—and delicious—bouquets and compositions.

Where you'll be pampered... At **Theresia P.C.,** you can admire the clothes Beatrix buys (yes, Theresia does dress the queen), and perhaps Theresia herself will be the one who escorts you over the polished marble of the ready-to-wear floor and up the spiral staircase to couture heaven. Across and down the street at **Edgar Vos,** matrons, mavens, and 45 ish businesswomen nod their approval as you don the pricey garden-party and socialite attire, while the stylish staff members listen and advise like the psychiatrists they really are. The master himself, **Panc Vergouw,** welcomes you into his tiny couture store near the Singel canal, and in no time you feel like a minor Grachtengordel socialite yourself, stunned by the magic of sequins and padded black-widow spider outfits suitable for noir society weddings. Across the street at **Dutch Design by Godelief,** Madame Godelief will help you into a white embroidered wedding dress or a tweedy suit.

Once you've outfitted yourself for serious spending, head to **Kolthoorn Kunst** antiques. You ring the doorbell of a 1662 Golden Bend mansion and are ushered into "the museum where every exhibit can become yours," as the company's slogan runs. The knowledgeable staff manage to make you feel like the owner of the place, and a much greater expert than they, as you gape at the museum-quality Old Dutch furniture, tapestries, and etchings (including several dozen by Rembrandt, for lease). Once you've made your purchase, stride up Rokin to **P.G.C. Hajenius** and celebrate with a cigar in Amsterdam's "last elegant tobacco shop." As you stand on a thick red carpet under the huge bronze chandelier in the landmark 1915 interior, the genial, portly staff will open a dozen humidors, pouches, and canisters to find you the perfect smoke—possibly the extraordinary house Sumatra cigars, which you can savor in the new backroom cigar bar and mini–tobacco museum.

Everything under one roof... The city's biggest and best-loved department store is **De Bijenkorf** on the Dam, called the Beehive by locals. It's a cross between Macy's and Bloomingdale's, with perfume-soaked salesladies and a strait-laced, moneyed feel. Everything under the Dutch sun is there for the taking, if you aren't fazed by steep prices. **Metz & Co.,** with an exclusive address at Keizersgracht and Leidsestraat, is worth a visit for the view from the panoramic top-floor cafe. It's a favorite among well-heeled locals in the market for silk scarves, china, art glass, and the like. **Vroom & Dreesmann,** better known locally as V&D *(fay en day),* is a mass-market outfit on both sides of busy, tacky Kalverstraat that's handy for all the things you forgot to pack (rain gear, notebooks, toothpicks, 220V converters, etc.).

Diamonds are a girl's best friend... To believe most guidebooks and promotional brochures, Amsterdam is synonymous with diamonds. Diamond factory tours (see the Diversions chapter) are, in fact, among the city's biggest tourist attractions, but several other cities around the globe, including Antwerp, outrank Amsterdam as diamond-processing centers. No matter. The industry does trace its roots here to the late 1500s, prices are competitive, and there are many long-established, reputable dealers who gladly guarantee in writing the so-called four Cs: carat (weight), cut, color, and clarity. During World War II, when Nazi atrocities wiped out countless other Jewish diamond dynasties, the Van Moppes family escaped to Brazil, returning after the war to reopen what has become probably the biggest operation in town, **Van Moppes Diamonds.** Their claim to fame is having cut the smallest brilliant in the world, weighing .24 milligrams. The **Amsterdam Diamond Center** was created after the war by several big families, including seventh-generation kingpin

Paul Asscher, whose family spent 8 months cutting the world's biggest diamond—a 3,106-carat rough—into nine gems, including the famed Cullinan I (530 carats) and Cullinan II (317 carats). **Coster Diamonds** won renown in the 1930s by restyling the 186-carat Koh-i-Noor ("Mountain of Light") into the 108-carat centerpiece of the British royal crown (now in the Tower of London). **Gassan** and **Stoeltie Diamonds** round out the list of the city's top five dealers (there are many others); though smaller, their tours are just as good. Be aware that all the tours end in the salesroom, where you can be made to feel like the least you could do in return is buy a precious stone or two.

Club gear... Clubbing is big in Amsterdam, and hardcore party fiends outfit themselves for it. Wild garments, plus wild hair styling, are on offer at **Housewives on Fire,** a split-level new-and-used clubgear store and hair salon. After your hair-raising spree, you might even stand a chance of getting into iT or Escape (gee, what a privilege), provided, of course, that your shoes meet the bouncers' standards. When it comes to outrageous footwear—towering clogs, marvelously silly spike heels, and other un-PC items for the tootsies—try **Antonia by Yvette** or **Shoebaloo.** Further down the club-fashion food chain is **Chill Out,** on the top floor of De Bijenkorf department store. The best thing about Chill Out isn't the neobourgeois, teeny-bopper wear; it's the view. For leather, plastic, and S&M club garb, check out **Wasteland,** an aptly named boutique near Spui.

Royal fashions... Yes, everyone knows Amsterdam's worst-kept secret: **Theresia P.C.** dresses Queen Beatrix. Classic but fun, regal but discreet, conservative yet liberal, Theresia's clothes are a miracle of paradox and oxymoron. Even if you can't afford them, go to experience the majesty of her P.C. Hooftstraat premises. Apparently that other P.C. Hooft straat institution, **Edgar Vos,** has *not* had the privilege of a royal commission. Nonetheless, the reigning lady would doubtless approve of the colorful, classic, richly kitschy creations favored by rich Amsterdam businesswomen and socialites. The same crowd motors over to **Dutch Design by Godelief** for tweedy suits and Orientalist evening wear. In a pinch, both the women's and men's floors at **De**

Bijenkorf, really the only full-fledged department store in town, would provide the kind of proper, upstanding, practical, yet noble clothes that would suit the royals. The feel is more English than Dutch at **De Jager Country Shop,** but in a sporty moment, Dutch princeling Willem Alexander might find De Jager's stylishly waterproof, laudably masculine clothes suitable for a damp country trot, a canalboat ride, or a spot of urban cycling. Though there are no women's fashions per se, much of the rain gear and sports clothes, like Barbour raincoats, are unisex. **Metz & Co.,** on the corner of Keizersgracht and Leidsestraat, is the kind of perfumed, exclusive, and specialized department store where moneyed matrons shop for silk scarves and other accessories with aristocratic flair.

Wacky and one of a kind... You'd think a freewheeling cosmopolis and the gay capital of Europe would be teeming with them, but **De Condomerie** is the city's first and still its lone condoms-only boutique. To prove that there's more to a rubber than meets the eye, this Red-Light District specialist also sells condom souvenirs, condom T-shirts, edible condoms (try passionfruit), and condom samplers specially designed for anal penetration. Nearby, try the edibles at **Jemi Bloemsierkunst,** a floral art boutique where you munch on tulips and other botanical eye candy. **Trunk Interior Decorators** is an exercise in kitsch, popular with hipsters who've grown allergic to Philippe Starck and his legions of hyper-design Euro imitators. This store down an alley near Spui is crammed with wacky furnishings and objects, mostly from Morocco and India, including plastic Oriental carpets, suitcases made from recycled tin cans, and mock-silver teapots straight from the souk.

For nautical instruments, or anything you ever wanted for your canal boat, try **Andries de Jong,** the city's most handsome chandler's store, on Muntplein near the flower market. The Maritime Museum's gift store is another great source for ship-related flotsam and jetsam (models, books, posters, accessories; see p. 182 for business hours). At the **Brilmuseum** the spectacles are the spectacle: Every imaginable type of eyeglass frame and lens is on show and for sale at this unusual boutique-museum. No one in town can hold a candle to **Pontifex,** located between the Jordaan and the royal palace, which sells only candles, many handmade

SHOPPING

right there. The other side of this same U-shaped store, **Kramer** is where a Mr. Kramer runs his celebrated doll hospital, working wonders on ragged Raggedy Anns and beheaded Barbies. **Gone With the Wind** is a wonderland of sculptural mobiles, and **Frozen Fountain** showcases plenty of impractical but irresistible *objets* by young Dutch designers. "Dive into the pool of fantasy," say the owners of the colorful Grachtengordel **Blue Gold Fish** gift store and gallery. There's no real rhyme or reason to the items for sale. They cover a wide range of ceramics, jewelry, household items (including colorful lamps in the "Aladdin's Corner"), and textiles, all of them running the stylistic gamut from kitsch to chic. Still, there's unity in diversity in the more-or-less fantastic design sensibility that goes into each piece.

Bags and beans... The Dutch, among the world's earliest and most active coffee and tea drinkers, continue to import, roast, and consume some of the world's finest aromatic caffeine sources. **Wijs & Zonen** has been at its current location—among the gay bars, smoking coffee shops, and grubby hotels of the Red-Light District—since 1828, and little of the interior has changed. You can mix and match a dozen kinds of coffee beans, or choose the house blends; tea comes in 24 loose-leaf varieties, as well as in packaged form. **Simon Levelt Koffie & Thee** is almost as old (1839) and just as good. This coffee-roasting and tea store on the edge of the Jordaan—remodeled in 1999—is still full of old coffee grinders and paraphernalia and offers dozens of fragrant blends. The other equally venerable Simon Levelt store, facing Centraal Station, is always packed. At age 140 in 2004, the Red-Light District's **Geels & Co.** is a relative newcomer on the coffee and tea scene, but it's right up there in quality and atmosphere and it has a charming coffee and tea museum on its second floor. Try **Brandmeester's** for a contrast: This sleek, ultramodern coffee-roasting store and tasting bar in glitzy Van Baerlestraat, around the corner from P.C. Hooftstraat, has palsy service to counter its hard-edged decor. Its American-style brownies would pass muster stateside.

Fashion forward... **Carla V**, a custom ladies' leather boutique run by irrepressible Carla Van der Vorst, is one of the big draws at the new Cornelis Schuytstraat shopping area.

Choose the color and length of your posh lamé coat, guaranteed "as soft as your own skin." Skinflints should abstain. If silk is what turns you on, **McLennan's** kimonos, ties, scarves, and accessories are for you, artfully displayed in a chic silk-only boutique between the Jordaan and royal palace. At nearby **Van Ravenstein,** twin Dutch/Belgian designer boutiques, you're likely to bump into media stars, gallery owners, and the moneyed creative crowd of both sexes buying camelhair urban safari suits, vests made from zippers and embroidered evening wear, retro-hip felt or woolen garments, and discreet, darkly hip suits or pantsuits by Dries van Noten et al.

SHOPPING

Everything you always wanted to know about sex... De Condomerie is the first place slavering sex tourists go in the Red-Light District to gawk at the window displays, much to the irritation of the staff of this exuberant condom boutique. You can pick up more than just flavored rubbers here; there are T-shirts, toys, key rings, and underwear decorated with or incorporating condoms. The Red-Light District isn't the only—or even the best—place to stock up on goodies made from rubber, leather, and the like. At **Female & Partners,** near the royal palace, you'll find all sorts of women's lingerie and charming sex articles for women who like women, women who like men, and those who like both. If the vibrators make you hesitant to enter this chic store, you can order your goodies by phone, mail, or over the Internet. Leather is the name of the hardcore game at **Vero-Over,** an extraordinary store in the old center. Expect made-to-order leather couture items (the mind boggles), S&M accessories, pigskin pants, leather undies, plus all the usual off-the-rack leather paraphernalia fresh from the tannery. Closer in to the Center but just as outlandish is **Wasteland,** where, when it comes to getting into this boutique's club nights and raves, "the decision of the bitch is final" (their words). Leather, uniforms, plastic, rubber, metal, cross-dress, and fetish-glam. What fun!

For foot fetishists... Finding Dutch-designed shoes is a challenge not always worth the trouble, but **Panara,** a pricey, chic store on P.C. Hooftstraat, sells seriously attractive, classic, and elegant footwear for well-heeled women, designed by Hans van Paridon but made in Italy. Trendies clatter over to **Antonia by Yvette,** a Grachtengordel boutique, for Dutch designer Lola Pagoda's fanciful shoes and clogs. At P.C. Hooftstraat's **Shoebaloo,** the decor may be by celebrated architect/artist/designer Borek Sipek, a Czech who has been in Holland for decades, but the Dutch and European women's footwear itself is surprisingly midmarket conventional.

Home designs... At **Frozen Fountain,** a stylish Grachtengordel showroom near Nieuwe Spiegelstraat, contemporary Dutch designer furniture and other *objets* by Marcel Wanders—and a dozen other fashioners of the gorgeous-but-impractical—draw the media crowd and beautiful people from surrounding canal houses and converted warehouses. At Peter van Kesteren's and Helene van Ruiten's **Galerie Binnen,** another name-dropper's Grachtengordel address, you'll find Italian, Dutch, and international interior and industrial design: furniture, vases, jewelry, and more. Less pricey but still chic is **Koot Light & Design,** a pair of stores favored by Jordaan yuppies seeking sleek halogen lamps by Dutch designers Gerard van den Berg or Anette van Edmund, or vaguely Art Deco furniture and housewares, including Italian tea kettles and flatware. Koot's chief competition is **Wonen 2000 International Design Centrum,** another set of stores distributed around several multistory buildings on the same busy Jordaan street. This international design store might be in New York except for the Dutch appliances and garden furniture.

The art scene... Once you've shown at **Galerie Paul Andriesse,** your reputation as an artist is pretty much made. Established avant-garde abstract and figurative artists, international and Dutch, make this Jordaan gallery the Leo Castelli of Amsterdam. Younger, hungrier talents show at Adriaan ten Have's **Torch** gallery, a prime venue for progressive contemporary art. The occasional international name makes this hip Jordaan gallery *the* place to hobnob with the young, beautiful, and creative. Nearby at **De Praktijk,** Dirk Vermeulen, a dentist until the early 1990s, has converted his practice into a forum for contemporary Dutch artists and is the exclusive agent for the furniture art of the late monk Dom van der Laan. **Galerie**

Fons Welters and Galerie de Expeditie are the quintessential Jordaan and Grachtengordel galleries, specializing in functional art and contemporary work by young Dutch and other artists. In a relatively new gallery area on the southern end of Lijnbaansgracht is Galeriecomplex, a grouping of five showrooms in adjoining buildings with connecting doors. Each gallery is different in style, taste, and quality, showing trendy Dutch and international contemporary works. Back in the Grachtengordel, Galerie Binnen, the world-class interior and industrial design gallery, showcases Dutch and European artists and artisans—its owners, Peter van Kesteren and Helene van Ruiten, are local art-world movers and shakers. Amsterdam's premier photography foundation, Huis Marseille, in the Grachtengordel, shows top international art photographers (p. 187). *Note:* Most Amsterdam galleries are on the Internet (see www.akka.nl).

Very old things... At Rokin, near Muntplein, you'll come across two equally grand dealers for serious spenders. One, Premsela & Hamburger, is arguably Amsterdam's most reliable antique silver dealer. Poise and polish are the operative words here, with authentic silver baubles ranging from 19th-century English saltcellars to 18th-century tea strainers and Art Deco silverware. Next door, the suave staff at V.O.F. Mathieu Hart, discreet antiquarians since 1878, will help you fall in love with rare old prints, lithographs, and 18th-century delftware or grandfather clocks. Kolthoorn Kunst is an antiques store made to look and feel like a museum, and even the Rembrandt etchings are available for lease. Persnickety but knowledgeable, Martin Ex at Ex Antiquiteiten specializes in textile artworks (needlepoint) from the 17th through 19th centuries. His tiny Grachtengordel store is also crammed with priceless furniture and objects. As for the city's premier antiques quarter, there are almost 100 reputable dealers in the Nieuwe Speigelstraat alone—far too many to list. Just stuff your wallet and stride out.

Kid stuff... When the kids clamor for their fair share of conspicuous consumption, head to Magna Plaza, a mall housed in the turn-of-the-20th-century former Post & Telephone office facing the royal palace at the Dam;

upstairs is Bam Bam, one of the city's chic-est kiddie-clothes boutiques. **De Looier Kunst & Antiekcentrum,** ostensibly an antiques and art market, is actually a covered flea market in the Jordaan where the kids will flip over the junk, especially the old Barbie dolls, teddy bears, pocket knives, Zippo lighters, and maybe even the Aretha Franklin 45s. There's a Renaissance-fair atmosphere on Saturdays at the organic food market at **Noordermarkt** in the Jordaan (see "Outdoor Markets," earlier in this chapter), where you can get all sorts of healthful treats for the children and entertain them with a lively Dutch version of the Punch 'n' Judy show. **Mechanisch Speelgoed,** an old-fashioned toy store just down the street from Noorderkerk, again in the Jordaan, is stuffed with wooden toys, traditional games, teddy bears, masks, and costumes. The countless colorful mobiles at **Gone With the Wind** are sure to lift your darling's heart. And should your sprout's favorite doll bust its arm or head in your travels, **Kramer,** a delightfully creepy doll hospital not far from the Jordaan, has a kind surgeon named Mr. Kramer ready to Cabbage-Patch things up.

Incredible edibles... Three of the city's friendliest and best-stocked deli and cheese stores, with all the cheeses, young and old, meats (smoked beef), and specialty foods you'll want for your picnics, are **Ron's** in the Jordaan near Westerkerk; **De Kaaskamer** on Runstraat, 5 minutes from the flower market; and **Loekie,** with two locations, one on Utrechtsestraat south of Rembrandtplein, the other on Prinsengracht near Leidestraat. A new, upscale catering and takeout joint with adjoining brasserie, **Van Dam** is *the* place for Dutch-French delicacies at premium prices. Chocoholics will appreciate **J.G. Beune,** an old (1882) and old-fashioned confectionery store west of Centraal Station. Don't miss the Amsterdammertjes—liquor- or chocolate-filled sweets suggestively modeled on the phallus-shaped no-parking poles that line Amsterdam's streets. **Holtkamp** is a feast for both palate and eyes: The gorgeous Piet Kramer interior is a 1923 Art Deco masterwork; Cees and Petra Holtkamp's chocolates, pastries, and croquettes (there are 12 pastry chefs in the basement) are possibly the best in town. Amsterdam is famous for its salted licorice, known as *dropjes*—you'll either drop-dead love or hate it—and **The Natural Health Company** is an excellent source for it.

This old store off Muntplein has a wide selection of the sticky stuff, an equally wide selection of cheesy delftware, plus a grab bag of homeopathic cures in case you get indigestion. The brainchild of larger-than-life *jenever* and liquor distiller Cees van Wees, **De Admiraal** (p. 163)—a *proeflokaal* (tap house) on Herengracht—is a wonderful place to stock up on Amsterdam's only locally made gin. Tasty tulips with salmon or strawberries are on offer at **Jemi Bloemsierkunst,** a floral art boutique specializing in edible flowers.

Smokes... Tobacco smoking has been the national pastime since Holland's Golden Age. **P.G.C. Hajenius** is a city landmark on Rokin, a venerable tobacconist whose slogan is "the last of the elegant tobacco stores." Even if you're allergic to smoke and feel like kicking fat cats who puff away on smelly cigars, peek into the lovely 1915 interior: thick red carpet, marble and wood paneling, a huge bronze chandelier hanging from gilt beams. Dozens of wooden cigar boxes, humidors, and canisters of pipe tobacco hold some of the world's best tobaccos, including the celebrated hand-rolled house Sumatra cigars. The back rooms house a cigar bar, library, and minicigar museum. **J.N. Andringa Tabak** is the other serious tobacconist in town, and has been purveying top-quality products at Muntplein since 1902. The interior is simple compared to the competition's, but the handmade cigars and specially selected pipe tobaccos are just as good. If pipes are your thing, check out **Smokiana,** a pipe museum-store with tribal, antique, and ultramodern puffing equipment.

Book nooks... If you've forgotten to pack reading material, don't despair: Most Dutch bookstores carry books in English. The best source, however, is the **American Book Center,** a vast discount operation near the Dam, with everything you'd find at home, and at reasonable prices. **Athenaeum Boekhandel,** at central Spui, is both a bookstore and an experience: Some local intellectuals seem to live here, eternally browsing the excellent selection of English-language books, novels, and magazines. **The English Bookshop** is a

SHOPPING

small, cozy Jordaan store favored by English expats; the mid- or highbrow novels and literature on its shelves reflect the chatty English owner's taste. The upscale British chain **Waterstone's** near Spui has a wide selection from U.K. and U.S. publishers, including literature on Amsterdam and Holland. Henk Brinkman, part-owner of atmospheric **Antiquariaat Brinkman,** is the leading light in Amsterdam's antique book trade. One of just a handful of booksellers in the 1950s, Brinkman has seen the trade flourish, turning Amsterdam into a European center for bibliophiles, historians, collectors, and researchers. Today, more than 125 stores specializing in everything from musical scores to medieval medical texts, early cookbooks, 18th-century travel guides, and everything else ever printed anywhere in the world are scattered around the center of town, but concentrated around Spui. Many of these books are in English. A detailed map of antiquarian and secondhand bookshops is on sale all over town, and from the publisher, DE KAN (Binnenkadijk 237; Tel 020/627-5794). Check www.nwa.nl for a complete listing of booksellers. **Evenaar,** off Singel, is a travel-only specialist, with a good selection of new and used books in English.

Clogs, china, and kitsch... Dozens of souvenir boutiques around town sell delftware with a small "d" (i.e., junk). At **Galleria d'Arte Rinascimento,** near Westerkerk, you can buy the junk and the real thing, too: Royal Delftware with a capital *D.* Both the knockoffs and genuine articles come in sublimely ridiculous shapes: ceramic clogs, Christmas ornaments, contorted vases, and the like. **Gassan,** a diamond-polishing house, has a Royal Delftware painting workshop and boutique. You're just gonna love the high-camp atmosphere at **De Klompenboer,** Amsterdam's celebrated cloggery, just a few hundred yards south of Nieuwmarkt; live chickens peck at the wood shavings from the *klompen* (clogs) made by Ye Olde Shoemaker, and a woman in "traditional" costume paints these works of contemporary art before your very eyes. Over at the Bloemenmarkt, **Laddrak** stuffs brightly painted wooden clogs with U.S.-certified tulip bulbs.

Map 10: Central Amsterdam Shopping

A.H. Abels en Zoon **51**
American Book Center **43**
Amsterdam Diamond Center **24**
Andries de Jong **45**
Antiquariaat Brinkman **29**
Antonia by Yvette **22**
Athenaeum Boekhandel **39**
Aviflora **50**
Blue Gold Fish **14**
Brilmuseum **31**
Chill Out **17**
De Bijenkorf/Chill Out **17**
De Condomerie **64**
De Jager Country Shop **21**
De Kaaskamer **37**
De Klompenboer **65**
De Looier Kunst & Antiekcentrum **36**
De Praktijk **25**
Dutch Design by Godelief **10**
The English Bookshop **27**
Evenaar **28**
Ex Antiquiteiten **23**
Female & Partners **12**
Frozen Fountain **41**
Galerie Binnen **3**
Galeriecomplex **59**
Galerie de Expeditie **6**
Galerie Fons Welters **13**
Galerie Paul Andriesse **5**
Galleria d'Arte Rinascimento **7**
Gassan **66**
Geels & Co **61**
Gone With the Wind **54**
Holtkamp **56**
Housewives on Fire **11**
Huis Marseille **42**
IVY **58**
Jemi Bloemsierkunst **62**
J.G. Beune **1**
J.N. Andringa Takab **46**
Kolthoorn Kunst **68**
Koot Light & Design **15**
Laddrak **49**
Loekie **57, 69**
M.M.C. Roozen **48**
Magna Plaza **16**
McLennan's **20**
Mechanisch Speelgoed **2**
Metz & Co **53**
The Natural Health Company **47**

Map key continues at right

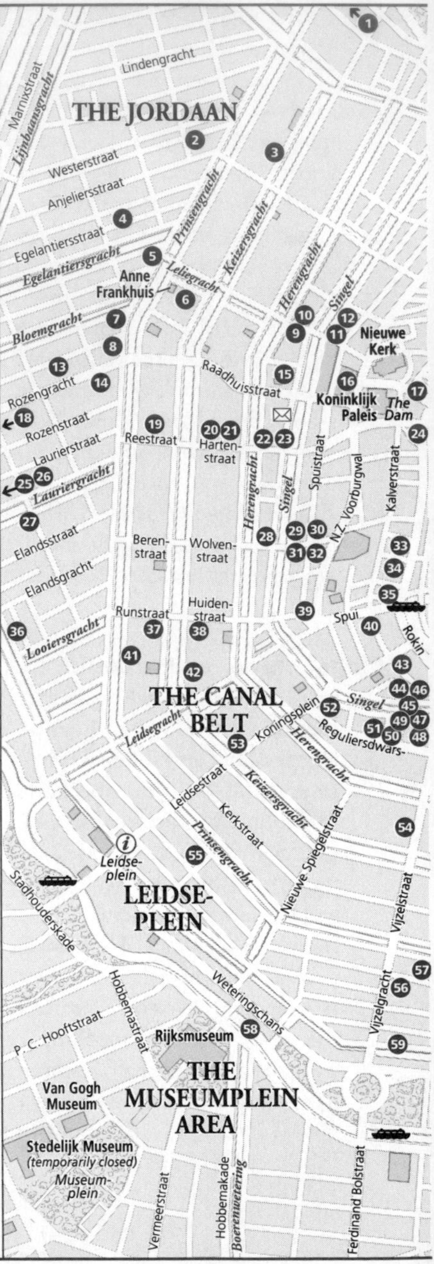
THE JORDAAN
THE CANAL BELT
LEIDSEPLEIN
THE MUSEUMPLEIN AREA
Lindengracht
Marnixstraat
Lijnbaansgracht
Westerstraat
Anjeliersstraat
Egelantiersstraat
Egelantiersgracht
Prinsengracht
Keizersgracht
Herengracht
Singel
Leliegracht
Anne Frankhuis
Bloemgracht
Nieuwe Kerk
Raadhuisstraat
Koninklijk Paleis
The Dam
Rozengracht
Rozenstraat
Reestraat
Hartenstraat
Lauriersstraat
Lauriergracht
Spuistraat
N.Z. Voorburgwal
Kalverstraat
Elandsstraat
Elandsgracht
Berenstraat
Wolvenstraat
Runstraat
Huidenstraat
Spui
Rokin
Looiersgracht
Leidsegracht
Koningsplein
Reguliersdwars-
Leidsestraat
Kerkstraat
Nieuwe Spiegelstraat
Vijzelstraat
Leidseplein
Stadhouderskade
Weteringschans
Hobbemastraat
P. C. Hooftstraat
Rijksmuseum
Vijzelgracht
Van Gogh Museum
Stedelijk Museum
(temporarily closed)
Museumplein
Vermeerstraat
Hobbemakade
Boerenwetering
Ferdinand Bolstraat

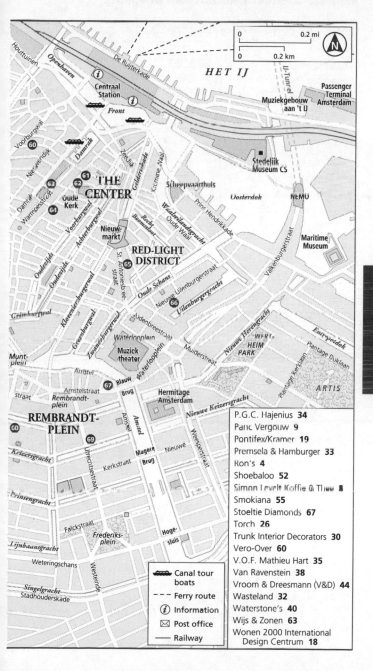

SHOPPING

P.G.C. Hajenius **34**
Paric Vergouw **9**
Pontifex/Kramer **19**
Premsela & Hamburger **33**
Ron's **4**
Shoebaloo **52**
Simon Levelt Koffie & Thee **8**
Smokiana **55**
Stoeltie Diamonds **67**
Torch **26**
Trunk Interior Decorators **30**
Vero-Over **60**
V.O.F. Mathieu Hart **35**
Van Ravenstein **38**
Vroom & Dreesmann (V&D) **44**
Wasteland **32**
Waterstone's **40**
Wijs & Zonen **63**
Wonen 2000 International
  Design Centrum **18**

Canal tour boats
Ferry route
Information
Post office
Railway

Map 11: Southern Amsterdam Shopping

Brandmeester's **1**
Carla V **9**
Coster Diamonds **6**
Edgar Vos **2**
Menno Kroon **7**
Panara **3**
Shoebaloo **4**
Theresia P.C. **5**
Van Dam **8**
Van Moppes Diamonds **10**

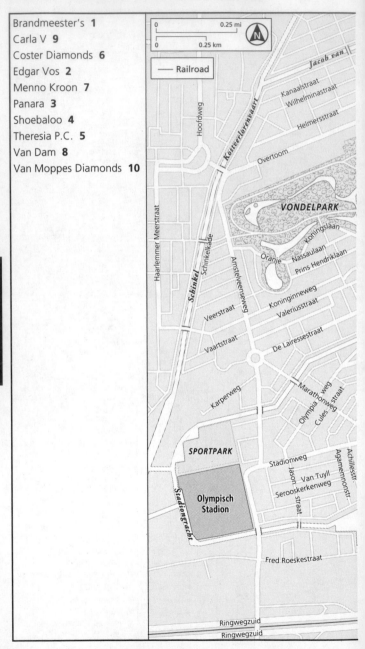

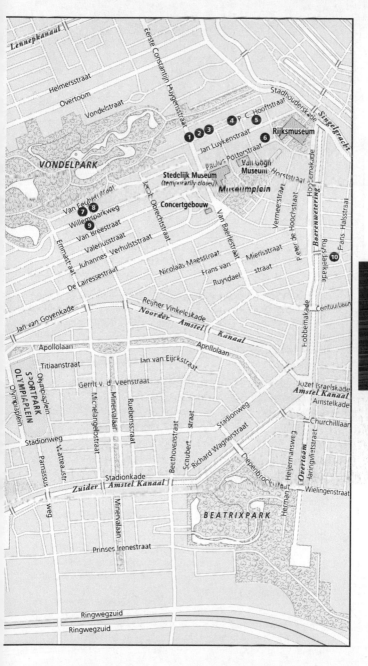

SHOPPING

The Index

A.H. Abels en Zoon (p. 166) CANAL BELT Fragrant flower and plant store in the floating market. Health-certified bulbs, no shipping.... *Tel 020/622-7441. Singel 490–494 at Muntplein. Trams 4, 9, 14, 16, 24, or 25 to Muntplein. Mon–Sat 10am–6pm.*
See Map 10 on p. 178.

American Book Center (p. 176) CENTER Multistory discount bookstore.... *Tel 020/625-5537. www.abc.nl. Kalverstraat 185 at Muntplein. Trams 4, 9, 14, 16, or 24 to Muntplein. Mon–Wed and Fri–Sat 10am–8pm, Thurs 10am–10pm, Sun 11am–6pm.*
See Map 10 on p. 178.

Amsterdam Diamond Center (p. 168) CENTER Serious gem complex on the Dam founded by seventh-generation diamond kingpin Paul Asscher.... *Tel 020/624-5787. www.amsterdamdiamond center.com. Rokin 1–5 at the Dam. Trams 4, 9, 14, 16, 24, or 25 to the Dam. Daily 10am–6pm, Thurs 7–8:30pm.*
See Map 10 on p. 178.

Andries de Jong (p. 170) REMBRANDTPLEIN Amsterdam yachtsmen drop anchor at this pricey chandler's store.... *Tel 020/ 624-5251. www.andriesdejong.nl. Muntplein 8. Trams 4, 9, 14, 16, 24, or 25 to Muntplein. Mon–Sat 10am–6pm.*
See Map 10 on p. 178.

Antiquariaat Brinkman (p. 177) CANAL BELT Leading antique bookstore.... *Tel 020/623-8353. www.nvva.nl/brinkman. Singel 319 at Oude Spiegelstraat (across the canal). Trams 1, 2, or 5 to Spui. Mon–Sat 11am–6pm.*
See Map 10 on p. 178.

Antonia by Yvette (p. 169) CANAL BELT Grachtengordel boutique for wild or merely hip Dutch shoes and clogs.... *Tel 020/320-9443. www.antoniabyyvette.nl. Gasthuismolensteeg 18–20, 12, and 16 at Singel. Trams 1, 2, 5, 6, 13, 14, or 17 to the Dam. Mon 1–6pm, Tues–Sat 11am–6pm.*
See Map 10 on p. 178.

Athenaeum Boekhandel (p. 176) CENTER The ultimate Amsterdam bookstore, at central Spui, with a wide selection of books, novels, and magazines in English.... *Tel 020/622-6248.*

www.athenaeum.nl. Spui 14–16. Trams 1, 2, or 5 to Spui. Mon–Wed and Sat 9:30am–6pm, Thurs 9:30am–9pm, Sun noon–5:30pm.

See Map 10 on p. 178.

Aviflora (p. 166) CANAL BELT One of the few flower market stores with U.S.-certified bulbs and Internet ordering.... *Tel 020/622-6592. www.aviflora.nl. Singel 522 at Muntplein (and several places at Schiphol Airport). Trams 4, 9, 14, 16, 24, or 25 to Muntplein. Mon–Sat 10am–6pm.*

See Map 10 on p. 178.

Blue Gold Fish (p. 171) CANAL BELT A gift store with a taste for fantasy and a wide-ranging collection *Tel 020/023-3134. Rozengracht 17 at Prinsengracht. Trams 6, 13, 14, or 17 to Westermarkt. Mon–Sat 11:30am–6:30pm.*

See Map 10 on p. 178.

Brandmeester's (p. 171) MUSEUM DISTRICT Trendy, updated coffee-roasting store.... *Tel 020/572-0811. www.brandmeesters.nl. Van Baerlestraat 13 at Pieter Cornelisz Hooftstraat. Trams 2, 3, 5, or 12 to Van Baerlestraat. Mon–Sat 9am–6pm.*

See Map 11 on p. 180.

Brilmuseum (p. 171) CENTER Museum-store for eyeglass aficionados.... *Tel 020/421-2414. www.brilmuseumamsterdam.nl. Gasthuismolensteeg 7 at Singel. Trams 1, 2, 5, 6, 13, 14, or 17 to the Dam. Mon–Sat 10am–6pm.*

See Map 10 on p. 178.

Carla V (p. 172) OLD SOUTH Dutch designer Carla van der Vorst's new leather clothing boutique: coats, skirts, bags, and belts. You choose the style and length; Carla dyes the duds whatever color you like.... *Tel 020/672-0404. Cornelis Schuytstraat 45 at Willemsparkweg. Tram 2 to Cornelis Schuytstraat. Tues–Sat 11am–5:30pm.*

See Map 11 on p. 180.

Chill Out See De Bijenkorf.

See Map 10 on p. 178.

Coster Diamonds (p. 169) MUSEUM DISTRICT One of the biggest, glitziest diamond operations in town.... *Tel 020/305-5555. www.costerdiamonds.com. Paulus Potterstraat 2–8 at Museum District. Trams 2 or 5 to Hobbemastraat. Daily 9am–5pm.*

See Map 11 on p. 180.

De Bijenkorf/Chill Out (p. 168) CENTER "The Beehive," Amsterdam's biggest and best department store.... *Tel 0900/0919. www.bijenkorf.nl. Dam 1. Trams 4, 5, 9, 14, 16, 24, or 25 to the Dam. Mon 11am–7pm, Tues–Wed 9:30am–7pm, Thurs–Fri 9:30am–9pm, Sat 9:30am–6pm, Sun noon–6pm.*

See Map 10 on p. 178.

De Condomerie (p. 170) RED-LIGHT DISTRICT The city's first condom boutique.... *Tel 020/627-4174. www.condomerie.com. Warmoesstraat 141 at Beursplein (based at adjacent Sint-Jansstraat 33 until November 2006 while renovations are going on at the Warmoesstraat shop). Trams 4, 9, 14, 16, 24, or 25 to the Dam. Mon–Sat 11am–6pm.*

See Map 10 on p. 178.

De Jager Country Shop (p. 170) CANAL BELT Clothes and accessories for the shooting, fishing, and riding set in a proper little store near the flower market.... *Tel 020/624-7172. www.countryshop-dejager.nl. Herengracht 230 at Hartenstraat. Trams 1, 2, or 5 to Koningsplein. Tues–Sat 10am–6pm.*

See Map 10 on p. 178.

De Kaaskamer (p. 175) CANAL BELT Possibly Amsterdam's best cheese store, with deli delights to boot. Will vacuum-pack and courier cheese anywhere.... *Tel 020/623-3483. Runstraat 7 at Keizersgracht. Trams 1, 2, or 5 to Spui. Daily 9am–6pm.*

See Map 10 on p. 178.

De Klompenboer (p. 177) JEWISH QUARTER Kitschy tourist magnet store for clogs and other souvenirs.... *Tel 020/623-0632. Sint-Antoniesbreestraat 51 at Nieuwmarkt. Trams 9 or 14 to Waterlooplein. Mid-April to mid-Sept daily 10am–9pm; mid-Sept to mid-April daily 10am–6pm.*

See Map 10 on p. 178.

De Looier Kunst & Antiekcentrum (p. 175) JORDAAN Tacky but irresistible covered flea market.... *Tel 020/624-9038. www.looier.nl. Elandsgracht 109 at Lijnbaansgracht. Tram 6, 7, 10, or 17 to Elandsgracht. Sat–Wed 11am–5pm, Thurs 11am–9pm.*

See Map 10 on p. 178.

De Praktijk (p. 174) JORDAAN Gallery for contemporary Dutch artists; exclusive agents for Dom van der Laan's extraordinary furniture.... *Tel 020/422-1727. www.praktijk.nl. Lauriergracht 96 at Lijnbaansgracht. Trams 6, 13, 14, or 17 to Marnixstraat. Tues–Sat 1–6pm, 1st Sun in month 2–5pm.*

See Map 10 on p. 178.

Dutch Design by Godelief (p. 167) CANAL BELT The sign says NOT IN PARIS, MILAN OR LONDON. I wonder why. Tweedy suits, embroidered wedding dresses, and Orientalist evening wear for 45-ish businesswomen and socialites.... *Tel 020/623-2638. www.godelief.nl. Spuistraat 271 at Rosmarijnsteeg. Trams 1, 2, or 5 to Spui. Tues–Wed and Fri 11am–6pm, Thurs 11am–8pm, Sat 11am–5pm.*

See Map 10 on p. 178.

Edgar Vos (p. 167) MUSEUM DISTRICT Garden-party and socialite attire for 40-ish businesswomen and country-clubbers.... *Tel 020/671-2748. www.edgarvos.nl. Pieter Cornelisz Hooftstraat*

*136 at Van Baerlestraat. Trams 2, 3, 5, or 12 to Van Baerlestraat.
Mon noon–6pm, Tues–Fri 9:30am–6pm, Sat 9:30am–5pm.*
See Map 11 on p. 180.

The English Bookshop (p. 177) JORDAAN Friendly, intimate store specializing in British and American quality literature and travel books.... *Tel 020/626-4230. www.englishbookshop.nl. Lauriergracht 71 at Hazenstraat. Trams 6, 13, 14, or 17 to Marnixstraat. Tues–Sat 11am–6pm.*
See Map 10 on p. 178.

Evenaar (p. 177) CANAL BELT Small travel-only bookstore just off Singel. Good selection of new and used books in English.... *Tel 020/624-6289. Singel 348 at Oude Spiegelstraat. Trams 1, 2, or 5 to Spui. Mon–Fri noon–6pm, Sat 11am–5pm.*
See Map 10 on p. 178.

Ex Antiquiteiten (p. 174) CANAL BELT Tiny Grachtengordel antiques store selling rare needlepoint art, furniture, and objects.... *Tel 020/625-5180. www.exantiques.nl. Gasthuismolensteeg 8 at Singel. Trams 1, 2, 5, 6, 13, 14, or 17 to the Dam. Thurs–Sat 11am–6pm, or by appointment.*
See Map 10 on p. 178.

Female & Partners (p. 172) CENTER Chic retail and mail-order boutique for "sex articles for women"—lingerie, dildos, and other imaginative toys.... *Tel 020/620-9152. www.femaleandpartners.nl. Spuistraat 100 at Nieuwe Sparpotsteeg. Trams 1, 2, 5, 6, 13, or 17 to the Dam. Tues–Wed and Fri–Sat 11am–6pm, Sun–Mon 1–6pm.*
See Map 10 on p. 178.

Frozen Fountain (p. 171) CANAL BELT Dutch designer furniture and **objets** in a trendy showroom.... *Tel 020/622-9375. Prinsengracht 629 at Leidsegracht. Trams 16, 24, or 25 to Prinsengracht. Mon–Fri 10am–5pm, Sat noon–5pm.*
See Map 10 on p. 178.

Galerie Binnen (p. 173) CANAL BELT International interior and industrial design fills this serious Grachtengordel gallery.... *Tel 020/625-9603. Keizersgracht 82 at Prinsenstraat. Trams 1, 2, 5, 6, 13, or 17 to Nieuwezijds Kolk. Tues–Sat noon–6pm, 1st Sun of month 2–5pm.*
See Map 10 on p. 178.

Galeriecomplex (p. 174) CENTER Five galleries under the same roof, showing Dutch contemporary works.... *Lumen Travo: Tel 020/627-0883; www.lumentravo.nl. Metis-NL: Tel 020/623-9863; www.metis-nl.com). Akinci: Tel 020/638-0480; www.akinci.nl. Van Wijngaarden/Hakkens: Tel 020/626-4970; www.vanwijngaarden hakkens.nl. Vous Etes Ici: Tel 020/612-7979; www.vousetesici.nl.*

Lijnbaansgracht 314–318 at Weteringcircuit. Trams 6, 7, 10, 16, 24, or 25 to Weteringcircuit. Hours for galleries vary.

See Map 10 on p. 178.

Galerie de Expeditie (p. 174) CANAL BELT Grachtengordel contemporary art gallery with up-and-coming talents.... *Tel 020/ 620-4758. www.de-expeditie.com. Leliegracht 47 at Keizersgracht. Trams 6, 13, 14, or 17 to Westermarkt. Tues–Sat 10:30am–6pm.*

See Map 10 on p. 178.

Galerie Fons Welters (p. 174) JORDAAN Hip gallery showing functional and avant-garde art and top contemporary work by young artists.... *Tel 020/423-3046. www.fonswelters.nl. Bloemstraat 140 at Rozengracht. Trams 6, 13, 14, or 17 to Marnixstraat. Wed–Sat 1–6pm, 1st Sun of month 2–5pm. Closed mid-July to early Sept.*

See Map 10 on p. 178.

Galerie Paul Andriesse (p. 173) CANAL BELT Top gallery on the edge of the Jordaan for established avant-garde artists.... *Tel 020/623-6237. Prinsengracht 116 at Egelantiersgracht. Trams 6, 13, 14, or 17 to Westermarkt. Tues–Fri 11am–1pm and 2–6pm, Sat 2–6pm, 1st Sun of month 2–6pm.*

See Map 10 on p. 178.

Galleria d'Arte Rinascimento (p. 177) CANAL BELT Hand-painted Delftware of every conceivable type from De Porcelyne Fles is sold in this nondescript but well-stocked emporium in the shadow of Westerkerk.... *Tel 020/622-7509. Prinsengracht 170 at Bloemstraat. Trams 6, 13, 14, or 17 to Westermarkt. Mon–Sat 9am–6pm, Sun 10am–5pm.*

See Map 10 on p. 178.

Gassan (p. 169) JEWISH QUARTER One of the city's top five diamond houses. Good tours; also sells Royal Delftware.... *Tel 020/622-5333. www.gassandiamonds.com. Nieuwe Uilenburgerstraat 173–175 at Joodenbreestraat. Trams 9 or 14 to Waterlooplein. Daily 9am–5pm.*

See Map 10 on p. 178.

Geels & Co. (p. 171) A coffee-roasting and tea-importing establishment houses a tiny coffee and tea museum.... *Tel 020/624-0683. www.geels.nl. Warmoesstraat 67 at Oude Brugsteeg. Trams 4, 9, 14, 16, 24, or 25 to the Dam. Museum open Sat 2–4:30pm. Free admission.*

See Map 10 on p. 178.

Gone With the Wind (p. 171) CENTER Nearly 100 mobiles, plus traditional toys.... *Tel 020/423-0230. www.gonewind-mobiles. com. Vijzelstraat 22 at Herengracht. Trams 16, 24, or 25 to Herengracht. Sun–Mon noon–6pm, Tues–Sat 10am–6pm.*

See Map 10 on p. 178.

Holtkamp (p. 175) CENTER Homemade chocolates, pastries, and croquettes spread out in a gorgeous 1923 Art Deco interior.... *Tel 020/624-8757. Vijzelgracht 15 at Prinsengracht. Trams 16, 24, or 25 to Prinsengracht. Mon–Sat 10am–6pm.*

See Map 10 on p. 178.

Housewives on Fire (p. 169) CENTER Clubwear and hair-styling for serious house fiends.... *Tel 020/422 1067. Spuistraat 102 at Nieuwe Sparpotsteeg. Trams 1, 2, 5, 6, 13, or 17 to the Dam. Fri–Wed 10am–7pm, Thurs 10am–9pm.*

See Map 10 on p. 178.

Huis Marseille (p. 174) CANAL BELT The city's top photo exhibitions, at a nonprofit foundation ... *Tel 020/531-0989. www.huismarseille.nl. Keizersgracht 401 at Leidsegracht. Trams 1, 2, or 5 to Keizersgracht. Tues–Sun 11am–5pm*

See Map 10 on p. 178.

IVY (p. 167) LEIDSEPLEIN Creative, postmodern-baroque florist across from the Crowne Plaza Amsterdam-American.... *Tel 020/623-6561. Leidseplein 35. Trams 1, 2, 5, 6, 7, or 10 to Leidseplein. Tues–Sat 10am–6pm.*

See Map 10 on p. 178.

Jemi Bloemsierkunst (p. 167) RED-LIGHT DISTRICT Gorgeous bouquets, exotic plants, and the house specialty—edible flowers. In a historic landmark building in the Red-Light District.... *Tel 020/625-6034. Warmoesstraat 83A at Oude Brugsteeg. Trams 4, 9, 14, 16, 24, or 25 to the Dam. Mon–Fri 9am–6pm.*

See Map 10 on p. 178.

J.G. Beune (p. 175) WEST Old-fashioned chocolate store and bakery west of Central Station.... *Tel 020/624-8356. Haarlemmerdijk 156–158 at Haarlemmerplein. Tram 3 and buses 18 or 22 to Haarlemmerplein. Mon–Sat 8am–6pm.*

See Map 10 on p. 178.

J.N. Andringa Tabak (p. 176) CENTER A simple store founded in 1902, with excellent handmade cigars and pipe tobacco. Will ship anywhere.... *Tel 020/623 2836. Regulliersbreestraat 2 at Muntplein. Trams 4, 9, 14, 16, 24, or 25 to Muntplein. Mon–Sat 9am–6pm, Sun noon–5pm.*

See Map 10 on p. 178.

Kolthoorn Kunst (p. 167) CANAL BELT An antiques showroom in a 17th-century mansion with some of the city's finest Old Dutch furniture, Delftware, tapestries, and etchings.... *Tel 020/622-1010. Herengracht 518 at Vijzelstraat. Trams 16, 24, or 25 to Herengracht. By appointment only.*

See Map 10 on p. 178.

THE INDEX

SHOPPING

Koot Light & Design (p. 173) CENTER Two hip home-design bou-tiques west of the Dam.... *Tel 020/626-4830. Raadhuisstraat 52–54 and 55 at Singel. Trams 1, 2, 5, 6, 13, 14, or 17 to the Dam. Tues–Wed and Fri 9am–6pm, Thurs 10am–9pm, Sat 10am–5pm.*

See Map 10 on p. 178.

Laddrak (p. 166) CANAL BELT A Bloemenmarkt florist who will export your health-certified bulbs for you.... *Tel 020/625-4842. Singel 548 at Muntplein. Trams 4, 9, 14, 16, 24, or 25 to Munt-plein. Mon–Sat 9am–6pm.*

See Map 10 on p. 178.

Loekie (p. 175) CENTER AND CANAL BELT Two delis stuffed with delicious Dutch cheeses and specialty meats.... *Tel 020/624-3740. Utrechtsestraat 57 at Keizersgracht. Tram 4 to Keizers-gracht. Mon–Tues and Thurs–Sat 9am–5pm, Wed 9am–1pm. Tel 020/624-4300. Prinsengracht 705 at Leidsestraat. Trams 1, 2, or 5 to Prinsengracht. Mon–Tues and Thurs–Sat 9am–5pm, Wed 9am–1pm.*

See Map 10 on p. 178.

Magna Plaza (p. 175) CENTER Upscale five-level mall in the turn-of-the-20th-century Post & Telephone office building facing the royal palace.... *Tel 020/626-9199. www.magnaplaza.nl. Nieuwezijds Voorburgwal 182 at the Dam. Trams 1, 2, 5, 6, 13, 14, or 17 to the Dam. Mon 11am–7pm, Tues–Sat 10am–7pm, Sun noon–7pm.*

See Map 10 on p. 178.

McLennan's (p. 172) CANAL BELT Pure silk, by the yard or snipped into kimonos, ties, scarves, and other accessories.... *Tel 020/622-7693. Hartenstraat 22 at Herengracht. Trams 6, 13, 14, or 17 to Westermarkt. Mon 1–6pm, Tues–Fri 10:30–6pm, Sat 11:30am–6pm.*

See Map 10 on p. 178.

Mechanisch Speelgoed (p. 175) JORDAAN Old-fashioned toy store.... *Tel 020/638-1680. Westerstraat 67 at Violettenstraat. Trams 3 or 10 to Marnixplein. Mon–Tues and Thurs–Sat 10am–6pm.*

See Map 10 on p. 178.

Menno Kroon (p. 167) OLD SOUTH Hip new floral arts boutique where the beautiful people spend their euros on gorgeous blooms.... *Tel 020/679-1950. Cornelis Schuytstraat 11 at Willemsparkweg. Tram 2 to Cornelis Schuytstraat. Mon–Sat 10am–6pm.*

See Map 11 on p. 180.

Metz & Co. (p. 168) CANAL BELT Exclusive Grachtengordel depart-ment store. Panoramic cafe on top floor.... *Tel 020/520-7020. Keizersgracht 455 at Leidsestraat. Trams 1, 2, or 5 to Keizers-gracht. Mon 11am–6pm, Tues–Wed and Fri–Sat 9:30am–6pm, Thurs 9:30am–9pm, Sun noon–5pm.*

See Map 10 on p. 178.

M.M.C. Roozen (p. 166) CENTER Good source of U.S.-approved bulbs. At flower market.... *Tel 020/625-7176. Singel 496 at Muntplein. Trams 4, 9, 14, 16, 24, or 25 to Muntplein. Mon–Sat 10am–6pm.*

See Map 10 on p. 178.

The Natural Health Company (p. 176) CENTER Famous salted licorice, homeopathic cures, and tacky souvenirs are stuffed into this atmospheric store.... *Tel 020/624-4533. www.tnhc.nl. Vijzelstraat 1 at Muntplein. Trams 4, 9, 14, 16, 24, or 25 to Muntplein. Mon–Sat 9am–6pm, Sun 1–6pm.*

See Map 10 on p. 178.

Panara (p. 173) MUSEUM DISTRICT Elegant yet hip Dutch-designed shoes for women 30 and over.... *Tel 020/622-1908. www.panara-shoes.com. Pieter Cornelisz Hooftstraat 124 at Van Baerlestraat. Trams 2, 3, 5, or 12 to Van Baerlestraat. Mon 1–6pm, Tues–Wed and Fri–Sat 9am–6pm, Thurs 9am–9pm.*

See Map 11 on p. 180.

Panc Vergouw (p. 167) CANAL BELT Small couture store where businesswomen and socialites order sequined silks or more conservative, tailored woolens and cottons.... *Tel 020/428-0655. Oude Leliestraat 1 at Singel. Trams 1, 2, 5, 6, 13, or 17 to the Dam. Mon 1–6pm, Tues–Sat 1:30–6pm.*

See Map 10 on p. 178.

P.G.C. Hajenius (p. 167) CENTER Elegant 1915 tobacco store, cigar bar, and minimuseum. Will ship anywhere.... *Tel 020/623-7494. www.hajenius.com. Rokin 92–96 at Spui. Trams 4, 9, 14, 16, 24, or 25 to Spui. Mon–Wed and Fri–Sat 9:30am–6pm, Thurs 9:30am–9pm, Sun noon–5pm.*

See Map 10 on p. 178.

Pontifex/Kramer (p. 171) CANAL BELT Two stores in one: candles galore at Pontifex; toy repair at Mr. Kramer's doll hospital.... *Tel 020/626-5274. Reestraat 18–20 at Prinsengracht. Trams 6, 13, 14, or 17 to Westermarkt. Mon–Sat 10am–6pm.*

See Map 10 on p. 178.

Premsela & Hamburger (p. 174) CENTER Possibly the city's best source for buying or restoring antique or contemporary silver.... *Tel 020/627-5454. www.premsela.com. Rokin 98 at Spui. Trams 4, 9, 14, 16, 24, or 25 to Spui. Mon–Fri 9:30am–5:30pm, Sun noon–5pm, or by appointment.*

See Map 10 on p. 178.

Ron's (p. 175) JORDAAN Dutch deli and cheese store.... *Tel 020/624-8802. Tweede Tuindwarsstraat 3 at Tuinstraat. Trams 3 or 10 to Marnixplein. Mon–Sat 9am–6pm.*

See Map 10 on p. 178.

Shoebaloo (p. 169) MUSEUM DISTRICT AND CENTER Two chic boutiques, selling women's footwear that's not as outrageous as you'd expect from the decor.... *Tel 020/671-2210. www. shoebaloo.nl. Pieter Cornelisz Hooftstraat 80. Trams 2, 3, 5, or 12 to Van Baerlestraat. Mon noon–6pm, Tues–Wed and Fri–Sat 10am–6pm, Thurs 10am–9pm, Sun 1–6pm. Tel 020/626-7993. Koningsplein 7 at Herengracht. Mon noon–6pm, Tues–Wed and Fri–Sat 10am–6pm, Thurs 10am–9pm, Sun 1–6pm.*

See Map 10 on p. 178.
See Map 11 on p. 180.

Simon Levelt Koffie & Thee (p. 171) CANAL BELT An 1839 coffee-roasting and tea store in the shadow of the Westerkerk has expanded, with three other locations, but the same great coffee.... *Tel 020/624-0823. www.simonlevelt.nl. Prinsengracht 180 at Rozenstraat. Trams 6, 13, 14, or 17 to Westermarkt. Mon–Fri 10am–6pm, Sat 10am–5pm. Tel 020/489-5963. Kinkerstraat 109 at Tollensstraat. Trams 7 or 17 to Ten Katestraat. Mon–Fri 10am–6pm, Sat 10am–5pm. Tel 020/400-4060. Ferdinand Bolstraat 154 at Van Ostadestraat. Tram 3 to Ferdinand Bolstraat; 12, 16, 24, or 25 to Ceintuurbaan. Mon–Fri 10am–6pm, Sat 10am–5pm. Tel 020/428-5887. Stationsplein 15 inside Centraal Station. Trams 1, 2, 4, 5, 6, 9, 13, 16, 17, 24, or 25 and Metro to Centraal Station. Mon–Fri 8am–8pm, Sat 9am–8pm, Sun noon–7pm.*

See Map 10 on p. 178.

Smokiana (p. 176) CANAL BELT Pipe museum and store with pipes primitive to postmodern.... *Tel 020/421-1779. www.pijpenkabinet. nl. Prinsengracht 488 at Leidsestraat. Trams 1, 2, or 5 to Prinsengracht. Wed–Sat noon–6pm (at other times by appointment).*

See Map 10 on p. 178.

Stoeltie Diamonds (p. 169) REMBRANDTPLEIN Small, old, reliable diamond dealer near Rembrandtplein.... *Tel 020/623-7601. www.stoeltiediamonds.com. Wagenstraat 13–17 at Amstelstraat. Trams 4, 9, or 14 to Rembrandtplein. Daily 8:30am–5pm.*

See Map 10 on p. 178.

Theresia P.C. (p. 169) MUSEUM DISTRICT Luxurious boutique, where ready-to-wear (downstairs) ranges from 500€–5,000€ ($625–$6,250) for a dress.... *Tel 020/679-6225. Pieter Cornelisz Hooftstraat 55. Trams 2 or 5 to Hobbemastraat. Mon 1–6pm, Tues–Sat 10am–6pm.*

See Map 11 on p. 180.

Torch (p. 173) JORDAAN Progressive contemporary art, theme shows, and the occasional international name give this gallery its hipster cachet.... *Tel 020/626-0284. www.torchgallery.com. Lauriergracht 94 at Lijnbaansgracht. Trams 6, 13, 14, or 17 to Westermarkt. Thurs–Sat 2–6pm.*

See Map 10 on p. 178.

Trunk Interior Decorators (p. 170) CENTER This antidesign store in an alley near Spui has plenty of inexpensive wacky imports.... *Tel 020/638-7095. Rosmarijnsteeg 12 at Nieuwezijds Voorburgwal. Trams 1, 2, or 5 to Spui. Tues–Sun 11am–6pm.*

See Map 10 on p. 178.

Van Dam (p. 175) OLD SOUTH Franco-Dutch caterer with great takeout at regal rates. Also a hip brasserie.... *Tel 020/670-6570. Cornelis Schuytstraat 8–10 at Willemsparkweg. Tram 2 to Cornelis Schuytstraat. Daily noon–7:30pm.*

See Map 11 on p. 180.

Van Moppes Diamonds (p. 168) OLD SOUTH The biggest diamond operation in town. Draws crowds of tourists.... *Tel 020/676-1242. www.moppesdiamonds.com. Albert Cuypstraat 2–6 at Ruysdaelkade. Trams 16, 24, or 26 to Albert Cuypstraat. Daily 8:45am–5:45pm.*

See Map 11 on p. 180.

Van Ravenstein (p. 172) CANAL BELT Upscale Dutch/Belgian designer boutiques in the Grachtengordel, for women and men; good for handmade sweaters, leather pants, and two-piece suits.... *Tel 020/639-0067. Keizersgracht 359 at Huidenstraat. Trams 1, 2, or 5 to Spui. Mon 1–6pm, Tues–Wed and Fri 11am–6pm, Thurs 11am–7pm, Sat 10:30am–5:30pm*

See Map 10 on p. 178.

Vero-Over (p. 172) CENTRUM Off-the-rack and made-to-order leather and rubber couture, mostly for the hardcore S&M crowd.... *Tel 020/636-6486. Kolksteeg 2 at Nieuwezijds Voorburgwal. Trams 1, 2, 5, 6, 13, or 17 to Nieuwezijds Kolk. Mon–Wed and Fri–Sat 11am–7pm, Thurs 11am–9pm.*

See Map 10 on p. 178.

V.O.F. Mathieu Hart (p. 174) CENTER Polished century-old fourth-generation antiques dealer near Spui.... *Tel 020/623-1658. Rokin 122 at Spui. Trams 4, 9, 14, 16, 24, or 25 to Spui. Mon–Sat 10am–6pm.*

See Map 10 on p. 178.

Vroom & Dreesmann (V&D) (p. 168) CENTER Vast, mid- to downmarket department store scattered in several buildings on Kalverstraat.... *Tel 0900/235-8363. Kalverstraat 201–221 at Muntplein. Trams 4, 9, 14, 16, 24, or 25 to Muntplein. Mon 11am–6pm, Tues–Wed and Fri–Sat 9am–6pm, Thurs 9am–9pm.*

See Map 10 on p. 178.

Wasteland (p. 172) CENTER Kinky latex clubwear, plus all sorts of S&M "toys." Don't bring the kids.... *Tel 061/557-1306. www.wasteland.nl. Nieuwezijds Voorburgwal 332 at Spui. Trams 1, 2, or 5 to Spui. Tues–Wed 1–6pm, Thurs–Sun 1–9pm.*

See Map 10 on p. 178.

THE INDEX

SHOPPING

Waterstone's (p. 177) CENTER British chain bookshop near Spui with a wide variety of English and American books.... *Tel 020/ 638-3821. Kalverstraat 152 at Spui. Trams 1, 2, or 5 to Spui. Tues–Wed and Fri–Sat 9am–6pm, Thurs 9am–9pm, Sun–Mon 11am–6pm.*

See Map 10 on p. 178.

Wijs & Zonen (p. 171) RED-LIGHT DISTRICT One of Amsterdam's oldest (1828) and best coffee-roasting and tea-importing establishments, stuck in the seedy Red-Light District.... *Tel 020/624-0436. www.wijs-zonen.nl. Warmoesstraat 102 at Wijde Kerksteeg. Trams 4, 9, 14, 16, 24, or 25 to the Dam. Mon–Sat 9:30am–6pm.*

See Map 10 on p. 178.

Wonen 2000 International Design Centrum (p. 173) JORDAAN Dutch and international designer home furnishings distributed around several multistory buildings.... *Tel 020/521-8710. Rozengracht 219 at Lijnbaansgracht. Trams 6, 13, 14, or 17 to Marnixstraat. Mon 1–6pm, Tues–Wed and Fri–Sat 9am–6pm, Thurs 9am–9pm.*

See Map 10 on p. 178.

THE INDEX

SHOPPING

NIGHTLIFE

& CAFES

6

Basic Stuff

Amsterdam's reputation as Europe's sex, drugs, and rock 'n' roll capital is as solid as ever. A steady stream of European 20-somethings—particularly British and German—flows into the city solely for the nightlife. You can drink whenever you want; clubs usually open around 10pm, get lively at midnight, and buzz until 4am Monday to Thursday and Sunday (until 5am Fri–Sat). Cover charges are usually a low 4€ to 7€ ($5–$8.75), with drinks for 2€ to 5€ ($2.50–$6.25). If you're at least 18, you can buy and consume what you please, where you please. Erotic—i.e., porno—venues are rife. The city is rich with smoking coffee shops where you can puff dope and hash; most have ear-boggling live or canned music. The gay scene is world-class, with venues that cater to every taste, including hardcore S&M.

Hangouts range from tiny, laid-back cafes and bars to huge, exclusive 100 beats-per-minute dance clubs with *sui generis* dress codes and ferocious bouncers. For bureaucratic reasons, some clubs call themselves "societies" and theoretically require you to pay a "membership fee" (2.50€–5€/$3.15–$6.25), nearly always waived at the door. Clubwear boutiques (see the Shopping chapter) cater to serious clubbers keen to get into the top venues— iT, Sinners in Heaven, More, and Escape.

Rave parties, organized by professionals and usually held in warehouses or theaters, are no longer the thing unless you're into acid, spasm-inducing noise (i.e., "music"), and pushy creeps in smelly synthetic sweat suits. Raves and other "events" (such as "fetish fantasy" nights) are announced via leaflets distributed in clubs, bars, and cafes; the cover charge is usually about 20€ ($25). Clubs are hipper, and the harder it is to get into them the better they are. Admittance is based on your look, sexual orientation, and the people you hang out with. As elsewhere, clubs and star DJs spring up like proverbial mushrooms; trends in music come and go. What's hip today—a mix of pumping house, grunge, hypnotic techno and progressive trance, drum & bass, 100-bpm club house, rave, speed garage, R&B, soul, jazz-dance—will be passé tomorrow. Most venues listed here have been around awhile and look likely to last in one form or another.

Cafe Society

The city's cafes are better than its eateries, the saying goes. And the truth is, Amsterdam's more than 1,400 cafes and bars— among the most atmospherically smoky, friendly, cozy, pleasantly worn in the world—are a hard act to follow.

Cafe culture thrives here as it did 50 years ago in other European capitals, Paris in particular. A lot of Amsterdammers still start their day at their favorite cafe (usually a so-called brown cafe), have lunch there, return for drinks before dinner, and then go back for a bit of socializing, a game of snooker, and some live (or canned) music and a sing-along. Of course, all of this is lubricated by aperitifs. The bartender doesn't bother to ask what to pour, and the pool cues are as ubiquitous as the bentwood chairs. Since everyone goes to these cafes, they are the ultimate democratic institutions. You, the street sweeper, drink with the CEOs and politicos and speak your mind about everything from croquettes to geopolitics.

At last count there were more than 1,400 cafes and bars in Amsterdam proper; in this chapter, we list only a small selection. Of the four basic types, the most famous is the centuries-old *Bruine Kroeg* (brown cafe). These are brown because of tobacco stains (a red flag for rabid nonsmokers) and because the proprietors make a cult of never washing or painting the spectacularly fly-blown walls. How to recognize them? They are the quintessence of coziness *(gezelligheid)* and seem trapped in a time warp—anywhere from about 1600 (the Golden Age) to 1968 (Provos, hippies). They are amazingly interchangeable, whether authentically old or made to look that way—neo-browns. Standard trappings include: picturesque locals who feign surprise at the sight of a nonregular; a worn wooden or zinc bar; (empty) barrels of *jenever* or beer; a snooker table; sand—not sawdust—on the floor; a sidewalk terrace; and carpets on the worn wooden tables. The carpets absorb spilled beer, are optional, and seem to be going out of fashion (but not at places where the traditional style is more than a skin-deep affectation). Brown cafes often open in the morning (between 8 and 10am) and close late at night (between 1 and 3am). They're found all over town, with a high concentration between Spui and Centraal Station, and in the Jordaan. The standard lunch and snack menu features a selection of small bun sandwiches *(broodjes)* made with everything from *osseworst* (smoked beef sausage) to cheese, pastrami, vegetables, ham, and salami; *toost* (toasted white bread) with ham and cheese, smoked eel, or beef tartare; and a variety of simple salads. Occasionally omelets, croquettes, or quiches crop up.

The opposite of the brown cafes are the "white" or "grand" cafes: modern, spacious establishments that usually have big windows and terraces and more food on the menu (salad bar, quiches, sandwiches, daily specials, pasta, and so forth). They can be refreshingly anonymous and sunny after all those chummy, cheek-by-jowl brown-cafe conversations, though they're often just as smoky.

Falling between the extremes are the dozen or so "designer" cafes, frequented primarily by a self-consciously sophisticated crowd. They combine elements of the old (coziness, smoke patina, sand on the floor, regulars) and new (spaciousness, better food, a degree of anonymity). They're all in the center of town, and opening hours are generally 10am to 1 or 2am. Dozens of other cafes, tea salons, and diners don't fit into these categories; some resemble old-fashioned American bakeries or collegiate coffee shops.

Tap Houses

It's no coincidence that tap water in Amsterdam is called "municipal beer" *(gemeente pils)*—which perhaps explains the success of those unremarkable local brews Heineken and Amstel. Tap houses, *proeflokaalen*, are where *jenever* and beer are swilled from noon until about 8pm, usually by middle-age and older tipplers. Food is rarely available. The best ones are within stumbling distance of the Dam. (See p. 19 for more on Dutch gin and how to drink it.)

Smoke Houses

Here's Dutch ambiguity again: Officially, drug menus are illegal, but all smoking coffee shops have them (they are often small, and you must ask specifically to see one). A typical dope menu reads as follows: per gram cost: "Skunk," 5.70€ to 8.40€ ($7.15–$11); "Sauraica," 6.40€ ($8); "Morocco," hash 5.25€ to 13€ ($6.55–$16); "Afghanistan," hash 3.60€ to 10€ ($4.50–$13); "India," 11€ ($14). A single joint is about 4€ ($5). Even in smoking coffee shops, though, you are never limited to smoking the dope: You can eat and drink the stuff, too—in space cakes, brownies, or hash tea. So when ordering food or drinks, make sure you're getting what you want. If you don't partake, that's fine, but you might get a free contact high just eating a sandwich (some places serve health food) or drinking fruit juices or soft drinks that may have residual dope somewhere in them. The sale and consumption of alcohol in all smoking coffee shops is theoretically forbidden, part of a successful effort by city officials to bring down their numbers.

●●●

HOUSE OF ILL REPUTE WITH A GREAT REPUTATION

*There's prostitution, and there's prostitution. In Amsterdam, streetwalkers are illegal (most are desperate young addicts). Bordellos are not. The most celebrated one in town—a decades-old institution—is **Yab Yum**, owned and managed by affable Théo Heuft and Madame Monique, his Swiss friend. Everyone loves Yab Yum, especially taxi drivers, who get a hefty tip if they deposit you there. The name: a goddess of love heavily featured in the Kama Sutra. The location: a 17th-century mansion on Singel, far from the sleaze of the Red-Light District (plus there's a branch in Rotterdam and one at Schiphol Airport). The women: 20 nightly, all Dutch, well-educated, gorgeous, ages 18 to 24 (with one perfectly preserved 40-something). Most are reportedly stewardesses, nurses, students, and housewives—all strictly moonlighting: No one is twisting their arms. The clientele: businessmen, jet-setters, and kinky couples into threesomes or orgies.*

The setup: A musclebound bouncer leads you up the stairs and rings a buzzer. An elegant guy—a banker by day?—shakes your hand, and initiates you into the mysteries. You can change money in the lobby or use a credit card. The decor: quintessential cat-house stuff. There are stalagmite chandeliers, nudes, a lounge with a splashing Venus fountain, and a U-shaped bar where the ladies perch on stools. The price: 70€ ($88) to get in; about 160€ to 500€ ($200–$625) for champagne while you chat. Innocent entertainment can stop there. It's about 360€ ($450) per hour per woman should you decide to mount the faux leopard-skin carpet leading to the 11 luxury bedrooms, fitted out like the extravagant whorehouses of Hollywood westerns but with Jacuzzis and beds big enough for, well, use your imagination. Expensive? To paraphrase Sly and the Family Stone: The nicer the nice, the higher the price. (Yab Yum; Tel 020/624-9503; www.yabyum.nl; Singel 295; open daily 8pm–4am).

●●●

Sources

The up-to-the-minute entertainment info sources in English are Amsterdam *Day by Day,* the VVV tourism bureau's strait-laced monthly magazine; *Gay & Night Magazine,* an alternative entertainment monthly written by and for the gay community; and *Shark,* a giveaway with a 20-something, outlandish readership. Rave invitations are found in clubs, bars, shops, and cafes, while rave tickets and insider info are available from the city's top clubwear shops, including **Wasteland** (p. 172). For one-stop ticketing and information on music, parties, and the club scene, call or visit the **AUB Uitburo** (Leidseplein 26; Tel 0900/0191; www.uitlijn.nl; trams 1, 2, 5, 6, 7, 10 to Leidseplein; daily 9am–9pm).

The Lowdown

Kink on stage... If you're dreaming of breaking into the hardcore live Dutch porno scene and would like to leap onstage to display your prowess, **Casa Rosso**, the city's most famous erotic theater, is the place for you. (You'd better be well endowed.) Nearby, operated by the same pornomeisters, is the **Bananenbar,** where the classic Mexican donkey act has been replaced by a piece of artfully wielded fruit. Audience participation is welcome; fruit is distributed free, and the rest I leave to your imagination.

That arty, multiculti thing... Fun of a less obscene kind is at **Melkweg,** an Amsterdam institution that started in hippy days and has evolved into an international multimedia cultural center, with everything from a cafe and smoking coffee shop to music and dance spaces.

Dutch drinking songs... Sing-along cafes, where older locals belt beer and *jenever* and then break into old Dutch songs, are a dying breed, but a handful still exist, especially in the Jordaan. That's where you'll find both **Café Nol,** whose red-vinyl stools prop up local roisterers, and **Café De Twee Zwaantjes,** with famously tobacco-stained walls, full-throated singers, and live accordion music. In the same vein, though across town in the east, **Ruk & Pluk** is a neo-brown cafe run by a jovial gay couple, where mixed locals make merry against the Brazilian carnival backdrop, breaking into song when the spirit moves them.

Smoking out... If you'd sooner forget all of Amsterdam's other special attractions, you can enjoy its tolerant approach to soft-drug use by diverting yourself into oblivion at any one of the 200 or so smoking coffee shops found on practically every street (p. 198). Center-city establishments are almost exclusively frequented by tourists. City officials estimate that 90% of these supposedly laid-back, cool places are now owned by international organized crime, a thought to keep in mind as you plunk down your nice, clean euros. **The Bulldog,** a 28-year-old veteran—filled with bleary-eyed tourists oblivious to the deafening music and snarling staff—is the archetype. It has half a dozen locations downtown and in the Red-Light District.

The Grasshopper is strictly for curious tourists, because it's bright and clean and has a big terrace on Nieuwezijds Voorburgwal. **Paradox** and **Kadinsky** are among the only center-city places with a neighborhood feel. City and police authorities continue to eliminate as many dope-smoking establishments as they can, so these are here-today, possibly-gone-tomorrow addresses.

Painting the town pink... Lesbians only have a few night-club venues and tend to organize private parties, announced with leaflets. The lesbian community's most celebrated hangout is **Café Saarein II,** an old brown cafe in the Jordaan with a pool table, a woman-watching mezzanine, and a bulletin board where lesbian parties are announced. Saarein also welcomes gay men. Other, less lavender venues welcome lesbians, too. There's a women-only dance venue called **You II;** and some nights are women-only at the **GETTO** (a bar). One Sunday a month at **Melkweg** there's lesbian dancing-clubbing; the party moves to **Vrankrijk,** a wild "squatter's club," every third Sunday of the month ("Planet Pussy" is the lip-smacking name of these wild theme nights). **iT** is the city's hippest dance venue, followed by **More;** both are exclusively for gay men on Saturdays and Wednesdays, but mixed the rest of the week. Dress and act like a glamorous lunatic (feathers and sequins are big) and you'll probably get in. iT has heart-stopping techno house music, artificial smoke, lightning-storm spotlights, and a grandstand for voyeurs. More is less glam, though that's not what the owners think. Reguliersdwarsstraat is currently the hottest gay area in town; **April** bar, **Soho** bar, and **Exit** dance clubs are here. They're among the most fashionable venues for beautiful people, gay and lesbian, who begin their night with a drink at the modern-looking bars, then wander down or across the street for DJ dancing and other amusements. Nearby at **Havana,** a gay cafe-club, things get especially hot on Friday and Sunday nights. Hardcore is the specialty at **Cockring,** in the leather and S&M gay district on Warmoesstraat. There are the usual ear-splitting house music and blinding lights on the vast dance floor, as well as a particularly active back room where tough guys get up to all sorts of tricks. **Club COC,** on Rozenstraat, is tamer, appealing mostly to local guys in their 30s (Sat nights are women only).

NIGHTLIFE & CAFES

Dance fever... The postpubescents who like to wriggle and scream to deafening vintage hard rock or contemporary ear-exploding noise go to **ArenA,** a large venue in a former orphanage. Anyone and everyone dances at **Mazzo,** a big dance hall in the Jordaan with no dress code, where top DJs spin mostly cutting-edge stuff. The cultural center **Melkweg** has popular dance club nights on Thursday, Friday, and Saturday, where a mixed-age crowd dances to funk, jungle music, hip-hop, soul, R&B, and club-house. Sunday nights are Planet Pussy—women only. At nearby **Paradiso,** the DJ theme nights—so-called VIP club nights, like "Drum & Bass," "Big Beat," or "Speedgarage"—can be a big draw, filling the place to capacity. The in crowd, both gay and straight, dances near Rembrandtplein at exclusive venues like **Sinners in Heaven, Escape,** and **iT,** famous for its huge dance floor, sound system, and top DJ theme nights. Ditto **More,** a club in the Jordaan that considers itself on a par with iT and Sinners in Heaven. Gay-only dance clubs are **Cockring,** with a big dance floor and blinding lights, and **Soho** or **Exit,** fashionable, upscale dance clubs on Reguliersdwarsstraat, where you can dance or dress up for drag-queen balls. **Club COC,** a tame gay cafe-club, offers a variety of theme dance and DJ nights. Lesbians dance at **You II,** Amsterdam's sole women-only venue and at Planet Pussy theme nights at **Melkweg** and **Vrankrijk.**

All that jazz 'n blues... Jazz is big in Amsterdam, though performance quality isn't consistent. The biggest and unquestionably the best club is **Bimhuis,** the focus for top names and rapt audiences. Bimhuis was formerly based in a grungy old shipping warehouse but moved in 2005 to Space-Age-new premises in a kind of annex to the Muziekgebouw aan 't IJ (see below), in the harbor area just east of Centraal Station. Two less ambitious but good clubs near Leidseplein are almost interchangeable: **Alto Jazz Café**—the city's oldest—and **Bourbon Street.** They're smoky, cozy, and crowded with Americans, English expats, and locals 25 and up. As the names suggest, jazz and blues—most of it cool—is the name of the game. Similar, and nearby, the **Bamboo Bar** offers cocktail-lounge jazz and blues plus a grab bag of world music, Brazilian, folk, and country and western. The **Westergasfabriek** is a converted gas plant where trendies groove to jazz and a blend of everything but house; its motto, hanging on the wall: "Jazz is the teacher. Funk is the preacher. And with hip-hop it won't stop."

For experimental jazz, atonal chamber music, and all kinds of modern and experimental sounds, strap on your shades against the glare at the shiny new **Muziekgebouw aan 't IJ,** an astonishingly ambitious cutting-edge venue favored by intellectuals and the designer-stubble set (p. 242). The IJsbreker cafe remains in place at the operation's former stomping ground on the Amstel River waterside. De Engelbewaarder, a so-called literary brown cafe, is where intellectuals wearing "I'm Cool" badges hang out in a bluish fog and listen to live jazz on Sunday afternoons (and some nights). **Cristofori** (p. 241), a big piano repair and sales outfit with a fabulous Prinsengracht location, hosts jazz concerts regularly in its fifth-floor auditorium. For jazz info call 020/770-0660 or visit www.jazz-in-amsterdam.nl. When it comes to the blues, nobody does it better in Amsterdam than **Maloe Melo.** This small club features live blues most nights, interspersed with evenings of jazz and country, and jams on Tuesday and Thursday nights. The music's quality varies, from sounds lovingly created by capable amateurs to those cooked up by an occasional big name, but a pleasantly intimate setting and a zealous audience make for a good time.

For fabulous, beautiful people... You'll probably make it into **iT** if you spend enough on your clothes—plumes, sequins, foot-high spikes. This huge, nominally gay club is famous for its jet-setting crowd and wild theme nights. Spot the same jet-setters with mega-wardrobes at **Sinners in Heaven,** an outlandish place with mock-medieval decor fit for a torture chamber, and **Escape,** a vast old theater space done over regularly for theme nights. **More** is tamer, with a media-moneyed and fashion crowd. **Time,** with minimalist, distressed-iron decor and music to match (the gamut of club sounds), attracts a raunchier, tougher crowd. Intellectual and wannabe hipsters go to the **Westergasfabriek,** where everything but house music is on the sound system—funk, jazz, power soul, Latin, hip-hop, R&B, and boom-boom. Designer 25- to 35-year-olds who don't feel like dancing drift into the **Café Luxembourg** on Spui, or the **Wildschut,** where they meld with the worn leather armchairs and sofas, drink, and listen to mellow jazz and 1970s rock tapes.

For youthquakers... Grungy expats, pimply club crawlers, and the smoking-coffee-shop set love **ArenA Tonight,** an aptly named teenybopper-plus club in an old orphanage, soundproofed like an asylum, with an atmosphere to match (there's a hotel in the building, too; see p. 49). It's great if you like undiscovered DJs who blast out whatever is currently breaking eardrums. The same crew can also be spotted at **The Bulldog,** that celebrated chain of smoking coffee shops, with loud rock and gruff help. Glamorous youngsters dressed elaborately are welcomed at **iT,** a gay dance club with mixed nights, set in a dark, cavernous hall. House music throbs, and the stunning iT dancers flex on raised platforms at the command of demonic DJs. **Sinners in Heaven** has a medieval-theme interior that junior S&M practitioners will love. Depending on the night, **Escape,** on Rembrandtplein in a vast theater space, can be full of 20- to 30-year-old trendies. Rejects from the top clubs often drift over to **Mazzo,** a big dance venue with a nondescript interior in the Jordaan; it has no dress code and plays all kinds of music. **Paradiso,** in a deconsecrated church off Leidseplein, is where clubbers go for rock and new-music concerts. Most bands are local or unknown. Paradiso is also popular for warming up before heading out to dance. **Melkweg** has Friday and Saturday theme house parties.

For baby-boomers and up... It's not as if the bouncers won't let over-30s into iT, Escape, More, or Sinners in Heaven—the top venues—or any of the other 1,001 youth venues in town. But if you prefer to be around a crowd with more mature elements, head for any of the city's 1,400 cafes (see the Dining chapter). Or try a music club like **Bimhuis,** the city's top jazz venue, and the three smoky, crowded jazz and blues clubs around Leidseplein—**Alto Jazz Café, Bourbon Street,** and **Bamboo Bar. Westergasfabriek** is fine for the long-in-tooth types, provided they're still hip. Gray hairs are sometimes spotted at **De Engelbewaarder,** a literary cafe with classic cool jazz. **Mazzo** welcomes anyone—no matter how old or infirm—willing to pay. You're unlikely to see anyone under 30 at **Café De**

Twee Zwaantjes or **Café Nol;** ditto their wilder, eastern-Amsterdam counterpart **Ruk & Pluk.**

Vintage brown cafes... **Café Chris** is the oldest of them all (1624), a Jordaan institution with beer mugs hanging from the ceiling, a pool table, and an old chain-pull toilet that you actually flush from the main room (now there's atmosphere for you). **De Karpershock,** across from Centraal Station, comes in second (1629) and attracts a blue-collar crowd to its smoky, darkwood interior and sandy floor, while **De Druif,** the third-oldest (1631), out east near the Maritime Museum, claims to be older than them all. It's the archetypal neighborhood hangout, with old *jenever* and beer barrels piled high behind the bar, and a mezzanine where the regulars perch like voluble old parrots. **Papeneiland,** from 1642, is a Jordaan hangout near Noorderkerk, with beautiful delft tiles and a cast-iron stove. **Café Hegeraad,** another vintage Jordaan place, is especially lively on market days. **Hoppe** is favored by well-heeled locals and the Spui literary set; it's great for studying the human comedy from a lively terrace. **Café Mulder,** on the southern edge of central Amsterdam on Weteringlaan, has a gorgeous interior with etched glass, a hummy barkeep, and carpets on the tables. **De Sluyswacht** has a nondescript interior but panoramic terraces overlooking a lock on the Oude Schans canal; boats glide under your table. **'t Smalle,** a relative newcomer (founded in 1786), is among the Jordaan's most popular spots, with a tiny dock terrace under trees, packed with trendies and locals. **In de Wildeman** (1690), just off of Nieuwezijds Voorburgwal, really deserves to be stuffed and placed on exhibit for the astonishment of future generations—it has an entire room for nonsmokers, which (to state the proposition mildly) is remarkably un-Dutch.

Neobrowns... **Ruk & Pluk** is run by a famous gay couple of the same names; it's wild, festive, campy, and located way out east of Oosterpark. **Schaak Café Het Hok** is a smoky, friendly place near Leidseplein where fans of Amsterdam's soccer team, Ajax, play chess—there are stop clocks hung from the rafters. **Café Thijssen,** on the Jordaan's northern edge, could be in Paris, and so could the pretentiously hip clientele. **Café Daalder,** also in the Jordaan, has great apple pie, a nice terrace, and attracts a less self-important crowd. **Het Molenpad,** a Grachtengordel hangout, has a clubby, chummy feel inside, plus a wonderful canal-side summer terrace. **De Engelbewaarder,** full of cig and dope smoke, is a self-styled "literary cafe" east of the Red-Light District where self-styled intellectuals listen to jazz on Sunday afternoons. **De IJsbreker,** with a big tree-shaded terrace on the east bank of the Amstel River, is the trendy, neobrown section of the celebrated music club of the same name. At **Gambit**—one of a contingent of so-called "chess cafes"— regulars, and the occasional visitor, play chess, dominoes, and other board games in a cozy, smoky setting in the Jordaan.

White cafes... White cafes are the spiritual antithesis to brown cafes. They're modern, hip, and stylish—everything brown cafes aren't. They're sometimes referred to collectively as the "coketrail circuit." **Dantzig aan de Amstel** is a spacious place attached to city hall and the Muziektheater complex, with a library corner and a wraparound Amstel River terrace that's great for poseurs. **De Jaren,** on the Amstel 90m (98 yds.) north, is another big, sunny spot, with a panoramic upper-floor terrace where the young and hip survey the city in sweet, smoky anonymity.

Designer cafes... **De Kroon** is where media culture-vultures gather, either at the yard-wide zinc bar (flanked by bizarre displays of butterflies, bugs, and dusty bones) or on the enclosed, second-story terrace overlooking the rabble below on Rembrandtplein. **Café Luxembourg,** at Spui, draws much the same crowd (plus white collars) to its mock-old interior and enclosed terrace. **In de Waag,** inside a medieval tower, is a hip cafe/restaurant at Nieuwmarkt. **Wildschut,** near the Concertgebouw, features designer 25- to 35-year-olds in an early-1900s Amsterdam School building with stained glass, booths, armchairs, and a wraparound banquette.

Bar nosh... **Papeneiland,** a 1642 brown near Noorderkerk, serves the best hot-pastrami sandwich in town, plus a tasty onion soup. **Café Daalder,** a neobrown in the Jordaan, makes some of the best apple pie and sandwiches in town. **Het Molenpad,** another neobrown, has great sandwiches and daily specials to match its chummy atmosphere and classic jazz tapes. **De IJsbreker** serves Sunday breakfast, plus good soups and sandwiches.

Where to drink hard... Older intellectuals and literary types favor **Whisky Café De Still,** where owner Henk Eggens pours the world's best whiskeys in his tiny bar. Serious drinkers (and Amsterdam-American hotel guests) lounge at the **Bar Américain,** another time warp of a place where the bartender remembers your name and your favorite drink. **Mulligans** is a typical Irish bar, with live folk music and a friendly crowd that's both straight and gay, old and young.

Erotic play for gays... Scores of gay bars and dance clubs show porno films, and many have the kind of back rooms—also known as dark rooms—that disappeared elsewhere in the AIDS ravaged '80s. For example, **Cockring,** an aptly named hardcore club in the leather and S&M district, is renowned for its back room near the upstairs toilets. The biggest, most glamorous gay venue, **iT,** also has a back room, reportedly very feral on Saturday nights. **Exit,** the fashionable gay place on Reguliersdwarsstraat, hosts drag-queen balls and shows gay films that whip the boys into a frenzy. Lesbians head instead to **You II,** a women-only joint; or "Planet Pussy" theme nights (Sundays, once a month each) at **Melkweg** and **Vrankrijk;** or Saturday nights at **Club COC,** a gay cafe-club-dance setting.

Life is a gamble... The **Holland Casino,** the city's only legit casino, is a slice of Vegas. Join the bus-tour and provincial-Dutch set for a bit of gaming in smoke-filled rooms overlooking the Singelgracht at Leidseplein.

Map 12: Central Amsterdam Nightlife & Cafes

Alto Jazz Café **30**
April **25**
April's Exit **26**
Bamboo Bar **28**
Bananenbar **44, 45**
Bar & Lounge Américain **31**
Bourbon Street **33**
The Bulldog **32**
Café Chris **11**
Café Daalder **2**
Café De Twee Zwaantjes **8**
Café Hegeraad **4**
Café Luxembourg **22**
Café Mulder **37**
Café Nol **6**
Café Saarein II **18**
Café Thijssen **3**
Casa Rosso **45**
Club COC **13**
Cockring **43**
Danzig aan de Amstel **56**
De Engelbewaarder **47**
De Jaren **49**
De Karpershoek **39**
De Kroon **52**
De Sluyswacht **48**
Escape **51**
Gambit **9**
GETTO **42**
The Grasshopper **41**
Havana **24**
Het Molenpad **23**
Holland Casino **34**
Hoppe **21**
In de Waag **46**
In de Wildeman **40**
iT **54**
Kadinsky **19**
Maloe Melo **17**
Mazzo **12**
Melkweg **29**
More **14**
Mulligan's **50**
Papeneiland **5**
Paradiso **36**
Paradox **10**

Map key continues at right

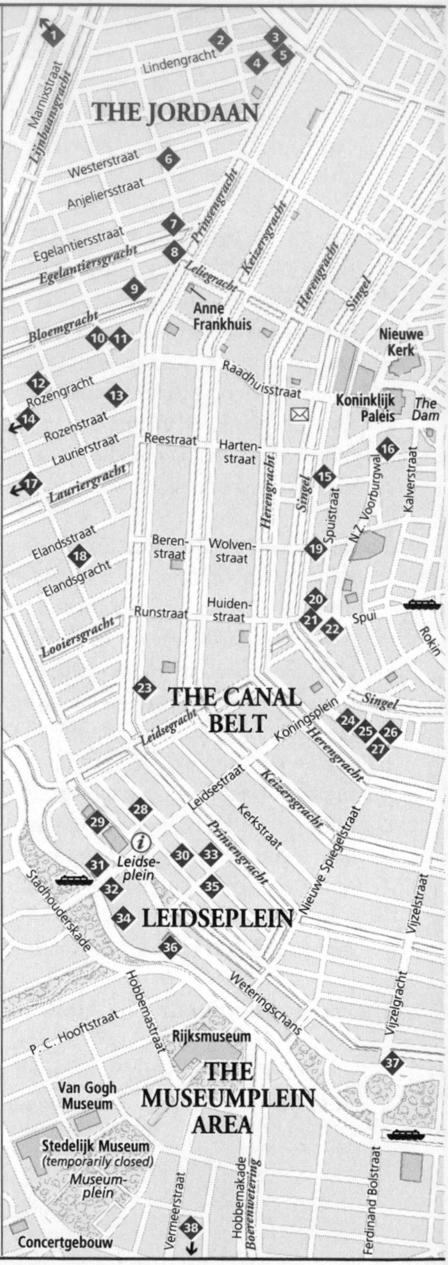

THE JORDAAN
Lindengracht
Marnixstraat
Lijnbaansgracht
Westerstraat
Anjeliersstraat
Egelantiersstraat
Egelantiersgracht
Prinsengracht
Keizersgracht
Herengracht
Singel
Leliegracht
Anne Frankhuis
Nieuwe Kerk
Bloemgracht
Raadhuisstraat
Koninklijk Paleis
The Dam
Rozengracht
Rozenstraat
Reestraat
Harten-straat
Laurierstraat
Lauriergracht
Spuistraat
N.Z. Voorburgwal
Kalverstraat
Elandsstraat
Elandsgracht
Beren-straat
Wolven-straat
Runstraat
Huiden-straat
Spui
Rokin
Looiersgracht
THE CANAL BELT
Leidsegracht
Koningsplein
Leidsestraat
Kerkstraat
Nieuwe Spiegelstraat
Vijzelstraat
Leidse-plein
Stadhouderskade
LEIDSEPLEIN
Weteringschans
Hobbemastraat
P. C. Hooftstraat
Rijksmuseum
Vijzelgracht
Van Gogh Museum
THE MUSEUMPLEIN AREA
Stedelijk Museum
(temporarily closed)
Museum-plein
Vermeerstraat
Hobbemakade
Boerenwetering
Ferdinand Bolstraat
Concertgebouw

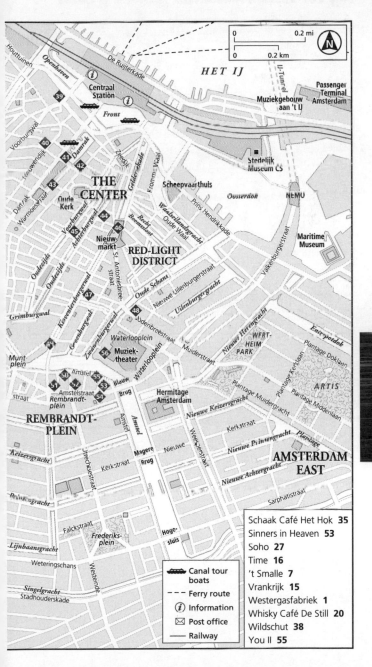

Schaak Café Het Hok **35**

Sinners in Heaven **53**

Soho **27**

Time **16**

't Smalle **7**

Vrankrijk **15**

Westergasfabriek **1**

Whisky Café De Still **20**

Wildschut **38**

You II **55**

Map 13: Eastern Amsterdam Nightlife & Cafes

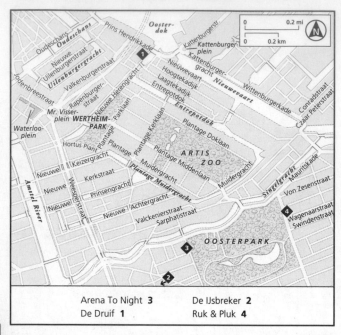

Arena To Night **3**	De IJsbreker **2**
De Druif **1**	Ruk & Pluk **4**

The Index

Alto Jazz Café (p. 202) LEIDSEPLEIN American and English expats, plus locals, crowd into this smoky, cramped club, the oldest jazz venue in town. Modern and classic tunes are played by the Alto Jazz Ensemble.... *Tel 020/626-3249. www.jazz-cafe alto.nl. Korte Leidsedwarsstraat 115 at Leidseplein. Trams 1, 2, 5, 6, 7, or 10 to Leidseplein. Daily 5pm–3 or 4am (jazz from around 10pm). No cover.*

See Map 12 on p. 208.

April, Exit, and Soho (p. 201) CENTER The most famous—and fashionable—gay bars and dance venues in town, in the heart of the Reguliersdwarsstraat gay district. Condoms available at all three spots (same owner).... *Tel 020/625-9572 and 020/625-8788. www.reguliersdwars.nl. Reguliersdwarsstraat 36, 37, and 42 at Koningsplein. Trams 1, 2, or 5 to Koningsplein. Daily; bars 10pm–1 or 2am, dance floor 10pm–4 or 5am. Cover.*

See Map 12 on p. 208.

ArenA Tonight (p. 202) EAST Huge club on various levels of an old orphanage, where international up-and-comers play very loud crossover rock—or whatever else is breaking—for a decidedly young crowd.... *Tel 020/850-2400. www.hotelarena.nl. 's Gravesandestraat 51 at Mauritskade. Trams 7, 9, 10, or 14 to Mauritskade. Thurs Sun 10pm–3am. Cover.*

See Map 13 on p. 210.

Bamboo Bar (p. 202) LEIDSEPLEIN A mix of jazz, world music, Brazilian, folk, country and western, and blues at this smoky, crowded club.... *Tel 020/624-3993. Lange Leidsedwarsstraat 66. Trams 1, 2, 5, 6, 7, or 10 to Leidseplein. Mon–Sat 10pm–2 or 3am. No cover.*

See Map 12 on p. 208.

Bananenbar (p. 200) RED-LIGHT DISTRICT Uniquely appalling places where scantily clad ladies use bananas to surprising effect. Porno emporium crowd; sticky floors.... *Tel 020/627-8945. Oudezijds Achterburgwal 106 at Stoofsteeg and Oudezijds Achterburgwal 37 at Molensteeg. Trams 4, 9, 14, 16, 24, or 25 to the Dam. Nightly 8pm–2 or 3am. Cover, but drinks are free.*

See Map 12 on p. 208.

Bar & Lounge Américain (p. 207) LEIDSEPLEIN Classic drinker's bar, just off the lobby of the Amsterdam-American Hotel.... *Tel 020/556-3116. Leidsekade 97 at Leidseplein. Trams 1, 2, 5, 6, 7, or 10 to Leidseplein. Daily noon–2 or 3am. No cover.*

See Map 12 on p. 208.

Bimhuis (p. 202) See review on p. 240.

Bourbon Street (p. 202) LEIDSEPLEIN More spacious and mainstream than Alto Jazz or Bamboo Bar, this live blues and jazz venue draws a tame crowd.... *Tel 020/623-3440. www.bourbon street.nl. Leidsekruisstraat 6 at Prinsengracht. Trams 1, 2, 5, 6, 7, or 10 to Leidseplein. Sun–Thurs 10pm–4am, Fri–Sat 10pm–5am. No cover.*

See Map 12 on p. 208.

The Bulldog (p. 200) LEIDSEPLEIN An institution among smoking coffee shops.... *Tel 020/627-1908. www.bulldog.nl. Leidseplein 15. Trams 1, 2, 5, 6, 7, or 10 to Leidseplein. Daily 9am–1am. No cover.*

See Map 12 on p. 208.

Café Chris (p. 205) JORDAAN The oldest of the old browns, founded in 1624, and a local institution. Famous for Sunday afternoon opera tapes.... *Tel 020/624-5942. www.cafechris.nl. Bloemstraat 42 at Prinsengracht. Trams 6, 13, 14, or 17 to Westermarkt. Mon–Thurs 11am–1 or 2am, Fri–Sat 10am–2 or 3am. No cover.*

See Map 12 on p. 208.

Café Daalder (p. 206) JORDAAN A neobrown—go on market days for the view.... *Tel 020/624-8864. Lindengracht 90 at Eerste Goudsbloemdwarsstraat. Trams 1, 2, 5, 6, 13, or 17 to Martelaarsgracht. Mon–Thurs 10am–1am, Fri–Sat 10am–2am. No cover.*

See Map 12 on p. 208.

Café De Twee Zwaantjes (p. 200) JORDAAN Famous sing-along brown cafe, with famously tobacco-stained walls.... *Tel 020/ 625-2729. Prinsengracht 114 at Egelantiersgracht. Trams 6, 13, 14, or 17 to Westermarkt. Daily noon–1am. No cover.*

See Map 12 on p. 208.

Café Hegeraad (p. 205) CANAL BELT/JORDAAN A vintage brown behind Noorderkerk, with carpets on the tables.... *Tel 020/ 624-5565. Noordermarkt 34 at Prinsengracht. Trams 1, 2, 5, 6, 13, or 17 to Martelaarsgracht. Mon–Thurs 11am–1 or 2am, Fri–Sat 10am–2 or 3am. No cover*

See Map 12 on p. 208.

Café Luxembourg (p. 204) CENTER A slick crowd blends into the designer decor.... *Tel 020/620-6264. www.luxembourg.nl. Spui 22–24 at Spuistraat. Trams 1, 2, or 5 to Spui. AE, DC, MC, V. Sun–Thurs 9am–1am, Fri–Sat 9am–2am. $*

See Map 12 on p. 208.

Café Mulder (p. 205) MUSEUM DISTRICT A handsome old brown on the southern edge of central Amsterdam.... *Tel 020/623-7874. Weteringschans 163 at Vijzelgracht. Trams 6, 7, 10, 16, 24, or 25 to Weteringcircuit. Mon–Thurs 11am–1 or 2am, Fri–Sat 10am–2 or 3am. No cover.*

See Map 12 on p. 208.

Café Nol (p. 200) JORDAAN There's a U-shaped bar, velvet stools, and lace on the windows at this legendary brown cafe. Older crowd, and very, very few tourists. A campy blast from the past.... *Tel 020/624-5380. Westerstraat 109 at Eerste Anjeliersdwarsstraat. Trams 3 or 10 to Marnixplein. Daily 11am–2 or 3am. No cover.*

See Map 12 on p. 208.

Café Saarein II (p. 201) JORDAAN Amsterdam's most famous (and notorious) lesbian cafe now welcomes gay men.... *Tel 020/623-4901. Elandsstraat 119 at Hazenstraat. Trams 7, 10, or 17 to Elandsgracht. Daily 8pm–1am. No cover.*

See Map 12 on p. 208.

Café Thijssen (p. 205) JORDAAN This hip neobrown on the Jordaan's northern edge is best on Lindengracht market days.... *Tel 020/623-8994. Brouwersgracht 107 at Lindengracht. Trams 1, 2, 5, 6, 13, or 17 to Martelaarsgracht. Mon–Thurs 11am–1 or 2am, Fri–Sat 10am–2 or 3am. No cover.*

See Map 12 on p. 208.

Casa Rosso (p. 200) RED-LIGHT DISTRICT A bordello-like erotic theater with live sex on stage (audience participation welcome; you'd better be well hung). Brought to you by the same folks who run the Erotic Museum (see the Diversions chapter).... *Tel 020/627-8945. Oudezijds Achterburgwal 106 at Stoofsteeg. Trams 4, 9, 14, 16, 24, or 25 to the Dam. Nightly 8pm–2 or 3am. Cover.*

See Map 12 on p. 208.

Club COC (p. 201) JORDAAN Gay and lesbian cafe-club and dance venue favored by clean-cut locals. No hardcore.... *Tel 020/626-3087. www.cocamsterdam.nl. Rozenstraat 14 at Prinsengracht. Trams 6, 13, 14, or 17 to Westermarkt. Opening hours vary; Sat nights women only. No cover.*

See Map 12 on p. 208.

Cockring (p. 201) RED-LIGHT DISTRICT A hardcore gay club in the center of the leather and S&M district. Condoms available.... *Tel 020/623-9604. Warmoesstraat 96 at Wijde Kerksteeg. Trams 4, 9, 14, 16, 24, or 25 to the Dam. Daily 11pm–4 or 5am. No cover.*

See Map 12 on p. 208.

Dantzig aan de Amstel (p. 206) WATERLOOPLEIN A spacious white cafe with a river terrace, at city hall; tasty food.... *Tel 020/620-9039. Zwanenburgwal 15 at Waterlooplein. Trams 9* *or 14 to Waterlooplein. AE, DC, MC, V. Mon–Thurs 11am–1am, Fri–Sun 11am–2am. $*

See Map 12 on p. 208.

De Druif (p. 205) EASTERN DOCKS Though it claims an even earlier pedigree, Druif is the third-oldest brown, dating to 1631. Far-flung, near the Maritime Museum, and probably the friendliest, most authentic of them all.... *Tel 020/624-4530. Rapenburger-plein 83. Buses 22 or 32 to Kadijksplein. Mon–Thurs 11am–1 or 2am, Fri–Sat 10am–2 or 3am. No cover.*

See Map 13 on p. 210.

De Engelbewaarder (p. 206) CENTER A literary neobrown east of the Red-Light District—wonderfully pretentious, surprisingly seedy.... *Tel 020/625-3772. Kloveniersburgwal 59 at Raam-gracht. Metro to Nieuwmarkt. Daily 11am–2am. No cover.*

See Map 12 on p. 208.

De IJsbreker (p. 206) EAST A neobrown on the east bank of the river, formerly attached to the celebrated music club of the same name (which has decamped to the harborside Muziekgebouwge-boue aan 't IJ, just east of Centraal Station; see the Entertainment chapter). Great Amstel-side terrace.... *Tel 020/668-1805. Weesperzijde 23 at Ruyschstraat. Tram 3 to Wibautstraat. Daily 10am–1 or 2am. No cover, except for occasional legacy performances at the in-house theater.*

See Map 13 on p. 210.

De Jaren (p. 206) CENTER A postmodern, big, and sunny white cafe overlooking the Amstel near Muntplein, where beautiful young Amsterdammers lounge on the terrace.... *Tel 020/625-5771. www.cafe-de-jaren.nl. Nieuwe Doelenstraat 20–22 at Kloveniers-burgwal. Trams 4, 9, 14, 16, 24, or 25 to Muntplein. V. Sun–Thurs 10am–1am, Fri–Sat 10am–2am. $*

See Map 12 on p. 208.

De Karpershoek (p. 205) CENTER The second-oldest brown, from 1629. Prototypical, and within shouting distance of Centraal Station.... *Tel 020/624-7886. Martelaarsgracht 2 at Prins Hen-drikkade. Trams 1, 2, 5, 6, 13, or 17 to Martelaarsgracht. Mon–Thurs 11am–1 or 2am, Fri–Sat 10am–2 or 3am. No cover.*

See Map 12 on p. 208.

De Kroon (p. 206) REMBRANDTPLEIN A vast designer cafe with a great view of Rembrandtplein from its big picture windows. The media crowd hangs out here.... *Tel 020/625-2011. www.dekroon. nl. Rembrandtplein 17. Trams 4, 9, or 14 to Rembrandtplein. AE, MC, V. Sun–Thurs 10am–1am, Fri–Sat 10am–2am. $$*

See Map 12 on p. 208.

De Sluyswacht (p. 205) CENTER A 1695 brown with canal-side terraces, bordering the Jewish Quarter.... *Tel 020/625-7611. Joodenbreestraat 1 at Waterlooplein. Trams 9 or 14 to Waterlooplein. Mon–Thurs 11am–1 or 2am, Fri–Sat 10am–2 or 3am. No cover.*
See Map 12 on p. 208.

Escape (p. 202) REMBRANDTPLEIN This cavernous club is favored by hip 20-somethings in silly clothes who flutter like demented butterflies between the other self-consciously cool clubs—Sinners in Heaven and iT. The decor and sounds change with every party, though the register remains industrial-chic and house. Saturday "Chemistry" theme night is hot. Top DJs. Clubwear and attitude essential.... *Tel 020/622-1111. www.escape.nl and www.chemistry.nl. Rembrandtplein 11. Trams 4, 9, or 14 to Rembrandtplein. Wed–Sun 10pm–4 or 5am. Cover.*
See Map 12 on p. 208.

Gambit (p. 206) JORDAAN One of Amsterdam's most competitive "chess cafes".... *Tel 020/622-1801. Bloemgracht 20 at Prinsengracht. Trams 6, 13, 14, or 17 to Westermarkt. Mon–Thurs 11am–1 or 2am, Fri–Sat 10am–2 or 3am. No cover.*
See Map 12 on p. 208.

GETTO (p. 201) RED-LIGHT DISTRICT Popular gay bar-restaurant; Tuesday nights women only.... *Tel 020/421-5151. www.getto.nl. Warmoesstraat 51 at Oude Brugsteeg. Trams 4, 9, 14, 16, 24, or 25 to the Dam. Daily 7pm–1am. No cover.*
See Map 12 on p. 208.

The Grasshopper (p. 201) CENTER Clean, well lit, and on the cusp of the Red-Light District, this smoking coffee shop with a regular cafe and steakhouse on the upper floors is a tourist magnet.... *No phone. Nieuwezijds Voorburgwal 59. Trams 1, 2, 5, 6, 13, or 17 to Nieuwezijds Kolk. Mon–Thurs and Sun 8am–1am, Fri–Sat 7am–3am. No cover.*
See Map 12 on p. 208.

Havana (p. 201) CENTER Gay cafe-club and dance venue in the Reguliersdwarsstraat gay district, patronized by the same friendly 20s and 30s crowd as April, Soho, and Exit nearby.... *Tel 020/620-6788. Reguliersdwarsstraat 17–19 at Koningsplein. Trams 1, 2, or 5 to Koningsplein. Sun–Thurs 6pm–1am, Fri–Sat 6pm–2am. Cover.*
See Map 12 on p. 208.

Het Molenpad (p. 206) CANAL BELT Neobrown neighborhood cafe with clubby atmosphere, jazz tapes, and some of the best cafe food in town day and night (sandwiches, daily specials). Canalside terrace.... *Tel 020/625-9680. Prinsengracht 653 at Leidsegracht. Trams 1, 2, or 5 to Prinsengracht. Mon–Thurs 11am–1 or 2am, Fri–Sun 11am–2 or 3am. No cover.*
See Map 12 on p. 208.

Holland Casino (p. 207) LEIDSEPLEIN Amsterdam's only officially recognized casino, full of bus-tour groups and provincial Dutch.... *Tel 020/521-1111. www.hollandcasino.com. Lido complex on Singelgracht at Leidseplein. Trams 1, 2, 5, 6, 7, or 10 to Leidseplein. Daily 11am–3am (gambling at tables from 1:30pm). Admission 3.50† ($4.40); free Wed and daily 11am–1pm.*

See Map 12 on p. 208.

Hoppe (p. 205) CENTER A vintage brown, from 1670, that's a great place to people-watch.... *Tel 020/420-4420. Spui 18–20 at Singel. Trams 1, 2, or 5 to Spui. Mon–Thurs 11am–1 or 2am, Fri–Sat 10am–2 or 3am. No cover.*

See Map 12 on p. 208.

In de Waag (p. 206) CENTER Trendy eatery in a centuries-old tower.... *Tel 020/422-7772. www.indewaag.nl. Nieuwmarkt 4. Metro to Nieuwmarkt. AE, DC, MC, V. Daily 10am–midnight. $$*

See Map 12 on p. 208.

In de Wildeman (p. 205) CENTER This beer bar, down an Old Amsterdam alley, started life in 1690 as a distillery; it serves more than 200 beers. Nonsmoking room.... *Tel 020/638-2348. Kolksteeg 3 at Nieuwendijk. Trams 1, 2, 5, 6, 13, or 17 to Nieuwezijds Kolk. Mon–Thurs 11am–1 or 2am, Fri–Sat 10am–2 or 3am. No cover.*

See Map 12 on p. 208.

iT (p. 201) REMBRANDTPLEIN Huge gay club-dance place with mixed nights Thursday, Friday, and Sunday. Saturday is strictly gay. There's room for 1,100 hipsters in the black-warehouse interior. Fancy dress required.... *Tel 020/421-6924. Amstelstraat 24 at Rembrandtplein. Trams 4, 9, or 14 to Rembrandtplein. Thurs–Sun 11pm–4 or 5am. Cover.*

See Map 12 on p. 208.

Kadinsky (p. 201) CENTER Relaxed, clean smoking coffee shop with neighborhood atmosphere (thick).... *Tel 020/624-7023. Rosmarijnsteeg 9 at Spuistraat. Trams 1, 2, or 5 to Spui. Daily 10am–1am. No cover.*

See Map 12 on p. 208.

Maloe Melo (p. 203) JORDAAN Amsterdam's smoky "home of the blues".... *Tel 020/420-4592. www.maloemelo.nl. Lijnbaansgracht 163 at Elandsstraat. Trams 7, 10, or 17 to Elandsgracht. Sun–Thurs 9pm–4am, Fri–Sat 9pm–5am (music from 10:30pm). Cover.*

See Map 12 on p. 208.

Mazzo (p. 202) JORDAAN Unpretentious, large club with nondescript interior. No dress code.... *Tel 020/626-7500. Rozengracht 114 at Akoleienstraat. Trams 13, 14, or 17 to Marnixstraat. Daily 9pm–4 or 5am. Cover.*

See Map 12 on p. 208.

Melkweg (p. 200) LEIDSEPLEIN An Amsterdam institution, this multimedia cultural center offers a maze of postindustrial-hip spaces in a former dairy (see the Entertainment chapter). There's a cafe and smoking coffee shop, a bar and restaurant, an art center, a dance and movement theater, a cinema, and lots of interesting music. There's also a dance club (Thurs–Sun 11pm–5am).... *Tel 020/531-8181. www.melkweg.nl. Lijnbaansgracht 234A at Leidseplein. Trams 1, 2, 5, 6, 7, or 10 to Leidseplein. Daily 3pm–5am. Cover plus membership.*
See Map 12 on p. 208.

More (p. 201) JORDAAN Glam club favored by fashion models, TV dolls and dudes, and other beautiful, self-conscious types. Theme nights Friday and Saturday; Wednesday gay night.... *Tel 020/344-6402. www.clubmore.nl. Rozengracht 133 at Tweede Rozendwarsstraat Trams 6, 13, 14, or 17 to Marnixstraat. Thurs–Sat 11pm–5am, Sun 5pm–midnight, 1st Wed of month 11pm–4am. Cover.*
See Map 12 on p. 208.

Mulligans Irish Music Bar (p. 207) REMBRANDTPLEIN The most appealing of Amsterdam's half-dozen beery Irish bars, with live folk music, spoon playing, and the like on Friday and Saturday. Crowded, noisy, smoky, friendly.... *Tel 020/622-1330. www. mulligans.nl. Amstel 100 at Bakkersstraat. Trams 4, 9, or 14 to Rembrandtplein. Daily noon–1 or 2am. No cover.*
See Map 12 on p. 208.

Muziekgebouw aan 't IJ (p. 203) See review on p. 242.

Papeneiland (p. 205) CANAL BELT A vintage brown (1642) near Noorderkerk.... *Tel 020/624-1989. Prinsengracht 2–4 at Brouwersgracht. Trams 1, 2, 5, 6, 13, or 17 to Martelaarsgracht. Mon–Thurs 11am–1 or 2am, Fri–Sat 10am–2 or 3am. No cover.*
See Map 12 on p. 208.

Paradiso (p. 202) LEIDSEPLEIN A deconsecrated church— the stairway to heaven for new-music and rock fiends. Occasional theme club nights, with DJs.... *Tel 020/626-4521. www. paradiso.nl. Weteringschans 6–8 at Leidseplein. Trams 1, 2, 5, 6, 7, or 10 to Leidseplein. Daily usually 10pm–3am. Cover plus membership.*
See Map 12 on p. 208.

Paradox (p. 201) JORDAAN A friendly neighborhood smoking coffee shop favored by English expats.... *Tel 020/623-5639. Eerste Bloemdwarsstraat 2 at Bloemgracht. Trams 6, 13, 14, or 17 to Westermarkt. Daily 10am–8pm. No cover.*
See Map 12 on p. 208.

Ruk & Pluk (p. 200) EAST One-of-a-kind neobrown way out east of Oosterpark, with a **Cage aux Folles** carnival spirit. Crowd and decor to match.... *Tel 020/665-3248. Linnaeusstraat 48 at Oosterpark. Trams 9 or 14 to Eerste Van Swindenstraat. Mon–Thurs 11am–1 or 2am, Fri–Sat 10am–2 or 3am. No cover.*

See Map 13 on p. 210.

Schaak Café Het Hok (p. 205) LEIDSEPLEIN A brown cafe favored by soccer fans and chess players.... *Tel 020/624-3133. Lange Leidsedwarsstraat 134 at Leidsekruisstraat. Trams 1, 2, 5, 6, 7, or 10 to Leidseplein. Mon–Thurs 11am–1 or 2am, Fri–Sat 10am–2 or 3am. No cover.*

See Map 12 on p. 208.

Sinners in Heaven (p. 202) REMBRANDTPLEIN Favored by jet-setters, Ajax soccer heroes, and visiting rock stars. Top DJs and theme nights.... *Tel 020/620-1375. www.sinners.nl. Wagenstraat 3 at Rembrandtplein. Trams 4, 9, or 14 to Rembrandtplein. Wed–Sun 10pm–4 or 5am. Cover.*

See Map 12 on p. 208.

Time (p. 203) CENTER Trendy, 20s–30s crowd. Minimalist decor with lots of bashed iron. The usual mix of house music, plus Dutch drum and bass. Strictly no sportswear.... *No phone. Nieuwezijds Voorburgwal 163–165 at Jonge Roelensteeg. Trams 1, 2, or 5 to the Dam. Thurs–Sun 11pm–3 or 5am. Cover.*

See Map 12 on p. 208.

't Smalle (p. 205) JORDAAN Founded as a distillery in 1786, this popular brown is near Westerkerk.... *Tel 020/623-9617. Egelantiersgracht 12 at Prinsengracht. Trams 6, 13, 14, or 17 to Westermarkt. Mon–Thurs 11am–1 or 2am, Fri–Sat 10am–2 or 3am. No cover.*

See Map 12 on p. 208.

Vrankrijk (p. 201) CENTER Gay-straight "squatters' club" with Queer Night on Monday and Planet Pussy lesbian nights every third Sunday. Rough 'n' ready scene. Closed for remodeling at this writing but should re-open in 2006.... *Tel 020/625-3243. www.vrankrijk.org. Spuistraat 216 at Wijdesteeg. Trams 1, 2, or 5 to the Dam. Daily 10pm–4 or 5 am. Occasional cover.*

See Map 12 on p. 208.

Westergasfabriek (p. 202) WESTERN DOCKS Converted industrial site on the western edge of town, now a hip club, bar, and restaurant (there's a barbecue in the middle of the room).... *Tel 020/586-0710. www.westergasfabriek.com. Haarlemmerweg 6–10 at Westerpark. Tram 10 to Van Limburg Stirumstraat. Daily 11:30am–1 or 2am; lunch 11:30am–3pm, dinner 6–10:30pm. Cover for some events.*

See Map 12 on p. 208.

THE INDEX

NIGHTLIFE & CAFES

Whisky Café De Still (p. 207) CENTER A tiny vintage bar in old Amsterdam. Affable Henk Eggens pours hundreds of the world's oldest and rarest whiskeys.... *Tel 020/620-1349. Spuistraat 326 at Spui. Trams 1, 2, or 5 to Spui. Mon–Sat 4pm–midnight. No cover.*

See Map 12 on p. 208.

Wildschut (p. 204) MUSEUM DISTRICT A designer cafe in an Amsterdam School building near the Concertgebouw.... *Tel 020/ 676-8220. www.goodfoodgroup.nl. Roelof Hartplein 1–3 at Van Baerlestraat. Trams 3, 5, 12, or 24 to Roelof Hartstraat. MC, V. Mon–Thurs 9am–1am, Fri 9am–3am, Sat 10:30am–3am, Sun 9:30am–midnight. $–$$*

See Map 12 on p. 208.

You II (p. 201) REMBRANDTPLEIN Amsterdam's only lesbian dance club.... *Tel 020/421-0900. Amstel 178 at Wagenstraat. Trams 4, 9, or 14 to Rembrandtplein. Thurs–Sat 10pm–4am, Sun 4pm–1am. Cover.*

See Map 12 on p. 208.

THE INDEX

NIGHTLIFE & CAFES

ENTERTA

INMENT

7

Basic Stuff

Unless you speak fluent Dutch or get your kicks by sitting through performances you can hardly understand, an Amsterdam theater is not the best place to spend your entertainment euro (and it doesn't help that the overall quality of the shows and performers is a bit less than world-class). Still, it's remarkable that a city of three-quarters of a million boasts some 60 theaters and concert halls. Such stats suggest a culture vulture need never sit at home cursing the language barrier.

The best time of year for the arts in Amsterdam is June, when the innovative Holland Festival (which runs simultaneously in Rotterdam, The Hague, and Utrecht) brings an abundance of international theater (in various languages, including English), dance, opera, and music to the city's stages. The Amsterdam Arts Adventure, running from late May through August, offers music and dance performances aimed primarily at tourists (no theater, no language probs). It, too, occupies a variety of venues. Music is, of course, a good bet year-round since it speaks all languages, but summer is a particularly musical time in the city's ancient but restless churches, whose frequent concerts make regular use of Amsterdam's 42 historical organs. Movies are a good choice, too, since most are in English; many, in fact, are American- or British-made.

Info Sources & Tickets

Amsterdam keeps no secrets about arts events from the uninitiated: There are posters up all over town all the time; fliers in bars, cafes, and restaurants; and a general sharing of knowledge that you don't necessarily find in other cities. Just walk into a bar, a cafe, or a club and ask whoever's on hand what's going on. Both the city tourist office, **VVV** Amsterdam (offices at Platform 2 inside Centraal Station and Stationsplein 10 in front of Centraal Station; and Leidseplein 1; Tel 0900/400-4040; 9am–5pm weekdays; .40€/50¢ per min.; see the Hotlines & Other Basics chapter, p. 253, for open hours), and the government-sponsored **AUB Uitburo** (Leidseplein 26; Tel 0900/0191; www.uitlijn.nl; daily 9am–9pm; .40€/50¢ per min.) give info by telephone or on the spot, and sell tickets to just about everything going on in town (advance telephone/Internet reservations cost 3€/$3.75 per ticket; 2€/$2.50 at the Uitburo ticket window).

Getting tickets in Amsterdam is a straightforward, democratic affair: Either they're available or they're not. Ticket scalping is practically unknown, so don't count on last-minute purchases on the steps of a concert hall. The best thing to do is to get hold of entertainment listings and make reservations before leaving the United States. You can do this by contacting either the VVV or the Uitburo.

The June **Holland Festival** (Tel 020/788-2100; www.holland festival.nl; see p. 222) publishes its own free newsletter in Dutch and English. Buy festival tickets through the Uitburo, VVV, National Reservations Center (Tel 0299/689-144), or at the venues where performances are held. Various season-ticket packages for the festival are sold and should be ordered before mid-April, preferably by mail, through the Uitburo or the NRC.

Three English-language magazines are good sources for entertainment listings: Amsterdam *Day by Day,* a strait-laced monthly tourism and entertainment magazine from the VVV; *Shark,* a fringe free-sheet; and *Gay & Night Magazine,* written by and for gay hipsters. For movie listings, buy a Dutch daily or pick up one of the leaflets or free movie magazines from the movie theaters themselves.

Though Amsterdam is an expensive city, ticket prices are reasonable compared to other European capitals. For example, Holland Festival tickets run about 12€ to 25€ ($15–$31) per event (or about 10€–15€/$13–$19 if you buy a season-ticket package). Movie prices average 10€ ($13), while rock concerts will set you back anywhere from 6€ ($7.50) for unknowns to 50€ ($63) and above for top names. Jazz and classical concerts average about 15€ ($19) at most venues, but can top 60€ ($75) at places like the Concertgebouw. For info on jazz, call Tel 020/770-0660 or visit www.jazz-in-amsterdam.nl (also see the Nightlife chapter). Opera tickets, at 15€ to 60€ ($19–$75) for most seats, are considerably cheaper than in London or Paris for performances of comparable quality (but you can pay up to around 150€/$188, for some seats).

The Lowdown

Classical sounds... Classical-music lovers will be in Beethoven's seventh heaven in Amsterdam, where concerts are abundant, relatively cheap, and of world-class quality. Musicians perform all over town—in parks, churches, clubs, concert halls, piano factories, etc.—and audiences are enthusiastic and savvy. Contemporary classical is a particular specialty, the Dutch being among Europe's greatest fans of new and challenging musical creations in the classical domain. The excellent **Koninklijk Concertgebouworkest (Royal Concertgebouw Orchestra;** www.concertge bouworkest.nl), currently under the baton of Latvian-born principal conductor Mariss Jansons, a former music director at the Pittsburgh Symphony Orchestra, plays at the **Concertgebouw,** an 1888 neoclassical hall just off of Museumplein, with acoustics so perfect you can hear every atonal instant of the contemporary pieces added to the repertoire. Guest performances by the world's best—from the Berlin and Vienna Philharmonic orchestras, to the Borodin Quartet or Frans Brüggen's Orchestra of the 18th Century—make this among Europe's most vibrant concert venues. Former principal conductor and current conductor emeritus Riccardo Chailly's taste for contemporary composers (Nono, Berio) was a breath of fresh air after the departure of his Brahms-obsessed predecessor, Bernard Haitink, but the ensemble has a vast range, and Bruckner and Mahler remain its fortes.

The **Nederlands Philharmonisch Orkest (Netherlands Philharmonic Orchestra)** and its spinoff **Nederlands Kamerorkest (Netherlands Chamber Orchestra),** potentially first-rate ensembles that had been handicapped by administrative struggles and constant shifts from one base to another, now have a permanent home in the **Beurs van Berlage,** Amsterdam's former stock exchange. This Dutch Art Nouveau landmark, just a few hundred yards up Damrak from Centraal Station, was successfully remodeled to improve acoustics. Though used almost exclusively for dance and opera, the **Muziektheater,** the artsy half of Amsterdam's 1980s city hall/opera complex, hosts free lunchtime chamber music concerts by the Netherlands Philharmonic, the Netherlands Ballet Orchestra, or the choir of the Netherlands Opera. Bach is the mainstay at the **Bachzaal,** part of the New South's Sweelinck Conservatorium, where accomplished students and professionals stage chamber music performances. At **Felix Meritis,** a 220-year-old theater on Keizersgracht, you can listen to a variety of classical and baroque music (and attend musico-cultural seminars and conferences). **Cristofori,** a vast piano showroom and restoration workshop with a fifth-floor concert hall, puts on classical and contemporary classical performances by an international mix of top-flight and fledgling musicians.

Music for the masses... Churches are particularly active venues for classical music. The **Waalse Kerk,** a rather unspectacular French Huguenot church in the Red-Light District, is now a vibrant venue for organ concerts (on a celebrated rococo Christian Müller organ) and baroque music, sometimes performed by top local and international talents. One of the most spectacular organs in town is at the **Nieuwe Kerk,** the 600-year-old Gothic "New Church" on the Dam. Architect Jacob van Campen designed the instrument in the mid 1600s, and it is played regularly by highly regarded resident organist Gustav Leonhardt as well as by visiting performers. The landmark **Westerkerk** has a gorgeous 1686 organ with scenes of David dancing before the Ark painted on its shutters, but its more modest choir organ is usually used for Bach cantatas and other performances. The city's only Golden Age wooden church, the **Amstelkerk,** overlooking Reguliersgracht and Prinsengracht canals, hosts chamber music, songs from the Middle Ages, and recitals, while the oldest church in town, the **Oude Kerk (Old Church),** in the middle of the Red-Light District, is another splendid setting for organ and classical music. Corelli, Bach, Handel, and Purcell are played regularly by local and visiting ensembles at the gorgeous and acoustically stunning 1392 **De Engelse Kerk (English Reformed Church)** in the Begijnhof, where in the summer months free lunchtime concerts are added to the musical calendar. (See the Diversions chapter for more about Nieuwe Kerk, Westerkerk, Oude Kerk, and De Engelse Kerk.)

Modern sounds... Wear black and don't shave when you visit the **Muziekgebouw aan 't IJ** (Piet Heinkade 1, Tel 020/788-2000; www.muziekgebouw.nl), a spectacular piece of modern architecture on the IJ waterfront just east of Centraal Station. Opened in 2005, this is the new home of the former Muziekcentrum De IJsbreker foundation for avant-garde and experimental music. From post-fusion jazz to concertos for pianoforte and tape to electrified 12-tone Schoenberg, this is 20th-and 21st-century, angular stuff. Some of it is outstanding, while much is strictly for initiates. You can also look for concerts of modern, jazz, electronic, and non-Western music, along with small-scale musical theater, opera, and dance. Tickets are 10€ to 40€ ($13–$50). Even if you don't pop for tickets, hang out in the cafe or on the terrace overlooking the IJ waterway and be entertained by the self-consciously arty regulars. **Cristofori,** a big piano repair and sales operation, offers contemporary music (and jazz) at its fascinating workshop-concert hall on Prinsengracht. Performers include Wong Wing Tsan, Niek von Dosterum, and Deborah Carter. One of the myriad activities at **Melkweg**—a groundbreaking, 28-year-old multimedia cultural center, theater, club, and art gallery just off Leidseplein (see "On the fringe," below)—is musical performance—everything from world music to indefinable contemporary works by local bands to classic or experimental jazz.

Paradiso, a deconsecrated church off Leidseplein, keeps you guessing with its eclectic lineup. Part dance club and major rock venue, it also books jazz, occasional classical music performances, and learned music conferences. **Westergasfabriek,** a converted gas plant in a former industrial complex in northwestern Amsterdam, is similarly eclectic, filling its music calendar with experimental jazz, pop, rock, and DJs. The cheapest, airiest concert venue of all is Vondelpark, a lovely 19th-century park where musicians of all kinds—from modern minstrels to execrable bongo players and tone-deaf guitarists—perform daily in summer among the greenery, especially at or around the domed Koepel music stand in the center of the park, about 137m (449.37 ft.) from the entrance on Van Eeghenstraat. When big crowds are anticipated for rock stars, teen idols, and so on, the **ArenA** soccer stadium in the southern suburbs is the top mega-venue.

All that jazz... Bimhuis, Amsterdam's prime jazz club for the last 30 years, once housed in a landmark old building, has upped the stakes and decamped to the new Muziekgebouw aan 't IJ at the harbor. The new arty, futuristic setting might not sit well with the alternative jazz scene, but American and international big names come here to play.

Kitsch concertos... The fantastically ornate **Tuschinski Theater,** a 1921 Art Deco cinema near Rembrandtplein that books mostly mainstream first-run features, spends many of its Saturday mornings mounting tributes to the cinema's glorious past. Typically, a great silent film from the 1920s fills the screen while an organist cranks up the old Wurlitzer to evoke the proper mood. Restored top to bottom in 2001 and 2002, the setting is Saturday-matinee opulence: marble panels, tiled floors, velvet seats, and lots of freshly polished brass and bronze. You can even reserve a special loge and sip champagne. Similar musical fare is served Sunday afternoons in the Jordaan at the Pianola Museum (p. 139), the coziest museum in town, where player-piano lovers congregate in a front-room brown cafe to listen to any of the 35 old pianolas.

Theater you can understand, sort of... At Badhuis Theater de Bochel, a former bathhouse near the Ooster-park, an evening can be exhilarating or baffling when experimental works are performed. A variety of languages are used—sometimes in the same performance—so unless you're polyglot, stick to the visiting American and British companies (though the quality of productions varies widely). Multiethnicity is the byword at the aptly named **Cosmic Theater** smack in the heart of Old Amsterdam, where some of the Third World companies (theater groups from developing world countries) perform in English. Visiting mainstream and experimental American or British theater troupes—some known, others up and coming—sometimes perform at **Westergasfabriek.** The setting is industrial-chic: a converted former electrical plant on the western edge of town. Most of these productions are not in English.

What's opera, doc?... The choice is simple: the **Muziek-theater,** a fascinatingly hideous complex built in 1986 and nicknamed "Stopera" (rhymes with "opera") when activists tried unsuccessfully to stop its construction, and that of the neighboring city hall, or Stadhuis. They combined the two in a brilliant slogan, "Stop the Stopera." The campaign's activists ultimately ran into clouds of CS gas and forests of vigorously wielded riot-police night sticks and retired from the field in defeat. Locals may rue the way the venue looks, but the **Netherlands Opera** company, reinvigorated by artistic director Pierre Audi, is winning kudos for every-thing from Monteverdi to world premieres by unknown

Dutch talents. The tickets are unusually cheap, considering the quality. Check Amsterdam *Day by Day* for visiting opera companies performing in a variety of Amsterdam venues.

Men in tights... The **Muziektheater** is also the city's top dance venue, home to the **Netherlands National Ballet** and its ballet orchestra and choir. This company is rated among Europe's best and has helped enhance the Muziektheater's status, making an unpopular building a success. Celebrated for performances of works by Balanchine, it also has a strong reputation in contemporary Dutch ballet (especially creations by choreographer Hans van Manen), as well as in classic crowd pleasers. The top international dance companies perform here, too, and the stage is vast. **Bellevue Theater,** a large theater near Leidseplein with three halls, features dance performances by up-and-coming local companies, with a slant toward minimalist modern works. Amsterdam's municipal theater, the **Stadsschouwburg,** has been opening its Leidseplein stage to cutting-edge Dutch contemporary dance. The setting is stunning: a gorgeous horseshoe-shaped auditorium with gilt colonnades, red velvet, and dozens of chandeliers. Another handsome late-1800s theater, the **Carré Theater,** on the Amstel River just south of the Magere Brug, is primarily for cabaret and musicals (in Dutch), but big-name dance companies (Pina Bausch, for example) and occasional folk-dancing groups make it a viable hall for non–Dutch speakers.

Fans of multicultural dance—African, Asian, South American, and combinations thereof—should head for one of two venues. At the **Cosmic Theater,** the multiethnic dance and movement program can be fascinating. Similar performances can be found at the beautiful **Tropeninstituut** and **Soeterijn**—two halls inside the Tropenmuseum (Tropical Museum) near Oosterpark. Amateurs and accomplished modern dancers perform their sometimes-inspired, sometimes-embarrassing creations at the **Dans Werkplaats Amsterdam (Amsterdam Dance Workshop),** just north of Vondelpark. More of the same goes on at **Veemtheater,** in a warehouse beyond Westerdok. It's great if you're keen on experimental dance, body movement, and mime theater, but the uninitiated will feel lost. Captivating contemporary dance performances are among the many things going on at **Melkweg,** a pioneering multimedia cultural center (see "On the fringe," below).

On the fringe... By their nature, fringe theater, music, dance, and combinations thereof pose a challenge in any language, so you may enjoy them even more in indecipherable Dutch (actually, some performances are at least partially in English). Forty years ago, **Melkweg** (its name, which means Milky Way, derives from its location in a former dairy) was the wildest, most cosmic club/theater/art gallery in Amsterdam. Over the decades it has grown ideologically away from flower power toward a savvy hipness, becoming part of an international network of multimedia cultural centers, and it has spilled into a series of separate spaces—a regular café and smoking coffee shop (where hash-laced goodies are sometimes available), a bar and restaurant, an art center, a dance and movement theater, a cinema, a music venue, and a dance club (p. 217). The scene is mixed: punks, artists, businesspeople, and the occasional lost socialite. And though it has moved steadily into the mainstream, Melkweg can still shock with lunatic dance, music, and performance art. **OCCII,** which in pregentrification days was one of many abandoned buildings near Vondelpark that had been seized by squatters, is now a bar, club, and performance venue where locals hash out electrified sounds and fling themselves into crazy cabaret or stand-up comedy acts. **Badhuis Theater de Bochel,** set in a reconverted bathhouse near Oosterpark, offers wild experimental theater, dance, and music that might leave you feeling wrung out. Out on the western edge of town, the former gas plant **Westergasfabriek** favors experimental theater that's hip but tame. Read *Shark* for the current, ever-changing roster of theaters and clubs on the fringe.

Life is a cabaret... The **Boom Chicago Theater,** an American improv troupe, landed in Amsterdam about 20 years ago, and contrary to everybody's expectations (and I mean *everybody*), it has not only survived but thrived by making fun of Dutch customs and language, and generally appealing to youngish tourists from America and Britain. They have a permanent venue, Leidseplein Theater, and even publish their own quarterly, *Boom!,* which they claim is written by "outsider insiders." Hmmm. We've all seen their brand of entertainment before: determinedly wild and wacky guys and gals riffing, rather tamely, off reactions of a mostly embarrassed and bemused audience (do they ever get repeat visitors?). The food (veggie sandwiches, Sunday brunch specials) will transport you right home. It's usually kind of fun and the food's quite good, but neither aspect is to die for, though some years back *Time* magazine compared it to Chicago's famous Second City comedy troupe. The competition, **Comedy Café Amsterdam,** hails and hah-hah-hahs from a modern shopping mall behind the Holland Casino. The standup- and improv-meisters here are American, British, or Dutch. It's a mixed bag of chuckles, guffaws, and groans, washed down by suds (and, if you're daring, accompanied by delicacies such as meat pastries or turkey tournedos swimming in mustard-dill sauce).

The sporting life... In Amsterdam, **Ajax** is neither a scrubbing powder nor a Trojan war hero: It's the name of the local *voetball* (soccer) club, which thrilled fans in 1995 by winning the European championship. A dominant European force in the early 1970s, the franchise slumped for about a decade before rejoining the game's elite in the late 1980s. Their 1995 title inspired fans to go on a rampage, breaking windows, looting, and attacking bystanders around Leidseplein, behavior that might send any team into a decade-long slump, maybe even intentionally. Indeed, Amsterdammers as a whole are enthusiastic boosters, and tend to go berserk—dancing in the streets, drinking even more than usual, and making lots of noise—whenever their local heroes win (be careful if you find yourself in the middle of one of these "celebrations"; Dutch riot police aren't picky about deciding which heads to break open). And win they sometimes still do—Ajax is among Europe's most unpredictable teams. The team has settled into its 51,000-seat, high-tech **ArenA** stadium, in the southwest suburbs, and regularly draws capacity-plus crowds. The stadium—now a tourist and soccer fan mecca—is like a minicity and shopping center. It features about 50 food stands (mostly burgers and pizza), the Soccer World restaurant (there's a giant soccer-ball pattern on the floor and a bank of TV monitors), a gift and souvenir boutique, and two giant video screens in the mall-like inner halls (so you won't miss a second of the action, even if you are on your way to the can). To pay for your fun, use cash or a credit card to buy an ArenA Card (you don't pay with cash at the stadium but must first buy an ArenA card, for 10€ ($13) or 20€ ($25), and use this to make purchases). The Amsterdam **RAI** still exists as a large conference and sporting hall about 2 miles south of central Amsterdam, though the ArenA has largely overshadowed its events.

Amsterdam also boasts professional teams in second-rate knockoffs of a few favorite American pastimes. The Amsterdam **Admirals** challenged for the 1995 championship title in the World League of American Football and have continued to perform admirably since. They have joined Ajax at the new Amsterdam ArenA. Nonetheless, the sport just doesn't seem to be catching on, golly gosh. Likewise, only a few thousand ticket buyers—mostly American expats and curious young locals—litter the stands any weekend from May to September when Amsterdam **Pirates,** among the top baseball teams in the Netherlands, take the field at Sportpark Jan van Galen in Bos en Lommer, out in the city's western boonies. Amsterdam's basketball team, the **Demon Astronauts,** also boasts of being among the best in the Netherlands. You can imagine what the competition's like. Their squad of American and European pros plays Saturday evenings, from September to April, at the Apollohal in the New South neighborhood, south of Vondelpark.

Map 14: Amsterdam Entertainment Orientation

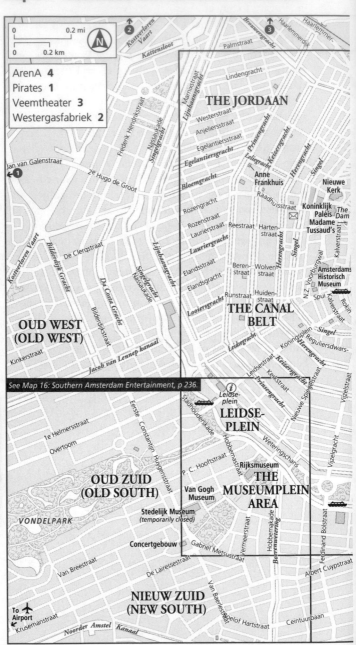

0	0.2 mi
0	0.2 km

ArenA **4**
Pirates **1**
Veemtheater **3**
Westergasfabriek **2**

THE JORDAAN

Marnixstraat
Lijnbaansgracht
Lindengracht
Westerstraat
Anjeliersstraat
Egelantiersstraat
Egelantiersgracht
Bloemgracht
Leliegracht
Prinsengracht
Keizersgracht
Herengracht
Singel

Brouwersgracht

Haarlemmer-
Haarlemmerdijk
Palmstraat

Kostverloren Vaart
Kattensloot
Kattensloot

Jan van Galenstraat
2e Hugo de Groot
Frederik Hendrikstraat
Nassaukade
Singelgracht

De Clercqstraat
Bilderdijkgracht
Kostverloren Vaart
Da Costa Gracht
Bilderdijkstraat
Singelgracht
Nassaukade
Lijnbaansgracht

Anne
Frankhuis
Raadhuisstraat
Rozengracht
Rozenstraat
Laurierstraat Reestraat
Laboratorium
Laurierstraat
Elandsstraat
Elandsgracht
Looiersgracht
Runstraat

Nieuwe
Kerk

Koninklijk
Paleis
Madame
Tussaud's

The
Dam

Kalverstraat

Berenstraat Wolven-
straat
Beren-
straat
Hartenstraat
Huiden-
straat

N.Z. Voorburgwal
Kalverstraat
Rokin

Amsterdams
Historisch
Museum

Spui

THE CANAL
BELT

Leidsegracht
Leidsestraat
Koningsplein
Singel
Herengracht
Keizersgracht
Prinsengracht
Nieuwe Spiegelstraat
Kerkstraat
Weteringschans
Regulersdwars-
straat

Vijzelgracht
Vijzelstraat

OUD WEST
(OLD WEST)

Kinkerstraat
Jacob van Lennep kanaal

See Map 16: Southern Amsterdam Entertainment, p 236.

LEIDSE-
PLEIN

Leidse-
plein

Stadhouderskade
Eerste Constantijn Huygensstraat

OUD ZUID
(OLD SOUTH)

1e Helmersstraat
Overtoom

P. C. Hooftstraat
Hobbemastraat

Rijksmuseum

THE
MUSEUMPLEIN
AREA

Van Gogh
Museum

Stedelijk Museum
(temporarily closed)

Concertgebouw

Gabriel Metsustraat
Vermeerstraat
Hobbemakade
Boerenwetering

Ferdinand Bolstraat

VONDELPARK

Van Breestraat
De Lairessestraat

Albert Cuypstraat

NIEUW ZUID
(NEW SOUTH)

To ✈
Airport
Krusemanstraat

Van Baerlestraat
Roelof Hartstraat
Ceintuurbaan

Noorder Amstel Kanaal

ENTERTAINMENT

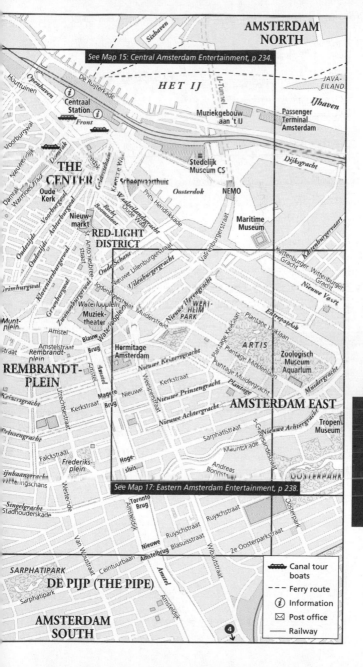

AMSTERDAM
NORTH

See Map 15: Central Amsterdam Entertainment, p 234.

HET IJ

JAVA-
EILAND

IJhaven

Centraal
Station

Muziekgebouw
aan 't IJ

Passenger
Terminal
Amsterdam

Dijksgracht

THE
CENTER

Oude
Kerk

Stedelijk
Museum CS

Oosterdok

NEMO

Scheepvaarthuis

Nieuw-
markt

RED-LIGHT
DISTRICT

Maritime
Museum

WERT-
HEIM
PARK

ARTIS

Zoologisch
Museum
Aquarlum

Munt-
plein

Muziek-
theater

Hermitage
Amsterdam

REMBRANDT-
PLEIN

AMSTERDAM EAST

Tropen
Museum

OOSTERPARK

See Map 17: Eastern Amsterdam Entertainment, p 238.

SARPHATIPARK

DE PIJP (THE PIPE)

AMSTERDAM
SOUTH

ENTERTAINMENT

Canal tour
boats

Ferry route

Information

Post office

Railway

234

Map 15: Central Amsterdam Entertainment

ENTERTAINMENT

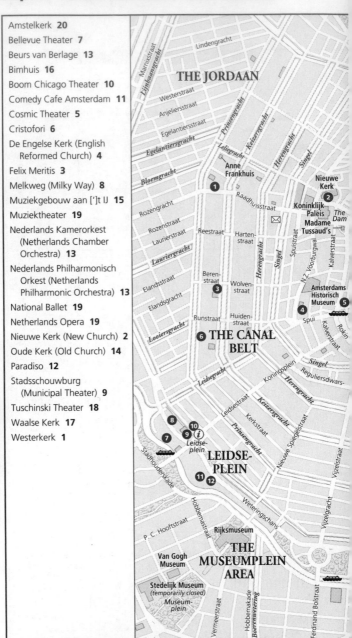

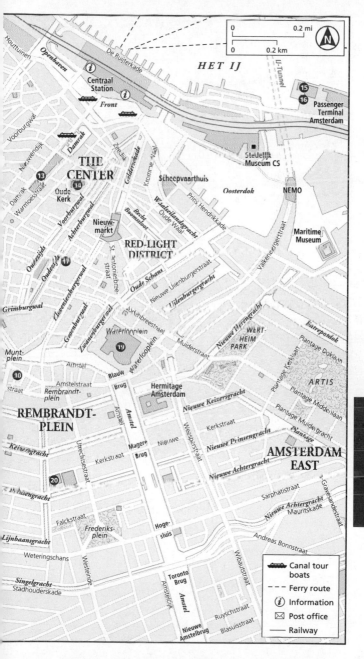

Map 16: Southern Amsterdam Entertainment

Bachzaal **4**

Concertgebouw **3**

Dans Werkplaats
  Amsterdam **2**

Demon Astronauts
  Amsterdam
  (aka Amsterdam) **5**

Koninklijk
  Concertgebouworkest
  (Royal Concertgebouw
  Orchestra) **3**

OCCII **1**

RAI **6**

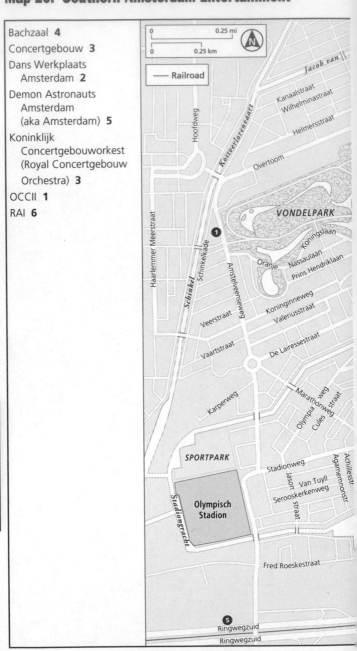

ENTERTAINMENT

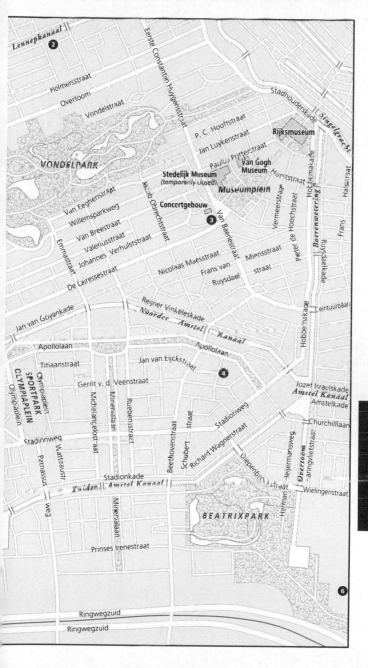

Lennepkanaal ②

Holmersstraat

Overtoom

Vondelstraat

Eerste Constantijn Huygensstraat

Stadhouderskade

Singelgracht

P. C. Hooftstraat

Jan Luykenstraat

Paulus Potterstraat

Rijksmuseum

VONDELPARK

Stedelijk Museum
(temporarily closed)

Van Gogh Museum

Horststraat

Hobbemakade

Hallstraat

Museumplein

Van Eeghenstraat

Willemsparkweg

Concertgebouw

③

Van Baerlestraat

Vermeerstraat

Pieter de Hoochstraat

Barentwetering

Frans

Van Breestraat

Valeriusstraat

Johannes Verhulststraat

Emmastraat

De Lairessestraat

Nicolaas Maesstraat

Frans van

Mierisstraat

straat

Rijsdaelkade

Ruysdael

Hobbemakade

Ceintuurbaan

Jan van Goyenkade

Reijner Vinkeleskade

Noorder — Amstel — Kanaal

Apollolaan

Apollolaan

Titiaanstraat

Jan van Eijckstraat

④

Jozef Israelskade

SPORTPARK OLYMPIAPLEIN

Olympiaplein

Olympiaplein

Gerrit v. d. Veenstraat

Michelangelostraat

Minervalaan

Rubensstraat

Beethovenstraat

Schubertstraat

straat

Stadionweg

Richard Wagnerstraat

Amstel Kanaal

Amstelkade

Churchilllaan

Stadinnweg

Wattstraat

Pernassus

weg

Stadionkade

Minervalaan

Zuider Amstel Kanaal

Diepenbrockstraat

Overtoom

Teijermansweg

aringvlietstraat

Wielingenstraat

BEATRIXPARK

Herman

Prinses Irenestraat

⑥

Ringwegzuid

Ringwegzuid

Map 17: Eastern Amsterdam Entertainment

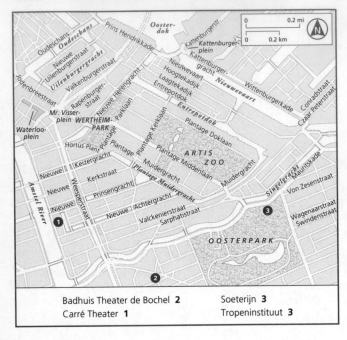

Badhuis Theater de Bochel **2**   Soeterijn **3**
Carré Theater **1**   Tropeninstituut **3**

The Index

Admirals (p. 231) SOUTHEAST The city's American-style football team plays home games on Saturdays April through June. They now play at the ArenA stadium complex.... *Tel 020/465 4545; ArenA Boulevard 73-76. See listing for ArenA below for directions. Tickets 22€-50€ ($28-$63).*

See Map 14 on p. 232.

Ajax (p. 230) SOUTHEAST Amsterdam's much-loved soccer team, winners of the 1995 European Cup and fully expected by optimistic locals to win again. They're at ArenA too... *Tel 020/311-1444. www.ajax.nl. See listing for ArenA below for directions. Tickets 22€-47€ ($25-$54).*

See Map 14 on p. 232.

Amstelkerk (p. 225) CANAL BELT This Golden Age church overlooking Reguliersgracht and Prinsengracht canals hosts classical music, recitals, songs from the Middle Ages, and chamber music.... *Tel 020/520-0070. Amstelveld 10 at Prinsengracht. Tram 4 to Prinsengracht. Tickets 10€-17€ ($13-$21).*

See Map 15 on p. 234.

ArenA (p. 226) SOUTHEAST A high-tech stadium with a sliding roof. Ajax and the Admirals play here. There are also major rock performances held here.... *Tel 020/311-1444. www.amsterdamarena.nl. ArenA Boulevard 1 at Amsterdam Zuidoost. Metro trains 50 or 54 to Strandvliet/ArenA or Bijlmer. Stadium complex open daily from 9am–6pm (hours vary on soccer or football match days and during rock concert performances). Ticket prices vary.*

See Map 14 on p. 232.

Bachzaal (p. 224) NEW SOUTH Part of the Sweelinck Conservatorium, this hall hosts regular chamber-music performances by students and professionals. The quality varies widely. Cheap.... *Tel 020/673-0303. Bachstraat 7 at Apollolaan. Trams 5 or 24 to Gerrit van der Veenstraat. Ticket prices vary.*

See Map 18 on p. 236.

Badhuis Theater de Bochel (p. 227) EAST Visiting companies, sometimes American or British, put on a variety of professional and amateur acts at this former bathhouse, but many productions are in Dutch.... *Tel 020/668-5102. Andreas Bonnstraat 28 at Mauritskade. Tram 3 to Camperstraat. Ticket prices vary.*

See Map 17 on p. 238.

Bellevue Theater (p. 228) LEIDSEPLEIN There are three halls in this theater, where the dance tends to be minimalist. You need to learn Dutch to appreciate most of its cabaret artists and theater companies.... *Tel 020/530-5301. Leidsekade 90 at Leidseplein. Trams 1, 2, 5, 6, 7, or 10 to Leidseplein. Ticket prices vary.*

See Map 15 on p. 234.

Beurs van Berlage (p. 224) CENTER The former stock exchange, this Dutch Art Nouveau landmark by Hendrik Petrus Berlage is now a concert venue, the permanent home of the Nederlands Philharmonisch Orkest and its offshoot, the Nederlands Kamerorkest.... *Tel 020/521-7520. www.berlage.com. Beursplein 1. Trams 4, 9, 14, 16, 24, or 25 to the Dam. Ticket prices vary.*

See Map 15 on p. 234.

Bimhuis (p. 226) CENTRUM Since 2005, a shiny metal box with windows that's an extension of the new Muziekgebouw aan 't IJ (see below), on the waterfront east of Centraal Station, has been home to the city's premier jazz, blues, and improv club.... *Tel 020/788-2188. www.bimhuis.nl. Piet Heinkade 3 on the IJ waterfront east of Centraal Station. Tickets 10€–25€ ($13–$31). Tram 26 to Muziekgebouw.*

See Map 15 on p. 234.

Boom Chicago Theater (p. 229) LEIDSEPLEIN This unsinkable American cabaret and improvisational theater company lives by a familiar formula: The audience dines, snacks, and drinks at candlelit tables while the fun-loving troupe plays for laughs in ever-changing yet predictable acts.... *Tel 020/423-0101. www. boomchicago.nl. Leidseplein Theater, Leidseplein 12. Trams 1, 2, 5, 6, 7, or 10 to Leidseplein. Tickets 6€–21€ ($7.50–$26).*

See Map 15 on p. 234.

Carré Theater (p. 228) EAST This 1887 wedding cake of a theater, long used as a circus venue, now hosts ribald Dutch cabaret and Dutch-language versions of British and American musicals. More comprehensible for English-only speakers are the big-name dance performances and the occasional high-spirited folk-dancing group.... *Tel 0900/252-5255. www.theatercarre.nl. Amstel 115–125 at Nieuwe Prinsengracht. Trams 6, 7, or 10 and Metro to Weesperplein. Ticket prices vary.*

See Map 17 on p. 238.

Comedy Café Amsterdam (p. 230) LEIDSEPLEIN Stand-up and improv routines by an international grab bag of funmeisters.... *Tel 020/638-3971. www.comedycafe.nl. Max Euweplein 43–45 at*

Leidseplein. Trams 1, 2, 5, 6, 7, or 10 to Leidseplein. Free admission.

See Map 15 on p. 234.

Concertgebouw (p. 224) MUSEUM DISTRICT This acoustically impeccable 1888 venue is the permanent home of the rejuvenated Koninklijk Concertgebouworkest. Visiting performers include the world's best, and their work ranges as far off the beaten path as obscure saxophone concertos. Monthly schedule in English. Guided tours Sunday mornings at 9:30 (4€/$5), in obligatory conjunction with a concert (13€/$16) at 11am. Reserve ahead because the tours are often fully booked.... *Tel 020/671-8345. www.concertgebouw.nl. Concertgebouwplein 2-6 at Museum District. Trams 2, 3, 5, or 12 to Van Baerlestraat; 16 to Museum District. Ticket prices vary.*

See Map 16 on p. 236.

Cosmic Theater (p. 227) CENTER Multiethnicity and multiculturalism are the grist for this multimedia mill, which offers avant-garde dance, theater, and combinations of same, mostly in Dutch, occasionally in English.... *Tel 020/626-6866. Nes 75 at Lange Brugsteeg. Trams 4, 9, 14, 16, 24, or 25 to Spui. Ticket prices vary.*

See Map 15 on p. 234.

Cristofori (p. 224) CANAL BELT Piano repair and sales outfit with a surprising fifth-floor concert hall (classical, contemporary, and jazz).... *Tel 020/626-8485. www.cristofori.nl. Prinsengracht 581–583 at Leidsegracht. Trams 1, 2, or 5 to Prinsengracht. Ticket prices vary.*

See Map 15 on p. 234.

Dans Werkplaats Amsterdam (p. 228) WEST A dance workshop where local performers do their robotic, serpentine, contortionistic thing, while sympathetic aficionados look politely on.... *Tel 020/689-1789. Arie Biemondstraat 107B at Nicolas Beetsraat. Trams 1, 7, or 17 to Jan Pieter Heijestraat. Ticket prices vary.*

See Map 16 on p. 236.

De Engelse Kerk (English Reformed Church) (p. 225) CENTER This handsome little 1392 church in the Begijnhof offers up to four classical concerts a week, performed by accomplished Dutch and foreign ensembles. The setting is beautiful and relaxed, the acoustics are good, and the ticket prices reasonable.... *Tel 020/624-9665. Begijnhof 48 at Spui. Trams 1, 2, 4, 5, 9, 14, 16, 24, or 25 to Spui. Ticket prices vary.*

See Map 15 on p. 234.

THE INDEX

ENTERTAINMENT

Demon Astronauts Amsterdam (p. 231) NEW SOUTH The city's basketball club, tops in the Netherlands, plays Saturday evenings from Sept to April.... *Tel 020/671-3910. Sporthallen Zuid, Burgerweeshuispad 54 at Amstelveenseweg. Trams 16 or 24 to Olympisch Stadion. Tickets 5€–15€ ($6.25–$19).*

See Map 16 on p. 236.

Felix Meritis (p. 224) CANAL BELT Classical music, seminars, and conferences have revived the fortunes of this 1780s neoclassical theater long celebrated for its acoustics and unusual architecture.... *Tel 020/626-2321. www.felix.meritis.nl. Keizersgracht 324 at Berenstraat. Trams 1, 2, or 5 to Spui. Ticket prices vary.*

See Map 15 on p. 234.

Koninklijk Concertgebouworkest (Royal Concertgebouw Orchestra) (p. 224) MUSEUM DISTRICT This top-notch orchestra, which excels at Bruckner and Mahler, has recently added contemporary atonal work to its broad repertoire. Find it at the Concertgebouw, the 1888 hall that lends the ensemble its name.... *Tel 020/671-8345. www.concertgebouw.nl. Concertgebouwplein 2–6 at Museum District. Trams 2, 3, 5, or 12 to Van Baerlestraat; 16 to Museum District. Ticket prices vary. See listing for Concertgebouw.*

See Map 16 on p. 236.

Melkweg (Milky Way) (p. 226) LEIDSEPLEIN A perpetually hip multimedia cultural center, which first opened its doors in 1970, with a smoking coffee shop, a bar and restaurant, an art center, a dance and movement theater, a cinema, a music venue, and a dance club.... *Tel 020/531-8181. www.melkweg.nl. Lijnbaansgracht 234A. Trams 1, 2, 5, 6, 7, or 10 to Leidseplein. Cover 5€–12€ ($6.25–$15); special events can cost up to 30€ ($36); plus 3€ ($3.75) monthly club membership.*

See Map 15 on p. 234.

Muziekgebouw aan 't IJ (p. 225) CENTER Opened in 2005 in a spectacular piece of modern architecture on the IJ waterfront, this is the new home of the former Muziekcentrum De IJsbreker, a grungy foundation for avant-garde and experimental music. This ocean of glass is far from grungy. The main hall seats around 750 and a smaller foyer hall 125, and you can look for concerts of modern, old, jazz, electronic, and non-Western music, along with small-scale musical theater, opera, and dance. A kind of next-door annex to the Muzeiekgebouw is the equally new home of the Bimhuis jazz and improvised music club. It's a powerful indicator of how Amsterdam is changing that these two "alternative" music operations should now be housed in such a futuristic setting. A visit to the concert hall's in-house cafe-restaurant, and in fine weather a seat outside on its waterfront terrace, would alone justify the short walk or tram ride here from the Center.... *Tel 020/788-2000. www.muziekgebouw.nl. Piet*

*Heinkade 1 on the IJ waterfront, just east of Centraal Station.
Tram 26 to Muziekgebouw. Tickets 10€ to 40€ ($13–$50).*

See Map 15 on p. 234.

Muziektheater (p. 227) WATERLOOPLEIN Multipurpose dance theater and opera house, home to the Netherlands National Ballet
and Orchestra and Pierre Audi's highly acclaimed Netherlands
Opera company. This is where top international dance and opera
companies perform. Each week, for most of the year, it also
hosts free lunchtime chamber music concerts (Boekmanzaal,
Tues 12:30pm, Oct–June).... *Tel 020/625-5455. www.muziek
theater.nl. Amstel 3 at Waterlooplein. Trams 9 or 14 and Metro to
Waterlooplein. Ticket prices vary.*

See Map 15 on p. 234.

National Ballet (p. 228) WATERLOOPLEIN This top-flight company,
most renowned for its stagings of Balanchine, makes its home at
the Muziektheater in the modern city hall complex.... *Tel 020/
551-8225, box office 020/625-5455. www.het-nationale-
ballet.nl. Waterlooplein 22. Trams 9 or 14 and Metro to Waterlooplein. Ticket prices vary. See Muziektheater.*

See Map 15 on p. 234.

**Nederlands Kamerorkest (Netherlands Chamber Orchestra)
(p. 224)** CENTER This offshoot of the Nederlands Philharmonisch Orkest often attracts top international soloists to concerts at its Beurs van Berlage homebase and other venues....
*Tel 020/521-7500. www.orkest.nl. Damrak 213 at Beursplein.
Trams 4, 9, 14, 16, 24, or 25 to the Dam. Ticket prices vary. See
Beurs van Berlage.*

See Map 15 on p. 234.

**Nederlands Philharmonisch Orkest (Netherlands Philharmonic
Orchestra) (p. 224)** CENTER This reputable ensemble boasts
world-class performances now that it's settled permanently at
the Beurs van Berlage, Amsterdam's former stock exchange....
*Tel 020/521-7500. www.orkest.nl. Damrak 213 at Beursplein.
Trams 4, 9, 14, 16, 24, or 25 to the Dam. Ticket prices vary. See
Beurs van Berlage.*

See Map 15 on p. 234.

Netherlands Opera (p. 227) WATERLOOPLEIN Everything from old
standbys to risky world premieres have won high praise since director Pierre Audi took over this company. The opera performs at the
Muziektheater.... *Tel 020/551-8922 info, box office 020/625-
5455. www.dno.nl. Waterlooplein 22. Trams 9 or 14 and Metro to
Waterlooplein. Ticket prices vary. See Muziektheater.*

See Map 15 on p. 234.

Nieuwe Kerk (New Church) (p. 225) CENTER This 600-year-old
Gothic church on the Dam is now primarily an art and cultural

center; its spectacular 17th-century organ is used regularly for concerts by top performers.... *Tel 020/638-6909. www.nieuwe kerk.nl. The Dam. Trams 1, 2, 4, 5, 6, 9, 13, 14, 16, 17, 24, or 25 to the Dam. Admission charged (price varies) to events.*

See Map 15 on p. 234.

OCCII (p. 229) VONDELPARK Laid-back fringe venue, beyond Vondelpark. You're likely to see off-the-wall cabaret or stand-up acts by unknowns, and hear unclassifiable music produced by young Amsterdammers.... *Tel 020/671-7778. Amstelveenseweg 134 at Vondelpark. Tram 2 to Amstelveenseweg. Ticket prices vary.*

See Map 16 on p. 236.

Oude Kerk (Old Church) (p. 225) RED-LIGHT DISTRICT A 13th- or 14th-century church that often holds organ and classical music concerts.... *Tel 020/625-8284. www.oudekerk.nl. Oudekerksplein at Oudezijds Voorburgwal. Trams 4, 9, 14, 16, 24, or 25 to the Dam. Ticket prices vary.*

See Map 15 on p. 234.

Paradiso (p. 226) LEIDSEPLEIN Among the city's top music venues, this deconsecrated old church has a cafe/club out front and a large performance area in what used to be the nave.... *Tel 020/ 626-4521. www.paradiso.nl. Weteringschans 6–8 at Leidseplein. Trams 1, 2, 5, 6, 7, or 10 to Leidseplein. Ticket prices vary.*

See Map 15 on p. 234.

Pirates (p. 231) WEST The city's baseball team plays Saturday and Sunday from May to September at a ball field in the western suburbs.... *Tel 020/616-2151. Sportpark Ookmeer, Herman Bonpad 5. Tram 13 to Geuzenveld. Tickets 4€ ($5).*

See Map 14 on p. 232.

RAI (p. 231) NEW SOUTH This vast exhibition center in the southern suburbs hosts everything from international boat shows to occasional rock and classical music concerts, though it has been largely eclipsed by the ArenA.... *Tel 020/549-1212. www.rai.nl. Europaplein 12 at Rooseveltlaan. Tram 4 to Europaplein. Ticket prices vary.*

See Map 16 on p. 236.

Soeterijn See Tropeninstituut.

Stadsschouwburg (Municipal Theater) (p. 228) LEIDSEPLEIN Unfortunately, all theater productions are in Dutch at Amsterdam's main theater, but there are frequent contemporary dance performances.... *Tel 020/624-2311. www.stadsschouwburg amsterdam.nl. Leidseplein 26. Trams 1, 2, 5, 6, 7, or 10 to Leidseplein. Ticket prices vary.*

See Map 15 on p. 234.

THE INDEX

ENTERTAINMENT

Toneelgroep Amsterdam (p. 229) WESTERN DOCKS This excellent municipal theater company plays at the **Westergasfabriek** on the western edge of town. Their performances are in Dutch, but the occasional visiting theater or dance company puts on works intelligible to English-speaking audiences.... *Tel 020/ 686-9735. Haarlemmerweg 8–10 at Westerpark. Tram 10 to Van Limburg Stirumplein; buses 18 or 22 to Haarlempoort. Ticket prices vary. See Westergasfabriek.*

See Map 15 on p. 234.

Tropeninstituut and Soeterijn (p. 228) EAST These Art Deco/Art Nouveau halls at the Royal Tropical Institute building (which houses the Tropenmuseum) stage dance, theater, music, and film dedicated to multiethnic, multicultural themes. Very PC.... *Tel 020/568-8215. www.tropenmuseum.nl. Mauritskade 63 at Singelgracht. Trams 7, 9, 10, or 14 to Mauritskade. Ticket prices vary.*

See Map 17 on p. 238.

Tuschinski Theater (p. 226) REMBRANDTPLEIN An opulent restored 1921 Dutch Art Deco cinema—still a first-run theater— where an organ from silent-movie days is used for occasional concerts and to accompany silent films.... *Tel 020/626-2633. Reguliersbreestraat 26 at Rembrandtplein. Trams 4, 9, or 14 to Rembrandtplein. Ticket prices vary.*

See Map 15 on p. 234.

Veemtheater (p. 228) WESTERN DOCKS No language barrier here. This converted warehouse way out beyond Westerdok and the Western Islands now hosts experimental dance, movement, and mime theater. For contemporary dance aficionados.... *Tel 020/ 626-0112. Van Diemenstraat 410 at Houtmankade. Tram 3 to Zoutkeetsgracht; bus 35 to Van Diemenstraat. Ticket prices vary.*

See Map 14 on p. 232.

Waalse Kerk (p. 225) RED-LIGHT DISTRICT This small, simple church set back from a canal is now a vibrant venue for organ concerts (on a celebrated rococo Christian Müller organ) and baroque music, sometimes performed by top names.... *Tel 020/623-2074. www.waalsekerk-amsterdam.nl. Oudezijds Achterburgwal 157 at Oude Hoogstraat. Trams 4, 9, 14, 16, 24, or 25 to the Dam. Admission charged (prices vary) to most events.*

See Map 15 on p. 234.

Westergasfabriek (p. 226) WESTERN DOCKS This converted gas plant on the western edge of town is now a venue for experimental theater, live pop and rock, and DJ theme nights. There's also a hip bar and dinerlike restaurant.... *Tel 020/586-0710. www.westergasfabriek.nl. Haarlemmerweg 8–10 at Westerpark.*

THE INDEX

ENTERTAINMENT

Tram 10 to Van Limburg Stirumplein; buses 18 or 22 to Haarlempoort. Admission charged for performances and dance nights
(prices vary); admission to bar free.

See Map 14 on p. 232.

Westerkerk (p. 225) CANAL BELT Organ music and Bach cantatas
are a regular feature at this Golden Age landmark.... *Tel 020/
624-7766. www.westerkerk.nl. Prinsengracht 281 at Westermarkt.
Trams 6, 13, 14, or 17 to Westermarkt. Ticket prices vary.*

See Map 15 on p. 234.

HOTLINES & OTHER BASICS

Airport... **Amsterdam Airport Schiphol** (pronounced *Skhip-ol*) is 13km (8 miles) from downtown Amsterdam—about 30 minutes by taxi or car, 20 minutes by train, or 15 to 55 minutes by hotel shuttle bus. It's one of the world's most convenient, efficiently run, and least unpleasant airports, handling more than 20 million passengers a year. It features hotels, a casino, sauna and meditation facilities, a vast shopping center, restaurants, business meeting rooms, and even a satellite of the city's famed Rijksmuseum, where you can peruse a few Old Dutch Masters before or after your flight. For general information, call Tel 0900/0141 (.10€/13¢ per min.) from inside the Netherlands. The website is www.schiphol.nl.

Airport transportation to downtown... Trains leave from the airport station to Amsterdam Centraal Station downtown 24 hours a day (every 15 min., 5am–1am; hourly 1–5am). Tickets cost 3.40€ ($4.25) one-way. Note that there are through trains to and from Rotterdam, Utrecht, and The Hague, as well as Amsterdam, so make sure you board a train to Amsterdam CS (Centraal Station), or whatever other Amsterdam station you need. Information: **Netherlands Railways,** Tel 0900/9292 for domestic trains; Tel 0900/9296 for international trains. **Connexxion Hotel Shuttle** (Tel 038/339-4741) runs a hotel **shuttle bus** daily every 10–30 minutes from 6am to 9pm between the airport and around 100 Amsterdam hotels. Buy tickets from the Connexxion desk inside Schiphol Plaza or on board from the driver (the fare is 11€/$14 one-way and 18€/$22 round-trip). It takes only 15 minutes to the Hilton from the airport, but almost an hour to the NH Barbizon Palace; going the opposite direction, the times are reversed. **Taxis** cost about 40€/$50 to central Amsterdam (Tel 020/ 653-1000; www.schipholtaxi.nl).

Babysitters... Only one organization is approved by Amsterdam's tourist information office (known as the VVV; see "Visitor information," later in this chapter): **Oppascentrale Kriterion** (Valckenierstraat 45; Tel 020/624-5848). It's been around since the 1950s, and employs male and female students over 18. Reserve by phone 5:30 to 7pm daily. Babysitters will come to your hotel, but charge a slightly higher fee for the inconvenience. Most four- and five-star hotels will book babysitters for you through the concierge's desk.

Banks and exchange offices... Banking hours are usually 9am to 4 or 5pm weekdays. Most banks either have foreign exchange counters or can handle these transactions at the regular counters. The **GWK** (Grenswisselkantoor) exchange offices in Centraal Station and at the main hall of the Schiphol Airport Railway Station are open Monday to Saturday 7am to 10:30pm, Sunday 9am to 10:30pm. In general, banks and GWK exchanges offer the best rates. Avoid other exchange offices (called Bureau de Change) charging high commissions. The most convenient GWK offices (open daily) are at Dam 23–25 (Mon–Sat 9:15am–7pm, Sun 10:15am–5:45pm), Damrak 1–5 (9am–8pm), Damrak 86 (10am–10pm), Leidseplein 1–3 (8:30am–10pm), Leidseplein 31A (Mon–Fri 10:15am– 5:45pm, Sat–Sun 10:30am–6pm), and Kalverstraat 150 (Mon–Tues and Wed–Sat 9am–6pm, Thurs 9am–9pm, Sun 10:30am–5pm). GWK offices also give cash advances on all major credit cards, and they are agents for Western

Union (handy for emergency money transfers). GWK also sells telephone cards and (until the new OV-chipkaart public transportation passes take over) *strippenkaart* tickets for city trams, buses, and the Metro. In a pinch, the often-crowded **Dutch Post Bank** at all post offices will exchange foreign currency. **ABN–AMRO** bank has an automatic banknote-exchange machine at Amsterdam's main central square, the Dam, at the corner of Damrak (open 24 hr. daily); **Fortis Bank** offers the same service at Singel 548; both these banks have ATMs, and in fact ATMs are pretty common around town.

Car rentals... Rental cars are listed in the Yellow Pages under *"Autoverhuur"*; international agencies are at Schiphol Airport. Book from the U.S. for the best rates. **Avis:** Tel 0800/235-2847 or 020/683-6061, Nassaukade 380. **Budget:** Tel **0900/1576** or 020/612-6066, Overtoom 121. **Europcar:** Tel **070/381 1812** or 020/683-2123, Overtoom 197. **Hertz:** Tel **020/201-3512**, Overtoom 333. (Also see "Driving and parking," below.)

Consulates and embassies... For most purposes, the large U.S. and British consulates in Amsterdam are likely to be the only resources visitors to the city who are citizens of these countries will need. **U.S. Consulate-General:** Museumplein 19, Tel 020/575-5309. **British Consulate-General:** Koningslaan 44, Tel 020/676-4343. All embassies are in The Hague, around an hour's train ride from Amsterdam. **United States Embassy:** Lange Voorhout 102, Tel 070/310-9209. **Canadian Embassy:** Sophialaan 7, Tel 070/311-1600. **British Embassy:** Lange Voorhout 10, Tel 070/427-0427. **Irish Embassy:** Dr. Kuyperstraat 9, Tel 070/363-0993. **Australian Embassy:** Carnegielaan 4, Tel 070/310-8200. **New Zealand Embassy:** Carnegielaan Mauritskade 10, Tel 070/346-9324.

Currency... One euro is worth around US$1.25 at this writing. Euro coins are: 1, 2, 5, 10, 20, and 50 euro cents and 1 or 2 euros. The paper denominations are: 5, 10, 20, 50, 100, 200, and 500 euros.

Doctors and dentists... Doctors are listed under *"Artsenhuisartsen: dokters"* in the Dutch Yellow Pages (the Yellow

Pages Visitors Guide, in English, is in most hotels). The **Centrale Doktersdienst** (Tel 020/592-3434) is a 24-hour-daily referral service. For medical emergencies call Tel 112, 24 hours daily. (See "Emergencies and police," below.) Consult the Yellow Pages under *"Tandarts"* for dentists. The **Dentists Referral Bureau** will refer you 24 hours daily to an approved practitioner (Tel 020/592-3434).

Driving and parking... The best advice on driving in Amsterdam is this: Don't drive in Amsterdam. Traffic is horrendous, the normally polite Dutch are demon drivers, and parking is nightmarish. If your car is parked illegally, it will be clamped or towed almost immediately by the dreaded Parkeerbeheer police, and you will need large amounts of cash to get it back (45€–99€/$56–$124 to remove the clamp, and from 220€/$275 per day if it gets towed; call 020/553-0333 around the clock to recover a towed vehicle). You can leave your car for 5.50€ ($6.90) a day at the Transferium (P+R) lot at Amstel Station, south of town, served by taxis and by tram 12 and bus 15 (both run 6am–midnight weekdays, 6:30am–midnight Sat, and 7:30am–midnight Sun; the bus also has limited night service after midnight), and at P+R lots at other public transportation hubs. For other P+R locations call Tel 020/553-0333. A handful of hotels have garages; many central hotels offer a 1-day (Mon–Sat 31€/$38, Sun 24€/$31) or 3-day (76€/$95) tourist parking pass allowing you to park on the street—if you can find a spot. You can also buy passes from the *Parkeerbeheer* (Parking Management Office): **Bakkerstraat 13** (near Rembrandtplein); **Nieuwezijds Kolk** (near Kolk garage); **Ceintuurbaan 159** (near Sarphatipark); **Kinkerstraat 17** (near police headquarters); and **Cruquiuskade 25** (on the northwest edge of town). A 1-day pass for the Center zone costs 20€ ($26). Parking meters are now ubiquitous: 3.40€ ($4.25) per hour in the Center zone Mon–Sat 9am–midnight, Sun noon–midnight. Times and charges vary in other zones; check the meter for details. Some central city garages are: **Europarking BV** (Marnixstraat 250; Tel 020/623-6694; Mon–Sat 6:30am–2am, Sun 7am–1am); **De Bijenkorf** (Beursplein/Damrak; Tel 0900/0919; Mon–Sat 9am–midnight); **Parking Plus** (Centraal Station, enter at Prins Hendrikkade 20A; Tel 020/638-5330; 24 hr. daily); **Kroon**

& Zn (Waterlooplein 1; Tel 020/551-0700;); and **Parking Byzantium** (Tesselschadestraat 1G; Tel 020/616-6416; 24 hr. daily). Rates are about 2.50€ to 5€ ($3.15–$6.25) per hour.

Electricity... Dutch plugs are the same 220-volt European model used in Italy and France, with two small round poles. Hotels are not equipped for American plugs or appliances that use 110 to 120 volts.

Emergencies and police... For accidents, medical emergencies, burglaries, or fire, call the police *(politie)*, fire department, and ambulance 24 hours daily at Tel **112.** The Amsterdam police central dispatcher is 0900/8844 (24 hr daily). The main police station is at Elandsgracht 117. Other police stations are at Lijnbaansgracht 219, Nieuwezijds Voorburgwal 118, Prinsengracht 1109, Singel 455, Van Leijenberghlaan 15, and Warmoesstraat 44. The dark-blue–uniformed regular Dutch *politie* are by and large quite polite, tolerant, and reasonably efficient. Only the last adjective, with the qualification raised to "hyper," could be applied to the special para-military "riot police," who deal with soccer hooligans, black-flag anarchists and other radicals, and race riots (a new Dutch phenomenon). They provide convincing proof that there's a steel fist within the velvet glove of even the most liberal European state. The less you have to do with these gentlemen—and their Amazon helpmeets—the better.

Events information... AUB **Uitburo** (Tel 020/621-1288 or 0900/0191 [.40€/50¢ per min.]; www.uitlijn.nl; Leidseplein 26; daily 9am–9pm) is a one-stop entertainment ticketing agency and information office for music, dance, theater, and special events. The VVV **(Amsterdam Tourist Office;** see "Visitor information," later in the chapter) has an English-language info line that charges .40€/(50¢) per minute inside the Netherlands (Tel 0900/400-4040; from outside the Netherlands dial 31-20/201-8800).

Festivals & Special Events

FEBRUARY: **Carnaval Mokum,** a popular festival, draws big crowds; the **1941 Dockers' Strike** is commemorated February 25.

MARCH: **HISWA te Water** national boat show at RAI convention center fills hotels (mid-month); the **Silent Procession (Stille Omgang)** of about 15,000 people marks the bizarre 1345 "Miracle of Amsterdam" of the fire-resistant Host (closest Sun to March 15).

APRIL: There's a 2-day celebration before and on **Queen's Day (Koninginnedag)**, April 30—book your hotel room several months ahead.

APRIL–MAY: **Tulip season.**

LATE MAY TO END OF AUGUST: The **Amsterdam Arts Adventure** features dance and music (p. 222).

JUNE: **RAI Arts Fair (KunstRAI)** is a major contemporary arts-and-crafts fair (early June); **Canal Run (Echo Grachtenloop),** the closest thing to a marathon, lopes along city canals (routes are 4.8, 9.7, and 17.7km/3, 6, and 11 miles; second Sun in June); the monthlong **Holland Festival** features theater, dance, and concert performances by major artists and companies (also in Rotterdam, The Hague, and Utrecht; see the Entertainment chapter for details).

AUGUST: **Uitmarkt,** held on the last weekend of the month, ushers in the fall concert/theater/opera season.

SEPTEMBER: **Flower Parade (Bloemencorso)** occurs the first week of the month, from Aalsmeer through town to the Dam (best review spots are Rembrandtplein and Vijzelstraat); on **National Monument Day (Monumentendag),** usually the second Saturday of the month, landmark buildings are open to the public; **Jordaan Festival** features arts, crafts, and entertainment (second and third week of the month).

NOVEMBER: **St. Nicholas Parade/Santa Claus (Sinterklaas),** a kiddies' parade, runs from Centraal Station to the Dam, with Santa Claus and his sidekick Black Peter (Zwarte Piet). Held the second or third week of the month.

Gay and lesbian sources... Europe's self-appointed (legitimately) gay capital has a pretty dense network of support, social, and cultural services for the gay and lesbian community—both indigenous and just-passing-through. The **Gay and Lesbian Switchboard** (Tel 020/623-6565; www.switchboard.nl; 10am–10pm daily) offers English-language info and advice. Tune into **MNS Radio** (106.8 FM, 6–9pm daily) for up-to-the-minute info on gay events and issues. For advice and info from the government-sub-sidized **COC** (the **Dutch Gay and Lesbian Organization**), call or visit the local branch at Rozenstraat 14 (Tel 020/626-3087; www.cocamsterdam.nl; open Mon–Fri 10am–5pm; English-speaking meetings; cafe). The COC's national branch is at Rozenstraat 8 (Tel 020/623-4596; open Mon–Fri 9am–5pm). Call **AIDS Infolijn** (Tel 0900/204-2040) for info on AIDS. *Gay News,* a monthly news and listings tabloid, is published in Dutch and English and is sold in bookstores, cafes, and clubs (www.gaynews.nl). *Gay & Night Magazine,* a monthly gay-events listings guide, is sold in many bookstores and at clubs and cafes. *Shark,* a twice-monthly giveaway, lists clubs, squats, music, film, and gay events.

Holidays... National holidays when businesses shut down are: **January 1** (New Year's Day); **Good Friday, Easter Sunday,** and **Easter Monday** (usually mid-April); **April 30** (Koninginnedag/Queen's Day, when the entire city goes gaga and wears orange clothes, for the House of Orange); **Ascension Day** (the 40th day after Easter); **Pentecost Sunday** and **Monday** (the seventh Sunday after Easter, and the following day); and **December 25** and **26** (Christmas).

Internet... Most hotels; many shops, museums, and galleries; and some restaurants and cafes are on the Internet. There are numerous Internet cafes or bars in town, some of them seedy (in smoking coffee shops). Three exceptions are: **The Internet Cafe** (Martelaarsgracht 11; www.internetcafe.nl) and **Freeworld Internetcafé** (Nieuwendijk 30; Tel 020/620-0902; www.freeworld-internetcafe.nl), and the **Lost in Amsterdam Lounge Café** (Nieuwendijk 19; Tel 06/2547-7333; www.lostinamsterdam.com), where you can smoke a water pipe before or after you surf. In the center, **easyEverything** (www.easyeverything.com) has three large locations: Damrak 33, Leidsestraat 24, and Reguliersbreestraat 22. There are dozens of blue **"Internet Pillars"** on sidewalks, usually near telephone booths. They use KPN telephone cards. Surf the Web or receive messages (you cannot send e-mails). Instructions are in English: Insert card, "start" page appears onscreen, surf or go to "e-mail."

Language... Natives speak Dutch, but will likely not respond in Dutch if you try to speak to them in Dutch; they speak better English than most native English speakers and are keen to demonstrate it. They cannot stand hearing their language miscoughed (coughing and spluttering are key to correct pronunciation; just try saying "Fan Ghchoaghch"— van Gogh). Most Dutch also speak French, German, and more.

Newspapers... There is no English-language daily in Amsterdam, but the monthly Amsterdam *Day by Day* is widely available, and free English-language weeklies seem to come and go. Major British and American dailies and Sunday papers are sold at many newsstands. Readily available papers include *USA Today, International Herald Tribune,* and the *Wall Street Journal.* The best sources for these publications are: **American Book Center** (Kalverstraat 185); **Waterstone's** (Kalverstraat 152); **Kiosk** (Stationsplein 13, and other locations); **Centraal Station** newsstands; **AKO** (Rozengracht 21, and other locations); **Athenaeum Nieuwscentruum** (Spui 14); and **Bruna** (Leidsestraat 89). If you are so starved of news that you need to get it somehow from a Dutch paper, the main dailies are *Het Parool* (center-left afternoon paper); *NRC Handelsblad* (centrist, intellectual evening paper); *De Volkskrant* (Catholic, left-liberal morning paper); and *De Telegraaf* (right-wing morning rag).

Opening and closing times... Most shops are open 1 to 8pm Monday; 9am to 8pm Tuesday, Wednesday, and Friday; 9am to 9pm Thursday; and 9am to 5pm Saturday. Many businesses and shops are now also open on Sundays from noon to 5pm. Food shops generally open between 8 and 9am and close at 5 or 6pm (3pm Sat). A local Avond-verkoop (evening sales) store is a resource not to be ignored for keeping you stocked with things to munch on after normal hours. Many can prepare takeout meals to about the same standard as you would find in a typical Dutch *eet-cafe* (literally "eat cafe"—a cafe with eats), for 10% to 20% less than the restaurant price, and they often sell fresh delicatessen items. Opening times are usually from 5pm to midnight.

Passports and visas... American, Australian, Canadian, New Zealand, British, and Irish citizens need only present a valid passport for stays of up to 3 months. No visas are required.

Post office... The main **TPG Post** office is at Singel 250 (Tel 020/556-3311; open weekdays 9am–6pm [Thurs to 9pm], 9am–1pm Sat); there are other post offices around town, though not actually all that many. For general information call Tel 0800/0402. Stamps are sold at newsstands and tobacco shops; coin-operated stamp dispensers are attached to some mailboxes. For mail sent outside Amsterdam, use the slot marked *overige bestemmingen* (sometimes labeled FOREIGN COUNTRIES).

Public transportation... There are trams, buses, and a subway system (the Metro) running 6am to midnight. Night buses run Monday through Friday from 1 to 5:30am, and weekends from 1 to 6:30am (buses 73 to 76 serve central areas). The subway, only marginally useful, runs from Centraal Station to eastern and southern suburbs (or dreary housing projects), with center-city stops at Nieuwmarkt, Waterlooplein, and Weesperplein. A new subway line, the Noord-Zuid (North-South) Metrolijn, is being dug out at this time and will have greater utility than the existing line when it opens—in 2011; meantime Amsterdam has about as many excavation sites as the Valley of the Kings, causing traffic headaches all around town. There are 17 tramlines (streetcars). Trams are the most useful, expedient, and popular form of transit. A minibus service, De Opstapper, links Centraal Station to the Muziektheater opera and dance theater, via Prinsengracht, on the otherwise hard to-access Grachtengordel (Canal Ring). During 2006, public transportation in Amsterdam—and by the end of 2008 around the Netherlands—will be using the new national electronic OV-chipkaart in place of tickets. The card is loaded up with a pre-selected amount of euros which can then be reduced automatically by electronic readers as you travel. Until the OV-chipkaart takes over fully, from 2008, a punch-as-you-go strip ticket, called a *strippenkaart*, valid on all types of transit (restricted on trains), is sold by drivers or conductors; at the GVB Tickets & Info office in front of Centraal Station; and at tobacco shops, and post offices. There are also passes for 1 hour, 1 day, multiple days, 1 week, or 1 month, sold at the same places as other tickets. On board the trams, a *strip-penkaart* costs 1.60€ ($2) for two strips, 2.40€ ($3) for three strips, and 6.40€ ($8) for eight strips. Buy strip tickets at railway stations or GVB offices and they cost less per strip: 6.50€ ($8.15) for 15 strips, and 19€ ($24) for 45 strips. There are 11 fare zones in greater Amsterdam. Central-city rides cover one zone, requiring two strips; two zones require three strips (always one strip more than the total number of zones). Fold the ticket and time-stamp the strip corresponding to the length of your trip. Once stamped, the ticket is valid for 1 hour or more from the time stamped, for transfers to other trams, buses, and Metro lines. Upon request, drivers or conductors will stamp tickets and tell you when your stop comes up. Drivers cannot sell or stamp tickets on trams with conductors. For transfers to buses, board in front and show the driver your ticket. Day passes for 1, 2, and 3 days cost 6.30€ ($7.90), 10€ ($13), and 13€ ($16), respectively (see the You Probably Didn't Know chapter for more on streetcars; also check out www.ov-info.nl and www.gvb.nl for more information). Ticket inspectors do spot checks; fines are 30€ ($38) plus the ticket price (info at Tel 0900/9292).

Radio and TV stations broadcasting in English...
Radio stations include **Voice of America for Europe,** at 99.1 MHz; **BBC World Service** at 101.3 MHz and 648 kHz on MW; and **BBC Radio 4** on 106.6 MHz, 198 kHz AM, and 1500 kHz LW. **CNN International, BBC 1, BBC 2, BBC World,** and **EuroNews** are available in most luxury hotels; some also offer **MTV** and **NBC Superchannel.**

Taxes and duty free... The murderously high value-added tax (VAT; here called BTW) of 19% is included in the sales price of most consumer goods (some include only 6% VAT, as do restaurant and hotel bills). Tax-free shopping is possible (though more complicated than you'd think) for non-E.U. residents: You've got to spend 137€ ($171) or more in one day at one participating shop, then take your purchases out of the country within 3 months. You're actually refunded 13.5% to 14%, less a variable commission fee. Look for the "Europe Tax-Free Shopping" blue-and-gray logo or the red-and-blue "Easy Tax Free" logo at shops. Ask for a Global Refund Cheque when you make your purchases, get a customs officer at Schiphol or Centraal Station to stamp the "cheques" as you leave the country, then rush to the refund office at one of the ABN-AMRO banks in airport departures halls 1 and 3, or the GWK exchange office at the train station or in Schiphol Plaza Shopping Center. For information: Tel 023/524-1909; www.info@globalrefund.com.

Taxis and limos... You can hail cabs in Amsterdam, but they are not obliged to stop. Best spots to flag a cab: an artery with a tram line, or central-city streets like Damrak, Rokin, Vijzelstraat, Nieuwezijds Voorburgwal, Raadhuis-straat, and Amstelstraat. Main taxi stands are at Centraal Station, the Dam, Leidseplein, Spui, Rembrandtplein, Westermarkt, and at the bus station on the corner of Marnixstraat and Kinkerstraat. **Taxi Centrale** (Tel 0900/677-7777; 24 hr. daily) is the central dispatcher for all of these. Radio taxis will pick you up anywhere; the meter runs once you board. Rates are 3.10€ ($3.90) to start, 1.90€ ($2.40) per kilometer (.62 miles) thereafter, and after 25km (15.5 miles) 1.40€ ($1.75) per kilometer (.62 miles); standing time is 35€ ($44) per hour. A ride from Centraal Station to a hotel within the Singelgracht costs 10€ to 15€ ($13–$18). Baggage is free. Limousines are listed under *"Autoverhuur met chauffeur"* in the Yellow Pages. **Business Limousines** (Tel 020/669-3889; www.business limo.com) uses luxury cars and limos. **Carey Chauffeur Drive** (Tel 020/659-5333; www.chauffeurdrive.nl) offers luxury cars and minivans. The **Water Taxi** dock is in front of Centraal Station; they will pick you up at your hotel or restaurant (Water Taxi Centrale, Stationsplein 8; Tel 020/535-6363; www.water-taxi.nl; daily 9am–1am). Rates for one to eight passengers: 85€ ($106) for the first half-hour, 70€ ($88) per additional 30 minutes.

Telephones... The Amsterdam area code for calls within the Netherlands is 020; don't dial it inside the city. When calling from abroad, dial 31 (Netherlands), 20 (Amsterdam), then the subscriber's number. Some 0900 numbers cost .10€ to .90€ (13¢–$1.15) per minute. **Telephone booths** are abundant and clearly marked KPN TELEKOM/TELEFOON

HOTLINES & OTHER BASICS

or TELFORT. All use telephone or credit cards. Phone cards are sold at post offices and telephone centers, plus GWK exchange offices (note that KPN and Telfort cards do not work with the other companies' phones). Operating instructions are given in English: To dial the United States or Canada, dial 001 plus the area code plus the subscriber's seven-digit telephone number. For Country Direct services press "special functions" and follow instructions displayed (the LCD screen allows you to select language and country code and displays the amount of credit on your phone card). To use a credit card, follow the same procedure, but dip your card. **Directory information:** Tel 0900/8008 for domestic; www.detelefoongids.nl or www.kpn.com; for the **Yellow Pages:** www.goudengids.nl; **international info:** Tel 0900/8418; **international collect calls:** Tel 0800/0410. **MCI:** Tel 0800/022-9122; **Sprint:** Tel 0800/022-9119; **AT&T:** Tel 0800/022-9111; **Canada Direct:** Tel 0800/022-9116; **British Telecom:** Tel 0800/022-9944; **mobile phone info:** Tel 0800/0106.

Time... Amsterdam's time zone is 6 hours ahead of Eastern Standard Time, 9 hours ahead of Pacific Time.

Tipping... Don't believe that the Dutch don't appreciate tips, but do believe that the Dutch themselves don't leave many, or much. Leave symbolic tips at cafes and bars (loose change, or 1€/$1.25 max). Leave about 10% at top restaurants. Service is always included in the bill, but as in most European countries, the service charge goes to pay the waiter's miserable salary, so it's good form to leave at least a token tip. Taxi drivers get 1€ to 3€ ($1.25–$3.75) max for a ride in the Center. Hotel bell staff: 2€ to 4€ ($2.50–$5). Bathroom attendants: .30€ to .50€ (38¢–63¢).

Trains... Centraal Station (CS) is an unmistakable major landmark—currently undergoing major refurbishment to make space for a new Metro line that's due in service in 2011—on Stationsplein (Tel 0900/9292 for info 6:30am–10pm daily; Tel 030/297-7240 for advance international tickets Mon–Fri 9am–6pm, Sat 10am–4pm, closed Sun). Lots of Continental destinations are served and (via Brussels and the Eurostar train through the Channel Tunnel) London too. For international train info contact Tel 0900/9296 or www.ns.nl.

Travelers with disabilities... Amsterdam is a difficult city for travelers with disabilities. It has uneven pavements, old buildings with narrow stairways, and buses and trams not equipped with "kneeling" apparatus (though the newer trams are being equipped). Metro cars are accessible unless your arms are immobilized. Most curbs are contoured for bikes, which means they're wheelchair-friendly. Museums, concert halls, and public buildings are generally accessible; phone ahead and assistance can be requested almost anywhere. Hotels that can accommodate travelers with disabilities are lamentably rare. Best bets are luxury/business establishments. Call the VVV (see "Visitor information," below) for hotel addresses; fax your chosen hotel for details. **IHD Schiphol Service** will pick up persons with disabilities from trains, buses, or taxis and take them to and from their flights (Tel 030/316-1415). **Netherlands Railways** (NS) distributes a free pamphlet on train travel for the disabled, plus timetables in Braille (sold at NS stations, or call Tel 0900/9292); for free escort service at a train station call 24 hours ahead (Tel 030/235-7822, 8:30am–2pm weekdays).

Visitor information... VVV (pronounced *fay-fay-fay*) is Amsterdam's official tourist office. VVV is what people say and what's on the official literature. No one—not even many locals—knows what it stands for. (If you must know, it's Vereniging voor Vreemdelingenverkeer, which roughly translates as the Association for Visitor Travel.) Its main info number (Tel 0900/400-4040; www.visitamsterdam.nl; 9am–5pm weekdays) at .40€ (50¢) per minute, often with a long wait, can get ridiculously expensive; if you are calling from outside the Netherlands, dial 31-20/201-8800. Go in person to the VVV offices at Stationsplein 10 (in front of Centraal Station; 9am–5pm daily); inside Centraal Station, platform 2 (Mon–Sat 8am–8pm, Sun 9am–5pm); and Leidseplein 1 (9:15am–5pm daily; July–Aug Fri–Sat to 7pm). Correspondence: VVV Amsterdam, Box 3901, 1001 AS Amsterdam. The **Netherlands Board of Tourism** (NBT) has offices in the **United States** at 355 Lexington Ave., 19th floor, New York, NY 10017 (Tel 212/557-3500, fax 212/370-9507); in **Canada:** 14 Glenmount Court, Whitby, Ontario, L1N 5M8, (Tel 905/666-5960, fax 905/666-5391); and in **Britain:** (mail inquiries) P.O. Box 30783, London, WC2B 6DH (Tel 020/7539-7950;

brochure-line Tel 0906/871-7777; fax 020/7539-7953).
The city of Amsterdam now has two websites with cultural/
municipal info: www.amsterdam.nl and www.visitamsterdam.
nl; and you can visit the Netherlands tourism website on
www.holland.com.

Weather... Amsterdam has an ideal climate—for tulips. Winter is windy, icy, and damp; fall is cold, foggy, and damp;
spring is rainy and damp; summer is brief but sticky. Rainy
days average 237 per year. February and June are the dry
months (17 days of rain on average). Average temperatures: January 36°F (2°C), February 37°F (3°C), March
41°F (5°C), April 46°F (8°C), May 54°F (12°C), June 59°F
(15°C), July 62°F (17°C), August 62°F (17°C), September
57°F (14°C), October 51°F (11°C), November 43°F (6°C),
December 38°F (3°C).

GENERAL INDEX

Accommodations

Restaurants

Notes

Notes

Frommer's® Complete Guides

The only guide independent travelers need to make smart choices, avoid rip-offs, get the most for their money, and travel like a pro.

Frommer's®

WILEY

Available at bookstores everywhere.

Frommer's® Portable Guides

Destinations in a Nutshell

FROMMER'S® COMPLETE TRAVEL GUIDES

Alaska
Amalfi Coast
American Southwest
Amsterdam
Argentina & Chile
Arizona
Atlanta
Australia
Austria
Bahamas
Barcelona
Beijing
Belgium, Holland & Luxembourg
Belize
Bermuda
Boston
Brazil
British Columbia & the Canadian
  Rockies
Brussels & Bruges
Budapest & the Best of Hungary
Buenos Aires
Calgary
California
Canada
Cancún, Cozumel & the Yucatán
Cape Cod, Nantucket & Martha's
  Vineyard
Caribbean
Caribbean Ports of Call
Carolinas & Georgia
Chicago
China
Colorado
Costa Rica
Croatia
Cuba
Denmark
Denver, Boulder & Colorado Springs
Edinburgh & Glasgow
England
Europe
Europe by Rail

Florence, Tuscany & Umbria
Florida
France
Germany
Greece
Greek Islands
Hawaii
Hong Kong
Honolulu, Waikiki & Oahu
India
Ireland
Italy
Jamaica
Japan
Kauai
Las Vegas
London
Los Angeles
Los Cabos & Baja
Madrid
Maine Coast
Maryland & Delaware
Maui
Mexico
Montana & Wyoming
Montréal & Québec City
Moscow & St. Petersburg
Munich & the Bavarian Alps
Nashville & Memphis
New England
Newfoundland & Labrador
New Mexico
New Orleans
New York City
New York State
New Zealand
Northern Italy
Norway
Nova Scotia, New Brunswick &
  Prince Edward Island
Oregon
Paris
Peru

Philadelphia & the Amish Country
Portugal
Prague & the Best of the Czech
  Republic
Provence & the Riviera
Puerto Rico
Rome
San Antonio & Austin
San Diego
San Francisco
Santa Fe, Taos & Albuquerque
Scandinavia
Scotland
Seattle
Seville, Granada & the Best of
  Andalusia
Shanghai
Sicily
Singapore & Malaysia
South Africa
South America
South Florida
South Pacific
Southeast Asia
Spain
Sweden
Switzerland
Texas
Thailand
Tokyo
Toronto
Turkey
USA
Utah
Vancouver & Victoria
Vermont, New Hampshire & Maine
Vienna & the Danube Valley
Vietnam
Virgin Islands
Virginia
Walt Disney World® & Orlando
Washington, D.C.
Washington State

FROMMER'S® DOLLAR-A-DAY GUIDES

Australia from $60 a Day
California from $70 a Day
England from $75 a Day
Europe from $85 a Day
Florida from $70 a Day

Hawaii from $80 a Day
Ireland from $90 a Day
Italy from $90 a Day
London from $95 a Day

New York City from $90 a Day
Paris from $95 a Day
San Francisco from $70 a Day
Washington, D.C. from $80 a Day

FROMMER'S® PORTABLE GUIDES

Acapulco, Ixtapa & Zihuatanejo
Amsterdam
Aruba
Australia's Great Barrier Reef
Bahamas
Berlin
Big Island of Hawaii
Boston
California Wine Country
Cancún
Cayman Islands
Charleston
Chicago

Disneyland®
Dominican Republic
Dublin
Florence
Las Vegas
Las Vegas for Non-Gamblers
London
Los Angeles
Maui
Nantucket & Martha's Vineyard
New Orleans
New York City
Paris

Portland
Puerto Rico
Puerto Vallarta, Manzanillo &
  Guadalajara
Rio de Janeiro
San Diego
San Francisco
Savannah
Vancouver
Venice
Virgin Islands
Washington, D.C.
Whistler

FROMMER'S® CRUISE GUIDES

Alaska Cruises & Ports of Call

Cruises & Ports of Call

European Cruises & Ports of Call

FROMMER'S® DAY BY DAY GUIDES

Amsterdam	London	Rome
Chicago	New York City	San Francisco
Florence & Tuscany	Paris	Venice

FROMMER'S® NATIONAL PARK GUIDES

Algonquin Provincial Park	National Parks of the American West	Yosemite and Sequoia & Kings
Banff & Jasper	Rocky Mountain	Canyon
Grand Canyon	Yellowstone & Grand Teton	Zion & Bryce Canyon

FROMMER'S® MEMORABLE WALKS

Chicago	New York	Rome
London	Paris	San Francisco

FROMMER'S® WITH KIDS GUIDES

Chicago	National Parks	Toronto
Hawaii	New York City	Walt Disney World® & Orlando
Las Vegas	San Francisco	Washington, D.C.
London		

SUZY GERSHMAN'S BORN TO SHOP GUIDES

Born to Shop: France	Born to Shop: Italy	Born to Shop: New York
Born to Shop: Hong Kong, Shanghai & Beijing	Born to Shop: London	Born to Shop: Paris

FROMMER'S® IRREVERENT GUIDES

Amsterdam	Los Angeles	Rome
Boston	Manhattan	San Francisco
Chicago	New Orleans	Walt Disney World®
Las Vegas	Paris	Washington, D.C.
London		

FROMMER'S® BEST-LOVED DRIVING TOURS

Austria	Germany	Northern Italy
Britain	Ireland	Scotland
California	Italy	Spain
France	New England	Tuscany & Umbria

THE UNOFFICIAL GUIDES®

Adventure Travel in Alaska	Hawaii	Paris
Beyond Disney	Ireland	San Francisco
California with Kids	Las Vegas	South Florida including Miami &
Central Italy	London	the Keys
Chicago	Maui	Walt Disney World®
Cruises	Mexico's Best Beach Resorts	Walt Disney World® for
Disneyland®	Mini Las Vegas	Grown-ups
England	Mini Mickey	Walt Disney World® with Kids
Florida	New Orleans	Washington, D.C.
Florida with Kids	New York City	

SPECIAL-INTEREST TITLES

Athens Past & Present	Frommer's Exploring America by RV
Cities Ranked & Rated	Frommer's NYC Free & Dirt Cheap
Frommer's Best Day Trips from London	Frommer's Road Atlas Europe
Frommer's Best RV & Tent Campgrounds in the U.S.A.	Frommer's Road Atlas Ireland
	Retirement Places Rated

FROMMER'S® PHRASEFINDER DICTIONARY GUIDES

French	Italian	Spanish